SOUL!

Fulfilling the Promise of

Your Professional Life

as a Teacher and Leader

Timothy D. Kanold

Foreword by Robert Eaker

Solution Tree | Press
a division of
Solution Tree

555 North Morton Street Bloomington, IN 47404
800.733.6786 (toll free) / 812.336.7700
FAX: 812.336.7790

email: info@SolutionTree.com
SolutionTree.com

Visit **go.SolutionTree.com/SOUL** to access materials related to this book.

Printed in the United States of America

Library of Congress Cataloging-in-Publication Data

Names: Kanold, Timothy D., author.
Title: SOUL! : fulfilling the promise of your professional life as a
    teacher and leader / Timothy D. Kanold.
Description: Bloomington, IN : Solution Tree Press, 2021. | Includes
    bibliographical references and index.
Identifiers: LCCN 2020040762 (print) | LCCN 2020040763 (ebook) | ISBN
    9781951075651 (paperback) | ISBN 9781951075668 (ebook)
Subjects: LCSH: Teachers--Professional relationships. | Reflective
    teaching. | Educational leadership.
Classification: LCC LB1775 .K283 2021 (print) | LCC LB1775 (ebook) | DDC
    371.12--dc23
LC record available at https://lccn.loc.gov/2020040762
LC ebook record available at https://lccn.loc.gov/2020040763

Solution Tree
Jeffrey C. Jones, CEO
Edmund M. Ackerman, President

Solution Tree Press
President and Publisher: Douglas M. Rife
Associate Publisher: Sarah Payne-Mills
Art Director: Rian Anderson
Managing Production Editor: Kendra Slayton
Copy Chief: Jessi Finn
Senior Production Editor: Christine Hood
Content Development Specialist: Amy Rubenstein
Copy Editor: Jessi Finn
Proofreader: Elisabeth Abrams
Text and Cover Designer: Laura Cox
Editorial Assistants: Sarah Ludwig and Elijah Oates

This book is dedicated to my family, our "FamBam";

to the memory of my colleague Becky DuFour;

and to all who choose our profession—

may your soul story search preserve your

good in order to create good in others,

each trip around the sun.

Visit **go.SolutionTree.com/SOUL** to access materials related to this book.

Table of Contents

About the Author

Timothy D. Kanold, PhD, is an award-winning educator and author. He is former director of mathematics and science and served as superintendent of Adlai E. Stevenson High School District 125, a model professional learning community (PLC) district in Lincolnshire, Illinois.

Dr. Kanold has authored or coauthored more than thirty books on K–12 mathematics, school culture, and school leadership, including his best-selling and 2018 IPPY award-winning book *HEART! Fully Forming Your Professional Life as a Teacher and Leader.* He also has authored numerous articles and chapters on school leadership and culture-care development for educational publications.

Dr. Kanold received the 2017 Ross Taylor / Glenn Gilbert National Leadership Award from the National Council of Supervisors of Mathematics (NCSM), the international 2010 Damen Award for outstanding contributions to education from Loyola University Chicago, and the 1986 Presidential Award for Excellence in Mathematics and Science Teaching.

Dr. Kanold earned a bachelor's degree in education and a master's degree in mathematics from Illinois State University. He received his doctorate in educational leadership and counseling psychology from Loyola University Chicago.

Dr. Kanold is committed to equity, excellence, and social justice reform for the improved learning of students and school faculty, staff, and administrators. He conducts inspirational professional development seminars worldwide with a focus on improving student learning outcomes through a commitment to the PLC process and a focus on living a well-balanced professional life by practicing reflection and self-care routines.

To learn more about Dr. Kanold's work, follow him @tkanold or #heartandsoul4ED on Twitter.

To book Timothy D. Kanold for professional development, contact pd@SolutionTree.com.

Foreword

By Robert Eaker

*Joy, feeling one's own value, being appreciated and loved by
others, feeling useful and capable of production are all factors of
enormous value for the human soul.*

—Maria Montessori

In an era of increased stress created by statewide testing of students, coupled with
the relentless pressure placed on teachers for improving student learning, it's time to take
a hard look at our cultural values reflected in such words as *caring* and *self-care, compassion
for others*, and *compassion for self* as educators search for and find passion for their work.

It is time to examine the *heart and soul* of what it means to be an educator.

What better person to write about educators' hearts and souls than Tim Kanold? For
more than four decades, I've had the pleasure of knowing Tim as he filled a variety of
roles across rural, urban, and suburban schools—teacher, division chair, assistant principal, superintendent, consultant, author, and most important, trusted friend. In each
of these roles, Tim has modeled and demonstrated the very best of our professional life,
which he wrote about first in *HEART!*[1], and now in this companion book, *SOUL!*

Regardless of their organizational structure, schools are composed of human beings,
with each person bringing his or her unique beliefs, attitudes, actions, dreams, and desires
to the school—his or her unique heart and soul.

Yet schools are more than a collection of individuals. Successful schools agree to unify
around ways of doing things, things that flow from a collective organizational *soul story*. It
falls to educators (administrators, teachers, and staff) to lead the *collaborative* development,

articulation, and promotion of core values and behaviors that, taken together, represent those good and right things for which the school stands—the values it will passionately promote, protect, and defend, such as belonging, community, intimacy, vulnerability, and validation.

As Tim illustrates through this book, we can create such school cultures—cultures that reflect a collective soul story that embraces our diversity and gives a focus to the collaborative efforts *everyone* makes to ensure the learning of *each* student.

Developing such schools requires more than mere structural changes. A school's collective soul story matters—a lot! It's what helps educators overcome obstacles to fully engage in their daily work life, practice self-care, and provide meaning to their work—how they behave today to create a positive legacy for tomorrow.

As Tim reminds us in A Note to Readers, "A healthy soul story feeds into the good you do for other human beings and embraces your professional responsibility to live a life of contribution as you help others flourish." Creating such school cultures is not only desirable but imperative, and Tim's *SOUL!* serves as a guidebook to help each of us on our individual, reflective, and collective journey.

Tim will help you search for and find your personal soul story, help you use it to overcome the professional obstacles sure to come your way, and help you become more confident, joyful, whole, and healthy as you live the soul story of your professional life.

In this book, he delivers a reflective self-care guide, providing wise advice for living an improved professional and personal life, and uses research, anecdotes, and stories to help create a powerful and positive culture in your school, for just such a time as this.

A Note to Readers

I wrote *HEART!* in 2017[2] to honor the work and character of my friend, mentor, and colleague for more than thirty years, Rick DuFour. As an original architect of the Professional Learning Community (PLC) at Work® process, Rick was the genius behind the clarity, beauty, and simplicity of its complex culture, expectations, actions, and beliefs. His passion focused on one primary purpose—creating and living an equity culture to significantly improve the learning of every child entrusted to us.

Rick, along with his colleague and close friend Bob Eaker, was the *heart* of the PLC movement.

From September 2014 to February 2017, Rick shared with the educational world his stage 4 cancer journey, and his battle to name the end of his professional seasons on his own terms. Walking hand in hand at every stage of that journey was his wife, Becky DuFour.

Becky was with Rick through all that comes with a cancer journey such as his, and she carried the PLC movement forward with remarkable grace and clarity. She was onstage at our major events, helped behind the scenes at meetings for all things PLC, and made sure everyone around her found a way to stay connected to their professional mission as educators, despite the pain and suffering that come with losing someone you love closely and deeply.

Fast-forward sixteen months, and Becky was leading the way as we started our summer 2018 PLC Institutes and series of teaching and leading events. If Rick DuFour represented the *heart* of the PLC life, then Becky DuFour was most assuredly its *soul*. Becky brought grace, compassion, humility, wisdom, kindness, goodness, and so much more to every person who crossed her path. When you spoke to her, she listened. Really listened. And she cared about *you*, and about nurturing the good that resides within you.

As late June 2018 approached, I was contemplating writing this book, and I needed to know her thoughts. Could and should I write this book about our responsibility to pursue our professional wellness and our moral good? I needed validation from a colleague and friend I could trust.

So I told Becky my idea.

"A healthy soul story," I said, "is reflected in the *good* person who chooses to treat those immediately around him- or herself (regardless of race, ethnicity, language, faith, gender identity, sexual orientation, or income) with respect, validation, compassion, and care. A healthy soul story feeds into the good you do for other human beings and embraces your professional responsibility to live a life of contribution as you help others flourish."

I finished with, "Look, sooner or later, your world will fall apart. What will matter then is the quality of the soul story you have lived and created over time!"

Then I asked Becky, "What do you think?" Becky's response was positive and swift. She asked me if she could write the foreword, and I told her it would be an honor to have her wisdom in the book.

Little did I know the simple and innocent statement *sooner or later, your world will fall apart* would personally resonate so soon. Just one week after this quiet dinner meeting with our colleague Bob Eaker (who graciously agreed to write the foreword to this book in Becky's place), I wouldn't speak with Becky ever again.

This dinner would represent my final conversation with her before she unexpectedly passed away. And like many, my struggle and choice of responses to make sense of it all have been part of my personal soul story construction these past few years.

Then, during the writing of this book about our *soul story* no less, and on a much bigger scale, like you, I got caught in the snare of the pandemic and protests of 2020. It was as if a book like this was not just for my personal suffering and stress, or your personal suffering and stress, but for the suffering and stress of so many in our profession. There was the sudden loss of students, friends, or family members to the isolation and death caused by COVID-19. This loss was further compounded by the anger and grief of racial discrimination and violence that persisted.

I wrote this book for you and for me. For all educators striving to do their best every day under often difficult, stressful, and overwhelming conditions; to find their own way of creating good in their students and colleagues; and to feel the joy and benefits of a life story emanating from a healthy and fully formed professional soul, like Becky's.

May we all fulfill the promise of our professional journey and become exemplars of *the good* demonstrated by the life of Becky DuFour.

—Timothy D. Kanold

Introduction

In a story I relate in chapter 2 of this book, I describe sitting down at the piano with my Uncle Al to play a 1938 Hoagy Carmichael song, "Heart and Soul."[3] It was 1958, and I was seven years old. And I became part of their soul story in that little house on 41st Street in Rock Island, Illinois. The personal journey that took me to that exact moment of my life story was riddled with difficulty and sadness for a young child of divorced parents. And the K–12 public school systems in the United States would have to figure out what to do with me from time to time.

Yet, what exactly is our *soul story*?

The late University of Southern California professor Dallas Willard provided a hint when he indicated the moral good of our profession, and subsequently our station in life, is rooted in the good person who "treats those immediately around himself or herself with respect and care. The good person then is a person of comprehensive and well-ordered virtues."[4] Socrates believed the most important good for a human being was the health of the soul.[5]

With these ideas in mind, and for the purposes of this book, I define your professional soul story as *the pursuit of your moral good in order to create good in others.*

In this book, we take a reflective yet forward-looking journey into why our professional soul story is so important to our professional well-being and our emotional health. What is the role our soul story plays in overcoming obstacles sure to occur, while also unifying our work as educators?

A closer look at the cover of this book reveals an insightful subtitle. Did you notice it? *Fulfilling the Promise of Your Professional Life as a Teacher and Leader.*

As educators, we agreed to become part of a profession. But not just any kind of profession; we chose a lifetime of work designed to contribute to the growth and development of others—our students and our colleagues. In that sense, we intuitively understand that we joined a helping profession of good persons for the creation of good persons.

And yet, that ideal—to thrive in our jobs in order to make positive contributions to others—is often very difficult to achieve, season in and season out. There are many obstacles, as described in part 2 of this book. The real obstacles to our professional fulfillment, as you will discover, are less outward and more inward. Our soul story is shaped from the inside out.

SOUL! is intentionally informal and written as if we were having a conversation together. Endnotes for resources are provided at the end of the book so as not to disrupt the flow of your thoughts and reflections as you read.

There is a flow to the book from one chapter to the next. In some chapters, you will be alerted to language and ideas from previous chapters, so you might need to go back and read those first should you choose to read ahead.

The book is filled with anecdotes and many of my favorite stories— some funny and some sad—which are always designed to make a point, connect you to your own soul story, and give you space to write about your progress as your career unfolds. Every story is true.

Please take your time working your way through the book. *SOUL!* takes you on a deep and purposeful walk through your professional life timeline, whether you are just starting our profession, nearing the end, or existing somewhere in between.

When I reference *you* in this book, I am including all adults responsible for educating students in your school or district. I am referencing each of us—the adults who have chosen the education profession, regardless of the role we play within the school organization.

If *HEART!* challenged you to live a more balanced and healthy professional life for the interfusion with others, then *SOUL!* takes you on a steeper mountain climb that encourages your interfusion with the good.

Hopefully, this book will help you choose a professional life of contribution, compassion, belonging, balance, and joy throughout your career. Our profession, our *vocation*, despite all its trials and tragedies, can lead to an incredible life fulfilled as we pay attention to and reflect on moments of stillness from the noise and seek to understand our soul story impact along the way.

SOUL! provides insights supported by research and various experts about ideas for pursuing a more meaningful teaching and leading career. I include thought leaders and researchers outside of the education profession such as: Daniel Coyle and Ryan Holiday, Chip Heath and Dan Heath, Brené Brown and Parker Palmer, David Brooks and Lisa Delpit, Emma Seppälä and James Clear, Tom Rath and Max De Pree, and Kristin Neff and Adam Grant, to name a few.

I also include reflections and wisdom from more than twenty-five teachers and leaders in our profession, including the voices of Anthony Muhammad, Julie Schmidt, Luis Cruz, Janel Keating, Brian Butler, Bill Ferriter, Regina Owens, Bob Eaker, Aaron Hansen, Bill Barnes, Jenn Deinhart, Jasmine Kullar, Linda Reusch, Mike Mattos, Tim Brown, and more. You will meet them too as you walk through your own soul story journey.

Each part of the book presents one of four unique actions derived from the word *SOUL*, as the title indicates: S is for *searching*, O is for *overcoming*, U is for *unifying*, and L is for *living*.

Part 1: S Is for Searching—Your soul story can be reclusive. You search for it. Your professional life thrives when you search for and use your soul story.

Part 2: O Is for Overcoming—You use it. Your professional life thrives when you use your soul story to overcome obstacles.

Part 3: U Is for Unifying—You develop it. Your professional life thrives when you develop your soul story in unity and community with others.

Part 4: L Is for Living—Your soul story reveals a life of contribution. You live it. Your professional life thrives when you live your soul story today to build your legacy for tomorrow.

To help your reflection throughout the book, I present My Soul Story spaces or margins, designed as a place to write down your thoughts and your responses, and examine your professional responsibility to help others flourish. Use the spaces as you deem fit for your personality and style. The chapters are reasonably brief and provide space for you to take notes and be more reflective as you read, if you so choose.

Despite all my efforts over the years to connect to my soul story and bring the best of who I am to each professional day, I have been overcome by tragedy. I have felt shallow, self-obsessed, insecure, isolated, and worse. I have been temporarily lost, hardened, and exhausted in my daily job and in the work life I have chosen. I have been overwhelmed

Did you choose our profession? Or, did our profession choose you? Briefly explain your response.

_____

_____

_____

_____

_____

_____

_____

_____

_____

_____

_____

_____

_____

_____

_____

_____

_____

_____

_____

_____

_____

_____

_____

_____

_____

_____

at times by life events. Off and on, I have lost contact with the joyful part of my soul story.

And so it is for you too. Sooner or later, the world of your professional life will experience difficulty; stretch you beyond your limits; pull you into moments of deep sadness, stress, pain, and suffering; and cause you to emotionally disconnect with your students and colleagues.

Yet it is in such stressful moments you realize you cannot abandon our profession, as it is so much more than your job. This profession is your *vocation*. What matters then is the quality of the soul story you have searched for, constructed, used, modeled, and enjoyed with others over time.

♥ MY SOUL STORY

It is my hope that *SOUL!* will be both affirming and challenging as your teaching and leading life unfolds. No matter where you may be in the wonderful journey of this remarkably rewarding and sometimes maddeningly frustrating profession, I hope this book will touch the story of *your* life and help you find your *voice for good* and fulfillment in the professional life you have chosen.

Or, did it choose you?

Join me, and let's take our soul story journey together!

PART 1

DEVELOPING YOUR
SOUL STORY

S

Is for Searching

Essential Soul Story Question: Your soul story can be reclusive. Are you searching for it?

The soul is the piece of your consciousness that has moral worth and bears moral responsibility. . . . Mostly, what the soul does is yearn. If the heart yearns for fusion with others, the soul yearns for fusion with the good.

—David Brooks

Your professional life thrives when you *search for and connect to* your soul story.

In part 1 of this book, you begin the search for your professional soul story. As I prepared to write *SOUL!* and spent more than a year in research, I discovered a common theme among everything I read across all authors regarding how to live a more meaningful and fulfilled professional life. It was overwhelmingly consistent, despite authors' diverse professional fields: psychologists, religious scholars, medical doctors, philosophers, educators, and researchers. The theme for part 1 and the entire book is this:

For your professional life to fulfill its full potential and promise, your life story becomes one of contribution to others, and not merely achievement to self.

In chapter 1, you consider moments in which your soul story often finds you and forces you to respond to the question, "Now what?" How do you and I become more intentional about staying connected to and knowing our soul story, which can indeed be reclusive?

In chapter 2, you dive into the definition of a soul story. How do you name it, and how do you differentiate between the *heartprint* and the *soul story* of your professional life?

In chapter 3, you come face to face with one of the most daunting aspects of our profession. We are to act *in loco parentis.* What a burden this is. It is a moral imperative, an unwritten code of trust between parent and teacher. By owning and knowing your soul story, you ensure this trust is rarely broken.

When we search for our soul story, we reflect on it and relentlessly pursue it. But to what end? Who and what will be the beneficiaries of our professional soul story pursuit? This question is partially answered in chapter 4.

You may or may not be familiar with the construct of a first and second mountain climb. Chapter 5 reveals the search for a second mountain professional life, as our soul story becomes *a story of contribution.*

Chapter 6 reveals a soul story secret for your professional life—compassion. The neuroscience about compassion is inescapable: no compassion, no soul. Without it, our professional life falls far short of its promise. Compassion is a challenging aspect of our work in our profession of emotional labor.

Finally, our part 1 soul story search ends in chapter 7 by looking at how to listen to the trusted voices that touch *your* soul story and then respond accordingly.

Searching to find, connect with, and live your soul story is just the beginning. Take your time, and know that each chapter propels you toward a more soul-filled professional life. Let it begin!

The Soul Asks, "Now What?"

S   O   U   L

Don't ask what the world needs. Ask what makes you come
alive, and go do it. Because what the world needs is people who
have come alive.

—Howard Thurman

Sometimes your soul story comes searching for you when you least expect it. The following is adapted from a blog I posted in the fall of 2018.[6]

It was one of those wonderful mid-fall afternoons early in a new school season as I walked to my car, crossing the quad of the university campus. Tree leaves were just starting to change color, and the air had that rare "higher temperatures than normal with crispness" smell.

I took off my suit jacket as I approached my car with the intense feeling that I had done this very act of *taking off my suit jacket and getting into the car* many times before. I was aware that these moments often left me feeling empty and wanting more. I knew it was a soul story moment, but I was having a hard time defining it.

It was a feeling similar to the one you sense right after spending hours with friends and family, saying goodbye, going on your way, but feeling a bit homesick for them in the wash of the aftermath.

This nostalgia for friends, family, and colleagues was lingering in my brain. You know, thinking, "Oh, just one more moment with them would be nice. Maybe I should send a text telling them I miss them already. Or better yet, send an email or Instagram photo letting them know how much they mean to me."

I wanted to hold on to the moment, as if letting go would leave me feeling lonely again. I wanted that *I belong* feeling: "I am connected with them, and they with me." And yet, there I was, arm out the window, driving off the campus. Life moves us forward, time does not stand still, and we stubbornly follow.

I could not escape how, as after other soul-filled events like this, I was once again left with the discomfort of "Now what?"

In reality, this particular event had that eerily familiar feeling of a wedding or a retirement party or a twenty-fifth wedding anniversary celebration. It was similar to an event in which family and friends, personal and professional, gather together to toast and celebrate the honoree or honorees. There is a reception and a luncheon, an agenda of speakers using both humor and story to mask feelings of disquiet about next steps to take once the bridge is crossed, and then the event is over and the chairs get folded up.

These events bring people together from all walks of life. People who perhaps saw each other yesterday or years ago, but no matter the time gap, hugs go all around. "It is *so* good to see you," we say. And we mean it. There is not only joy but also a little bit of caution in our eyes. A note of vulnerability. *Bridge moment* events like these always cause a stop to the madness of our hectic pace, from the noise, and the stuff of daily life. We take a forced time-out. We all sit and wonder, "Now what?"

You got your first teaching job—*now what?*

You are getting married—*now what?*

You are retiring—*now what?*

You are graduating high school or college—*now what?*

You are celebrating the life of a family member or friend—*now what?*

The *now what?* question is not just for the person or persons being honored at the event; it is for you and me too. Ending and beginning timeline moments in life do that to us. It seems to me that when we are connected to our soul story, we ask and actively answer the big and small *now what?* questions our entire lives.

MY SOUL STORY 💙

Consider a *now what?* moment you have faced in this or in past school seasons. Describe the event, and your subsequent actions.

_____

_____

_____

_____

_____

_____

_____

_____

_____

_____

_____

And then there are the really big transition moments. The soul story–shattering moments. Moments you often do not control. These are the ones that may cause you to change the direction of your personal life course and take action. They force you to dive deeper into the window of your soul story and again ask, "Now what?" The event I had just attended was the type that causes a soulful reality to surface in our brains and connect more deeply. We cannot control these events, but we can control our responses to the events.

And that is exactly how I was feeling as I took off my suit coat, got into my rental car, and left that beautiful Virginia campus in the late afternoon of September 29, 2018.

Friends and family, both professional and personal, had gathered together, not for a wedding or a retirement or a twenty-fifth anniversary but for a *celebration of life* for one of God's better angels indeed: Rebecca Burnette DuFour.

In the PLC at Work community, Becky was an educational rock star. In her family life and in every friendship, she was a beacon of grace. She had a way of leaning into you and demonstrating authentic care for you like no other colleague, friend, or family member you had known. Her wit, her calm, her commitment, her care, her compassion, her kindness, and her confidence were always on display for everyone to receive and observe. Becky exemplified *living with your soul story* on full display.

Becky taught us to see others without judging them. She had this remarkable ability to see inside of each person, listen to his or her concerns, and provide measured and sage advice about how to move forward. As attested by her Boones Mill Elementary School teacher colleagues that day, Becky was an inspiring teacher and principal, and they were the beneficiaries of her grace and commitment.

She was the type of person whose presence in your life increased your desire to respond with your own personal and *positive* commitment to pursue your moral good. To be better.

MY SOUL STORY 💜

Name a colleague or friend who best represents a Becky DuFour in your life.

Describe how that person has helped you be a healthier professional and contribute to the good in others, students or colleagues, even on your worst days.

New York Times best-selling author David Brooks reminds us, "The odd thing about the soul is that while it is powerful and resilient, it is also reclusive."[7] It does not always search for you. Sometimes, you need to search for and rely on it.

Sometimes it is in these moments when a close friend and colleague dies suddenly and completely unexpectedly that we and our soul story fuse together and a more intentional connection begins, or reconnects. We get a slap in the face to wake us from our settled selves.

We realize our soul story—that piece of us that yearns for moral good and moral responsibility—also yearns for us to sit up and notice.

Sometimes our "noticing" occurs during a really big event such as the coronavirus pandemic and all the parts of its unyielding and cruel interruptions. Sometimes we notice when there is a bright light shining on the social and racial suffering and injustices faced by so many of our colleagues, family members, and friends.

At other times, it requires much less. We don't need a family member, a friend, or a colleague to die unexpectedly or our job to be thrown into chaos. Maybe we notice a friend's divorce or maybe an addiction. Maybe it's just a struggle to feel confident at work. But we do need to first become *aware*.

So we become still, we quiet the noise of our lives (see chapter 21 on quietude, page 173), we seek to understand our emotions, and then we *take the right action* of contribution for *the good* as our soul story connection is revealed and unfolds.

Like Becky, you don't always get to name the end of your soul story, but you can build your soul story into each day as if the lives of your students and colleagues depended on it. In many ways, students' well-being has been entrusted to us and does depend on us.

What does that mean for you and me?

Consider Becky's soul story of contribution. Becky lived every day with less worry and fear than most, a lot less anger, a little less narrow-mindedness, and a little less self-importance, regardless of often difficult circumstances surrounding her life. Becky seemed to just stand taller, listen just a bit better, hold off her own judgments of others, and ask for and receive more grace than others—this was how her soul story contributed to her professional life story.

"Does my soul story matter?" you may ask.

It does matter, and we each have different platforms for connecting to and contributing to others.

Your platform as an educator is *yours*. Your soul story is uniquely yours, and you own it. No one else does. Whether you are a preK, elementary school, middle school, high school, or college educator, or a rural, urban, or suburban teacher and leader, your colleagues and your students—those who are closest to your actions and reactions—are hoping to get the best version of you, that your soul story has to offer, every day.

Take a moment to name what *you do* as an educational professional. What is the current platform you have been given for using the soul story of your professional life?

MY SOUL STORY ♥

Becky DuFour's platform changed significantly from her Boones Mill Elementary School days in Virginia. She spoke to more than twenty-five thousand educators a year, engaging them in discussions around the ideals and central tenets of the PLC at Work process.

Maybe, like those in attendance at the celebration-of-life event for Becky, you were the beneficiary of her words and moved by her inspiring message and life. Despite the celebrity, nothing about Becky's soul story changed. She treated everyone she met with the same dignity, care, humor, and compassion as she did her closest colleagues and community friends during her years at Boones Mill Elementary School.

I have promised myself to use Becky's inspiration to better inform my future *now what?* responses, and to better connect to the soul story of my professional life. I will not just drive away in my car, off that college campus, and keep living numb to the same tired and distant soul story. I can do better than let my professional soul story connections once again become reclusive.

What is the final lesson I take from the honor of knowing and being in Becky's life path?

When we lose the gift of someone who easily and positively brought us into a better version of ourselves, the least we can do is honor that person by choosing to live a good and meaningful life as we share and live

What grade level or levels do you teach and lead? Name the title of the role you serve in your school, district, or university. Why did you choose this specific grade band to teach and lead?

_____

_____

_____

_____

_____

Do you work in a more rural, urban, or suburban setting, or a mix? How did you choose your current community setting?

_____

_____

_____

_____

_____

Using your current platform, like Becky, how do you bring the best version of yourself to your profession each day?

_____

_____

_____

_____

_____

_____

our personal soul story. And so we charge forward to the next *now what?* moments waiting just down the road, past the next ending sure to come, and then on to a new beginning on the timeline of our professional life.

A Perfect Pair: Heart and Soul

 O   U   L

Claiming my heart and soul, taking away the stress of this day.
—RoseAnn V. Shawiak, "Claiming My Heart and Soul"[8]

From the moment I walked onto that Greyhound bus until ten months later, when I walked into my Aunt Dottie's house on 41st Street in Rock Island, Illinois, it had not occurred to my seven-year-old brain that I had been homeless. From my perspective, I had been on a ten-month vacation. Leaving my home in Chicago in January to travel with my mother and brother to the warmer climate and a motel room in Tucson, Arizona, had seemed fine with me.

Only it wasn't so fine. I wasn't on vacation. It was 1958, my parents had divorced, and I was supposed to be in second grade somewhere. Then the summer came and went in that tiny Tucson motel room, and third grade was about to begin—but not for me. Through a series of events, by late October, I arrived on the doorstep of my mother's sister, Aunt Dottie, in Rock Island, Illinois. My dad had remarried, and there just was no room for me in his blended family at that time.

Only years later, at a reunion event for my aunt's side of the family, I realized some of my relatives did not know I was an actual member of our family tree. I was casually introduced as my aunt's "foster child" by a relative, and I immediately felt like an outsider. I bristled at that phrase, yet when I was growing up, that is precisely what I was—an outsider to my family.

In the end, that home on 41st Street became the place where my *heart and soul* journey would begin, literally and figuratively. One of my first and favorite memories is sitting on an old piano bench to the right of my Uncle Al as he taught me the top hand to a famous Hoagy Carmichael song. It is a duet that many young piano players know quite well.

Heart and *soul*: How are
the two words the same or different for you? What do *heart* and *soul*
mean to you as an educator when
you hear or read them together?

_____
_____
_____
_____
_____
_____
_____
_____
_____
_____
_____
_____
_____
_____
_____
_____
_____
_____

The top hand has a familiar "Chopsticks" feel to it, and I often confused the two.

If you can't quite capture the tune in your head, check out a fun YouTube video where you *hear and see*, on a *really* large piano, the top (right hand) and bottom (left hand) parts my uncle taught me more than sixty years ago (http://bit.ly/2S06lxK). Carmichael wrote the music, but Frank Loesser supplied the words a few years later.[9] What was the new song title?

"Heart and Soul."

The words are indeed a famous pair. A *heart and soul* search on Amazon will yield more than 650 songs, books, poems, cards, and the like. iTunes reveals more than one hundred artists, like Huey Lewis, Otis Redding, the Cleftones, T'Pau, Kenny G, and more. *Heart and soul* moves across many musical genres: gospel, soul, country, rhythm and blues, alternative, and rock and roll. There is a *heart and soul* station on satellite radio as well.

A simple google of news stories on any random day will yield more than 150 headlines with the words *heart and soul*.

In short, the phrase *heart and soul* is ubiquitous. The words are intricately linked, forming an idiom, a phrase that takes on its own meaning: heart *and* soul.

When I was writing and researching about the *heartprint* of our professional life for *HEART!*, it wasn't difficult to notice the two words often tied together.

Author David Brooks describes our soul as "the piece of your consciousness that has moral worth and bears moral responsibility."[10] And he reminds us that "what the soul mostly does is yearn. . . ."[11]

Take a moment to reflect on your understanding of the differences between the words *heart* and *soul*.

 # MY SOUL STORY

Our professional heartprint longs for relationships with others, for building our capacity to connect to others' happiness or emptiness. In *HEART!*, I defined your professional heartprint as "the distinctive impression and marked impact your heart leaves on others."[12]

Yet our professional soul story yearns for more. It reveals the seat of our deepest thoughts and emotions. It is our essence and our purpose for creating a heartprint on others. It connects us to the good we are expected to do and subsequently create in others.

Thus, for the purposes of this book, I define your professional soul story as *the pursuit of your moral good in order to create good in others.*

In 1958, my Uncle Al worked two jobs. During the day, he worked at the Williams/White Steel Foundry across the street, and on weekends, he worked odd jobs to help pay the bills. A blue-collar World War II vet, Uncle Al was the soul of that house—he was a man dedicated to fusion with the good, wanting nothing but to create joy in those around him.

He loved to rock that beat-up piano with blues, soul, jazz, gospel, and something he called "boogie-woogie." And he could not read a single note! Uncle Al had an incredible ability to play any song by ear. He was kind and gentle by nature. It was just the essence of who he was—he was the soul story tone-setter of that home on 41st Street. More important, he was the first male adult in my young life who gave me unconditional affirmation. He helped jump-start my soul story and modeled for me how to be good and do good for others.

Aunt Dottie was the heart to Uncle Al's soul. She left her heartprint everywhere. As RoseAnn Shawiak mentions in the epigraph to this chapter, Aunt Dottie took away my seven-year-old stress of the day, claiming my heart and soul with a nurturing fusion to be with others. She removed my isolation and my sense of wanting to just be invisible and withdrawn.

I landed on my aunt's doorstep as a result of broken family relationships, neglect, poverty, and rough circumstances. I was a mess. I was shy, clumsy, illiterate for my age, and suffering from various health issues, and I had a severe loss of self-worth. Yet, I was in some ways no different from and perhaps in other ways better off than many other students who show up to school and enter into our professional path.

Sometimes, the problems of a child's home can be immediately obvious; more often than not, though, they can be well hidden from the day-to-day life of the school. Students are hungry, suffering from homelessness or abuse, and marginalized by others in the greater community or, worse, marginalized by the social constructs in our school community (learn more about these issues in chapter 4, page 23).

What are some highlights or lowlights from your years in elementary school? What do you most remember about how those moments and memories as a child began to forge who you are today as an educator?

_____

_____

_____

_____

_____

_____

_____

_____

_____

_____

_____

_____

_____

_____

_____

_____

_____

_____

_____

We should not forget: when we signed up for our profession, whether as public or private school educators, we tacitly agreed to act *in loco parentis*.[13] By joining our profession, we agreed to develop a soul story, which would bear the moral responsibility to treat every preK–12 student as if he or she were our own child. Thankfully, my little about-to-be-eight-year-old self ran into just such a teacher—a teacher who would treat me as if I was her own child.

So, I will leave this chapter with a question for you: Can you remember your elementary school days? Are there any highlights or lowlights you would like to share?

I don't remember a lot from that time of my life, but I do remember that upright piano crammed into that tiny room just off the kitchen. And I do remember sitting in the kitchen with Aunt Dottie and Mrs. Armstrong for a life-changing conversation during which I sat quietly.

♥ MY SOUL STORY

Mrs. Armstrong, as you will discover in the next chapter, was one of those silent heroes. She did so many things to help so many children, and none of it made the papers, or Instagram, or Facebook Live, or Twitch, or Twitter. In unison with Aunt Dottie, she worked to set me onto a path that changed my lifetime of learning. Mrs. Armstrong was a teacher, I suspect, a lot like you.

3

In Loco Parentis

 S   O   U   L

> *So much of America's tragic and costly failure to care for all its children stems from our tendency to distinguish between our own children and other people's children—as if justice were divisible.*
> —Marian Wright Edelman

Why do you need to *know your soul story as your professional seasons unfold?* This type of question feels deep, does it not? Most days, I am just trying to keep up with the day-to-day grind of my work life. How about you?

In the end, though, when most school seasons are complete, how well we are keeping up is how we are measured—measured not by others but by the positive impact we have (or don't have) on our students.

MY SOUL STORY

I like this My Soul Story activity because it forces you out of deficit thinking as you defend your rating. Instead of looking only at your deficits (the gap between you and a rating of 10), you end up illustrating much of your incredible work as a professional that *justifies* your current rating.

According to *Merriam-Webster, in loco parentis* is Latin for "in the place of a parent."[14] Exactly! We chose a profession that expects us to live the moral

Rank your current *positive impact* on students (from your perspective) on a scale of 1 to 10, with 1 being no positive impact and 10 being an awesome positive impact. Got a number in mind?

Answer this question: Why didn't you give yourself a *lower* ranking?

_____
_____
_____
_____
_____
_____
_____
_____
_____

imperative of acting responsibly *as if* we were in the place of the parent for each child.

That feels like a lot of responsibility. And, I am positive that during my first years as a high school mathematics teacher in my early twenties, acting as the parent of fourteen- to eighteen-year-olds was not what I had envisioned as part of my work-life responsibility.

During those Stillman Valley, Illinois, years, my annual teaching salary was so low I needed to take on a few "side hustles," as my colleague Bill Ferriter likes to say. So, to make some extra money, every morning, I drove a bus route for the district. This route included K–12 children dispersed over a wide expanse of very rural northern Illinois landscapes, with often dangerous conditions in the winter, our famous black ice sitting under the snow.

Parents watched their children get on that bus every day and trusted me to drive them to school with the same care, concern, and safety as they would. *In loco parentis.*

I would park the bus in the circle drive, run in, and teach my first-hour class to a group of thirty eager (mostly eager, and often tired) freshman algebra 1 students, and their parents trusted me to teach accurately, teach with care, and inspire my students to learn. *In loco parentis.*

In the winter, I would finish my teaching day, run to the gym, and coach the sophomore boys' basketball team. And those parents expected me to teach accurately, develop skills, create a positive culture of a team, win games, and play with their children, just as *they* would. *In loco parentis.*

I would create contest materials and coach our mathematics team on Saturdays and after school during my nonathletic coaching seasons. And those parents wanted me to care about developing their children's mathematics skills and prepare them for their college-bound opportunities in mathematics and science, just as *they* would. *In loco parentis.*

I had students with special education needs and English learners (ELs) in my classroom. And those parents expected me to understand their children's needs and care about helping them learn, just as *they* would. *In loco parentis.*

I had students who were homeless, living with other families, and perhaps suffering from trauma. Their parents or guardians, for so many reasons, were absent from their lives, and yet I had a moral imperative to treat their children (my students) as if they were my own children. *In loco parentis.*

Just like other helping professions, such as health care, our profession is not for everyone. It takes a certain willingness to embrace these and many more *in loco parentis* challenges, such as remote or blended student learning. It takes a special person to teach and lead in our profession.

Our profession is about *who you are becoming*, not just *what you do* for a living.

MY SOUL STORY 🩶

There is a special hard and soft wiring in your soul story that pushes you to embrace the moral responsibility to treat your students as if they were your own children.

The moment you emotionally disconnect from your teaching work life and just put in your time each day (see chapter 13, page 101), the disadvantaged child in the back of the class will suffer irreparable harm.

Let me explain.

Recall my Aunt Dottie's home on 41st Street in Rock Island, Illinois. Now imagine you are the third-grade teacher at the local elementary school five blocks from the house. It is late October, and here I come.

I enter your classroom on a gloomy late-fall day and show you a slip of paper that says I am a new student in your class. You think, "Great, just what I need right now, another student! Why didn't the office warn me he was coming?"

You need to get the day started, however, so you tell me to take a seat in the back of the room. I do. The desks are in rows (it is 1958, remember), and the open seat is in the far-left corner of the classroom.

Your day ends and is mostly uneventful, and now you head to the office to find out more about this new kid, a seven-year-old named Timothy Kanold, who is living in Dorothy Benoit's house just down the street. Then you get the bad news.

He has not been in school since the school year started, so he needs to get caught up. You think, "Okay,

Describe two or three current teaching and leading activities in which parents trust you to act *in loco parentis*.

_____

_____

_____

_____

_____

_____

_____

_____

_____

_____

_____

_____

_____

_____

_____

_____

_____

_____

_____

_____

that's about three months, but we can do this *if* he will work hard." Then you receive even worse news.

Apparently, he was not in school all of 1958, so he also missed the last five months of second grade. His parents are divorced, he is living with his mother's sister, and he is way behind in all reading and mathematics skills. Good luck. *In loco parentis.*

This was the news Mrs. Armstrong, my third-grade teacher, received when I became part of her class and instantly part of her professional life. As the weeks of November unfolded, I became one of those easily lost and slightly irritating students. I displayed a type of passive disobedience in her classroom.

You know the type of student I mean—the student who is well behaved, causes no discipline problems, demonstrates no aggressive behavior, and sits quietly. This student rarely pays attention, doesn't do any work in class, and just sort of checks out. In a class of thirty-four students, this particular student can easily get lost in the shuffle of the daily lessons and never chooses to read aloud publicly. And when it comes time to take a test, he or she is not able to do much of it with any proficiency but is polite when turning in a mostly blank set of answers or an incomplete writing response.

Right before Thanksgiving, Mrs. Armstrong, acting *in loco parentis*, came home with me to speak to my Aunt Dottie. To her credit, she was doing what she thought was best for me. If I were her child, she told my aunt, she would either have me sent immediately to second grade and fall a year behind or send me to the school for "slow children" (although back then she used a much harsher term).

Please keep in mind it was 1958. This was well before the Individuals with Disabilities Education Act (IDEA)[15] and the modern-day expectations for how we engage and include students with special needs. Mrs. Armstrong cited the facts to my aunt: I was slow to learn and almost seven months behind in the curriculum. I did not pay attention in class; I often did not respond to questions I was being asked; I could barely read; I could not write my name; and I seemed either lazy or just disinterested in the student work assigned.

And she was correct. These were all behaviors I was exhibiting. She was not exaggerating. I can still remember with great clarity sitting at the breakfast table in our small kitchen and watching my aunt, waiting for her response to Mrs. Armstrong. Although I could not know it then, *in loco parentis* was about to explode.

MY SOUL STORY ♥

Stop for a moment in the story, and imagine my second-grade self in your classroom. What would be your recommendation to my Aunt Dottie?

To Mrs. Armstrong's credit, she took the time to come to our house and consult with my aunt. What Mrs. Armstrong did not know, however, was my backstory or the passion my aunt had for me as her nephew. My aunt's concern for my well-being was just the same as her passion for her own children. In her eyes, I was like her son. *In loco parentis.*

Aunt Dottie was forceful and clear. I was not moving out of that elementary school. Moving me back a grade was also not an option. I could learn, and I would learn. I was a good child and well behaved in her home. She would do whatever was necessary to give me extra work at home to help me catch up. Together, she and Mrs. Armstrong would act *in loco parentis* on my behalf.

And their first act together was to put me through a hearing screening. Back then, at least in Illinois, hearing screenings at schools were not quite as common. My aunt took me to a doctor, had my hearing tested, and sure enough, I had been born completely deaf in my right ear. And it was not repairable. No one had known. Not even me.

Now, thinking back on my third-grade classroom seat assignment, I realize I had inadvertently been placed in a really bad place: in the far back left of the room. Mrs. Armstrong immediately moved me to the front right of the classroom. Instant participation! I became a lot smarter very quickly once Mrs. Armstrong moved me to a place in the classroom where I could see better and for sure hear what was going on.

Aunt Dottie relentlessly monitored my practice to catch up on what I did not know (which was vast). This happened every day after school and every Saturday morning. Together, Aunt Dottie and Mrs. Armstrong teamed up on me and acted *in loco parentis* and in my best interest. From my perspective, it was a long, slow slog. I just wanted to go outside and play catch. But by the next summer, I was reasonably ready for fourth grade.

Who needs you to lean into them *right now*? What actions can you take to lean into and discover the full story of a student who struggles in your class?

_____

_____

_____

_____

_____

_____

_____

_____

_____

_____

_____

_____

_____

_____

_____

_____

_____

_____

_____

_____

_____

_____

_____

Between their helping me hear what was taking place and their giving me additional time to learn essential skills I did not yet know, they chose to not select and sort me out or cast me off. They did not blame me and say it was my fault that I wasn't learning. They gave me the figurative intervention box of support to stand on and helped me over that second- and third-grade bar for the guaranteed and viable curriculum performance expectations.

On the surface, it might not seem like they did very much at the time. Who can predict what is to become of a third-grade child? There is always more to the story, far beyond our reach as teachers. And yet, sometimes, like Mrs. Armstrong, you become the teacher who starts a student on his or her way to a successful story. And that does not happen without intention to our theme in part 1: *your soul story becomes a story of contribution.*

Most of the time, that story unfolds one child at a time.

 # MY SOUL STORY

Think of three students who need you to lean into them *right now*, discover their backstory, and then step forward to make a contribution of support. Be sure not to blame or shame them for their current performance.

Finally, ask yourself, "What was going on in the lives of those two women, neither one of them my parent, that made them want to act on my behalf? Why did they treat me as if I were their own child? Why did they choose to act *in loco parentis*?" Why do *you* choose to act *in loco parentis*?

That answer lies in understanding the ultimate mission of why we chose our profession and our willingness to seek social justice and evidence of successful learning for each child or teenager who crosses our path, regardless of his or her race, ethnicity, language needs, gender, sexual orientation, faith, or disability different from our own.

That is next.

In the Name of Social Justice

  S   O   U   L

Power at its best is love implementing the demands of justice,
and justice at its best is power correcting everything that stands
against love.

—Martin Luther King Jr.

What do the words *social justice* mean to you? Imagine you had to share evidence that your classroom, your school, or your program is in pursuit of social justice; what would you show? How do the words *social justice* apply to our profession?

The *Oxford Reference Dictionary* provides a clue to the meaning of *social justice*, defining it as "the objective of creating a fair and equal society in which each individual matters, their rights are recognized and protected, and decisions are made in ways that are fair and honest."[16]

Social justice in education is about treating all students equitably so they feel safe and secure—physically, emotionally, and psychologically. Social justice actions start with the access and opportunity decisions we make to ensure the same well-rounded K–12 education, and end with a pedagogy that is respectful and culturally sensitive and provides intensive, on-task, relevant, and successful learning opportunities for all students.

Our profession demands a lot from us. Can we win with and for each student who enters our career path? Can we be more powerful than the devastating effects on students for knowing a language our society has deemed not as valid as English, or other forms of bias and abuse due merely to the color of their skin, their ethnicity, their language, their gender identity, or their sexual orientation? Perhaps not always, but it doesn't mean we should not try. Take a moment to complete the My Soul Story prompt on page 24.

Social justice is:

_____
_____
_____
_____
_____
_____
_____
_____
_____
_____
_____

The evidence of social justice in my classroom (remote learning or otherwise), school, or program is:

_____
_____
_____
_____
_____
_____
_____
_____
_____
_____
_____
_____
_____

 # MY SOUL STORY

And then try once again. But try *what?*

I have often wondered what was going on in my soul story development that caused me to not give up on Juan Gonzalez (not his real name), when in some ways he had already given up on himself.

Juan was mad at me and refused to look at me during my Spanish-speaking, fourth-period algebra 1 class. He hadn't liked me very much as his coach either over the past two weeks. He sat on the end of the bench for our sophomore boys' basketball team, but not because of his talent. He and I were in what I often called a tough-minded compassion moment, and I was determined to care enough about him to not give up.

We definitely had our differences. I was thirty-one and White. He was fifteen and Latino. I had 168 students; I coached two sports, had a young family, and taught two night classes during the week to supplement my teaching income. I spoke very little Spanish.

Juan spoke very little English, so words between the two of us often got lost in translation. He lived in our district, in a shared bedroom at his older sister's house on the high-poverty side of West Chicago, close to the high school where I worked. I had never met his parents. He had no phone at home, and he had hand-me-down clothes.

I had fought for his placement in my algebra 1 class, because as a player on my team, I knew he could do the work. I could *see* his talent and look past his attitude. At the time, his counselor told me Juan didn't belong in my class. He had failed basic mathematics (a discriminatory, below-level class offered mostly to our minority students back then) as a freshman; how could he possibly pass an algebra class? I could just hear the counselor saying, "I told you so."

My story with Juan is, of course, not unique. Over the years, many students just like Juan, of all ages (from prekindergarten to twelfth grade), pass through our professional life. We ask, "What does it mean to act *in loco parentis* with the Juans in our professional life?"

Ronald F. Ferguson is an adjunct lecturer at the Harvard Kennedy School. He addresses a unique predicament facing boys and young men of color (BYMOC) in a May 2016 research report to the Urban Institute, *Aiming Higher Together: Strategizing Better Educational Outcomes for Boys and Young Men of Color*:

> There is a tangled web of home, school, peer-group, and societal factors that place BYMOC *from every socioeconomic level* at risk for underperformance in school and life . . . a complex web of circumstances for which no individual is to blame and that no one person can unravel.[17]

Thankfully, Ferguson provides six specific soul story strategies to support young men of color in our schools.[18] The words in italics are my response to Ferguson's suggestions.

1. Teachers and administrators understand the key principles of high-quality instruction for all students and work hard to master and apply them. *Students must be engaged!*
2. Educators approach quality teaching as a moral obligation to each student. *See each student, and treat him or her as if he or she were your own child.*
3. Teachers are warm yet demanding with students, adapting their models and procedures to fit students' needs. *Be tough and loving, provide a safety net, and respect students' cultural heritage.*
4. Teachers deliver personalized, respectful, culturally sensitive, and intensive time-on-task learning opportunities to all students. *Provide timely, formative feedback every day that communicates to the child, "I have high expectations for you, I value you, and I will help you get there."*
5. Educators use data from regular student assessments to drive instructional decisions. *Use student learning data to inform and focus next steps for continued student support and learning at every collaborative meeting!*
6. Many students receive tutoring, with heavy doses for students who need it the most. *Provide tutoring that is targeted by student and by standard, that is required and provided at school, and that is just in time and designed to support successful student work during class time.*

MY SOUL STORY ♥

Review the suggested strategies from Ron Ferguson. Work with a colleague to record the depth at which these factors currently exist in your teaching response to students of color.

_____

_____

_____

_____

_____

_____

_____

_____

_____

_____

_____

When the river of our teaching life crosses the path of someone like Juan, someone who does not look or speak like us, we make soul story decisions. In this case, I had to ask myself, "Do I care for Juan enough to demand the same for him as I would for any of my other students, or even my own children? Is social justice something to which I give lip service, or is it something I take action on? Can I use my power as a teacher and a coach to care for this young man enough to correct the forces that stand against him? And can I, as a teacher and coach, listen to and connect to the heart of an angry, drifting student?"

Ferguson's suggestions bring me back to Juan—my student, my player, the thorn in my side. What to do about him? When he showed up to my algebra 1 class the next day, he turned in his basketball uniform. He was quitting the team. And then, as class was about to start, he walked out and walked off campus.

Gone.

I had a dilemma, right? I had every right to be mad at him, kick him off the basketball team, and fail him in my class. *Being right is different from doing the right thing.* When you connect to your soul story, it is never about being right. It is not about you. It is about doing the right thing for others. I needed to discover Juan's full story.

So, I recruited our Spanish-speaking guidance counselor during lunchtime, and together, we drove to Juan's sister's house. Juan wasn't there, but his sister informed us of the reason he lived with her. His parents' house had burned down earlier in the school year, and they had returned to Mexico with his younger brother.

I was his coach and his teacher, and I had no idea. I gave Juan's sister his basketball uniform and begged her to bring him to the school gym at the end of practice later that day. Using his sister as an interpreter, he and I talked for more than an hour. At one point, he asked why I cared. What was the big deal? I told him he was the big deal.

At the time, I did not know I was acting as a power in his life; and as Martin Luther King Jr. stated in the opening epigraph, "Justice at its best is power correcting everything that stands against love."[19] Juan needed me, at that moment, to be a power in his life who acted out of love.

And sometimes, tough-minded love with built-in compassion is the best answer.

The result was his reinstatement to the basketball team. A social worker, another teacher (Juan's English teacher), and I agreed to meet with him and an EL teacher in my room three days per week during his lunchtime until he got caught up on his work, with the expectation that he complete all assignments and miss no more tests or basketball practices. I made him sign a contract. I signed it too. *In loco parentis.*

Four weeks later, he passed my algebra class and played as my starting point guard against Glenbard South. He scored twelve points and hugged me after the game. A hug!

Small victories, indeed.

A colleague and reviewer for this book, Gina Rivera, indicated the first time she met me, I presented a vibe of being a *warm demander*. According to MacArthur Award winner Lisa Delpit, warm demanders are teachers who "expect a great deal of their students, convince them of their own brilliance, and help them to reach their potential in a disciplined and structured environment."[20]

I had not previously heard the phrase *warm demander*, much less in the context of an equity-centered approach to our work. Yet my colleague was right. Those two words summarized my teaching and coaching style perfectly. How about you? Are you a warm demander?

MY SOUL STORY 🩶

Not all attempts to positively influence my students were as successful as my interactions with Juan. I had 158 students in my classes, and only so much time and so many resources to give. There were too few victories during my West Chicago teaching days. But there were victories. And they kept me inspired in my work each day.

Who, then, are the *beneficiaries* of our efforts to reform school cultures that perpetuate social injustice? As we use our soul story to combat the powerful pull of systemic poverty, bias, and discrimination on our students and colleagues, *everyone* benefits.

We can find one of the best exemplars of a systemic call for social justice in the voice and actions of my PLC at Work colleague and author Luis Cruz. Luis is the former principal of Baldwin Park High School located in Los Angeles, California. He has been a teacher and administrator at the elementary, middle, and high

Name a student you know with a social justice story of struggle. How can you help contribute to his or her course correction by becoming a warm demander, using love, while also maintaining high expectations and standards for the quality of his or her work?

_____

_____

_____

_____

_____

_____

_____

_____

_____

_____

_____

_____

_____

_____

_____

_____

_____

_____

_____

_____

school levels and coauthored the 2019 best-selling book *Time for Change: Four Essential Skills for Transformational School and District Leaders* with Anthony Muhammad.[21]

Luis has achieved quite a bit of success as a school teacher and leader, yet this success does not fully reveal the soul story of *who he is*. His entire educational career, he has been a warrior for the mission and vision of a social justice culture in every school his life has touched.

In 2007, Luis led a collective effort to secure a $250,000 grant for Baldwin Park High School from the California Academic Partnership Program for the purpose of creating a more equitable and effective organization. Three years later, in 2010, Luis and a committee of teacher leaders at Baldwin Park subsequently received California's prestigious Golden Bell Award from the California School Boards Association for significantly closing the achievement gap between the general student population and students learning English as a second language.

His commitment to social justice began long before 2007, but it was galvanized and sharpened at Baldwin Park. When I interviewed Luis about the role our soul story plays in our professional life, he told me:

> I have always had a heart or a certain zest and a passion for my work. During my college days at Cal State Fullerton, sociology professor Dr. Isaac Cardenas, the chair of the Chicano Studies Department, invited me to come and speak to some high school kids at the local community college. I thought it would be a conversation about going to college with about five to ten students. It ended up becoming an onstage event in front of 120 students.

> They had faces that looked just like mine, and they were staring at me. My knees were buckling, unsure what to say exactly. So I started to tell them my growing-up soul story and how and why I made it to Cal State. I noticed they were riveted. I was just like them. They started laughing and listening, and there was a sense of hope and fear and future in the room.[22]

When Luis finished telling me this, he mentioned to me sometimes others (in this case, his professor) see your talent before you do. His professor knew Luis could *speak* to those students.

Luis was a *teacher*.

He went on to say:

> I quickly realized my story was not unique to me. They too were growing up in poverty. They too were growing up speaking a first language that was not English. They too were hearing voices in everyday life questioning whether optimal achievement was possible. A new generation of Latino

students found my message to be authentic and liberating, as I soon realized they saw in me a successful future that they too could have the power to grasp and call their own.[23]

Luis then said to me, "The power of the soul, when activated, sometimes with the help of others, liberates oneself from the chains that were created to limit your potential."[24]

I nearly jumped out of my skin when he said it. I felt validated that my professional life of more than a half century had been worth it. I did not tell him this, of course; I just continued on with my interview questions. Later that night, I was grateful Luis Cruz has such a gift for placing just the right words together.

MY SOUL STORY ♥

"The power of the soul, when activated, sometimes with the help of others, liberates oneself from the chains that were created to limit your potential."

Sit with this statement for a while and reflect. Then write your thoughts about what it means to you today.

_____

_____

_____

_____

_____

_____

_____

_____

_____

_____

_____

_____

_____

_____

_____

_____

_____

_____

_____

_____

_____

_____

I asked Luis how he knew when he was winning the soul story search at Baldwin Park. He indicated his faculty and staff were initially curious about a shift from the school's offering historically marginalized students the *opportunity* to learn toward a school *ensuring* high levels of learning for *all* students. And finally, the faculty and staff's hearts were on fire (they were emotionally invested) for the benefits of improved student learning and access to the school's best curriculum regardless of socially constructed impediments to learning such as race, poverty, language, and ethnicity. Once again, Luis's words:

> The gradual rise in graduation rates and test scores coupled with recognition from external agencies for our successful work as a school lifted our confidence as a staff. Yet, a deeper sense of satisfaction was felt on the day students learning English as a second language were overheard cheering and embracing each other in excitement over the news that they had successfully passed California's High School Exit Exam, a requirement to graduate, and given completely in English.
>
> Upon viewing the jubilee initiated by these students, our staff witnessed a true measure of success in the liberation celebrated and embraced by our students.[25]

Luis is an example of a soul *unifier*. He brought people together for a common social justice cause. He felt a certain moral outrage at the damaging acceptance that marginalized students can't learn as well as their White peers in other schools, much less his own school—and he instilled that moral outrage in others. He created a culture that defined the very essence of your soul story: *pursue your moral good in order to create good in others.* And he added the tagline "Do it together."

Social justice becomes one of the beneficiaries of your soul story search. Martin Luther King Jr. asked how long it should take to eradicate social injustice.

"Not long. Because the arm of the moral universe is long, but it bends toward justice."[26]

Above all else, our professional soul story search is, for sure, an arc-bending journey, and we are the arc benders. I am not sure what *how long* means in terms of time. Maybe my fifty years at searching and crying out for social justice in our schools is a short time in the big scheme of things.

I know this for sure: First, never ever give up. Never. The climb for social justice against the systemic suffering of so many students we encounter is just that—a long and arduous climb.

Second, in our profession, and within the society we send our children into, the hope lies inside our educational decisions toward contribution and compassion. These parts of our soul story are described in the next two chapters.

The Second Mountain

 S   O   U   L

Some time when the river is ice ask me
mistakes I have made. Ask me whether
what I have done is my life. Others
have come in their slow way into
my thought, and some have tried to help
or to hurt: ask me what difference
their strongest love or hate has made.

—William Stafford, "Ask Me"[27]

One of the primary ways you and I connect to and develop our professional soul story is through understanding the concept of *vocation* and its importance toward our professional maturity. Parker J. Palmer is the founder and senior partner emeritus of the Center for Courage and Renewal. In *Let Your Life Speak*, he provides wise insight into the meaning of the word *vocation*:

> I must listen to my life, and try to understand what it is truly about—quite apart from what I would like it to be about—or my life will never represent anything real in the world, no matter how earnest my intentions.

> That insight is hidden in the word *vocation* itself, which is rooted in the Latin for "voice." Vocation does not mean a goal I pursue. It means a calling that I hear. Before I can tell my life what I want to do with it, I must listen to my life telling me who I am. I must listen for the truths and values at the heart of my own identity, not the standards by which I *must* live—but the standards by which I cannot help but live if I am living my own life.[28]

Palmer speaks with a voice wise, deep, and insightful.

What is *your* initial response and connection to Palmer's description of our professional life as a *vocation*?

_____

_____

_____

_____

_____

_____

_____

_____

_____

_____

_____

Is your educational soul story a life story you cannot *help but live,* as Palmer mentions in his last sentence?

_____

_____

_____

_____

_____

_____

_____

_____

_____

_____

_____

_____

Early in my career, I did not think much about my professional life serving my identity or the voice of my vocation. I am now almost a half century beyond my first day as a teacher. It has been a soul story journey of figuring out what my professional life is demanding from me.

It took almost eight years of my teaching journey before I could fully claim that education was my *vocation*— the place where my inner voice was telling me *this is who I am.* It took time and a few seasons of teaching to realize I fulfill my vocation by understanding the contributions I am making and have made through my professional life.

♥ MY SOUL STORY

What are your initial thoughts on and connections to Parker Palmer's words about understanding your work life more as a vocation and less as a career? How has your own identity defined how you see and understand your work life?

In the spring of 1973, I was finishing my final semester at Illinois State University. Back then, job postings were paper announcements. You would go to the placement office, look up job postings (pink slips, believe it or not), decide whether the jobs were of interest, and then call the number listed. It sounds easy, but most students lived with multiparty phone lines, meaning you could not make a call from your phone unless the three other phones on your line, in other dorm rooms, were not currently in use.

Being from the Chicago area, I was hoping for a job near or in the city. I had the advantage of being high school mathematics qualified, so the job competition was limited. I also had help. There was an administrative assistant in the university jobs placement office who was like a mom figure to me. She would look out for job postings and then give me a call (if she could get through on the party line!).

One morning in late spring, she called me about a potential teaching job. That is the day I met the principal and superintendent from a small, rural mid-northern Illinois town, Stillman Valley. From my perspective, the job was a dream job! They wanted me to teach grades 7–12 mathematics, be the freshman boys' basketball coach and varsity boys' baseball coach, and, when it became state mandated in two years, be the health education teacher (health and music were my minors).

I really wanted to coach, and when offered the job, I immediately said *yes* to this validation of my four years in undergraduate school. It did not occur to me that the location wasn't really that close to Chicago. I would be expected to teach seven classes a day, with six separate preparations. I would be isolated, the salary would be considered below poverty level for that era, and some of my students would not be like me and highly value a post–high school education.

It did not matter. I had a job!

MY SOUL STORY ♥

Can you remember your very first year of teaching? It may not have been that long ago. How would you describe the *how* and *why* of your first job in our profession?

Teaching as a *vocation* is not necessarily the first thought we have at the moment we land our first job. Our first thoughts are usually more basic: "I can buy a car! I can pay rent! I can get ice cream whenever I want! I can pay off my student loans! I can help out my sister!" Doubts linger too. "What do people think of me? How do I look each day? How hard am I working? How am I doing? How will I ever be as good as that teacher? What will my students do? What does the principal think? What if I fail? What if I am not ready for tomorrow? What if the students don't like me? How will the parents respond to me? How will I keep up? Can we win a conference championship? Can we win some awards?"

I was climbing what author David Brooks would call the first mountain of my professional life.[29] The first mountain climb is one of achievement, ambition, and at times, competition with others. The first mountain is

Recall your first job as a teacher or in another role serving our profession. Describe how you got the job and why you decided to accept it. What were the interviews like?

about defining yourself professionally, partially based on what others think of you. This is what Brooks has to say:

> People climbing that first mountain spend a lot of time thinking about reputation management. They are always keeping score. How do I measure up? Where do I rank?
>
> The goals on that first mountain are the normal goals that our culture endorses—to be a success, to be well thought of, to get invited into the right social circles, and to experience personal happiness. It's all the normal stuff: nice home, nice family, nice vacations, good food, good friends and so on.[30]

But I wasn't enjoying all that I was taking on, despite pointing to several achievements and awards received by my players, my students, and our mathematics team. I was spread thin. There was no balance between my personal life and my professional life. My professional wellness was suffering.

Oddly enough, despite a major in mathematics during undergraduate school, I did not feel my ability to simplify the complex ideas of high school mathematics was a strength of mine. I felt overmatched by the content at times and wanted to become more expert as a high school mathematics teacher.

And finally, despite my outward demeanor of confidence and competence, I was not improving my skills and gaining the supporting experiences that would develop my career. Take another look at the Stafford poem that opened this chapter. The last part of that poem says, "And some have tried to help / or to hurt: ask me what difference / their strongest love or hate has made."[31]

At the end of my fourth year of teaching, the superintendent made it clear to me I should never consider leaving his school district. This was the best job I would ever have, he indicated. If I left, my teaching career would surely fail. And, he indicated I would not be welcome back to the school district once I finished my graduate school studies. At that stage in my professional life, I could not understand why he would want to hurt and not help my career path.

So, I left.

It took me two years to leave because I had such deep connections to the students and the community. But I was determined to climb that first mountain of achievement even higher. I would show him he was wrong about me. I finished a mathematics master's degree program in two summers and a full school year, while also teaching mathematics classes at the university. I said to myself, "*I'll show him.* Unlike my undergraduate grades, I'll get straight As. *I'll show him.* I'll get a great job in a bigger school district that values my teaching and my effort. *I'll show him.* I'll coauthor a national best-selling mathematics textbook someday and send him a copy. *I'll show him.*"

All first mountain, empty life stuff.

Pursuing my future career choices because of the hurtful words of a superintendent was not a soul story pursuit. It was a first mountain climb that left me exhausted, restless, and empty. *I'll show him* might supply temporary motivation, but it is not a *vocation*.

How did Parker Palmer advise us at the opening of this chapter? He indicated that a vocation is *not* a goal we pursue up that first mountain. That is called a *career*. Your *vocation* is revealed in your soul story life, centered on *who you are*.[32]

By the summer of 1980, something strange happened. My pending master's degree in mathematics was opening doors in non-education fields of work. I was at a crossroads. Would I take a job offer at West Chicago Community High School District 94, or would I go for a think tank–type mathematics job, located in the Chicago suburbs, for more than double the salary?

Although I did not know it at the time, I was entering into what David Brooks calls the second mountain moment in professional life.[33] I was entering into a time where I was challenged to know whether education was my vocation—*my voice.* David Brooks provides the following insights:

> The thing everybody knows about finding a vocation is that it's quite different from finding a career. When you have a career mentality, the frontal cortex is very much in charge. You take an inventory of your talents. What are you good at? What talent has value in the marketplace? Then you invest in your abilities by getting a good education. You hone your professional skills. . . . You strategize the right route to climb upward toward success.
>
> In the vocation mentality, you're not living on the ego level of your consciousness—working because the job pays well or makes life convenient. You're down in the substrate. Some activity or some injustice has called to the deepest level of your nature and demanded an active response.[34]

Although I was only twenty-nine at the time, this was one of those moments that forced me to think past what I wanted (more money, more prestige, and more career advancement) and ask, "What is my profession asking of me?" In my moments of stillness and reflection, I could not deny who I really was.

Can you think of a time when you moved from the first mountain climb ("What is my profession *giving* me?") to the second mountain climb ("What is my profession *asking* of me?")? Was it early on in your career? Later? Has your awareness of it occurred on more than one occasion?

_____

_____

_____

_____

_____

_____

_____

_____

If you are still mostly on your first mountain climb of achievement, how can you begin to think about a deeper purpose for your profession? What do you believe your profession is asking of you?

_____

_____

_____

_____

_____

_____

_____

_____

_____

_____

I was, and I am, a teacher. It is my voice. How about you?

MY SOUL STORY

There is a strange karma that exists in life-defining professional moments like this, understood only when we look in the rearview mirror of our life. In that summer of 1980, I made the decision to join the faculty and staff at West Chicago. I was following my soul story as an educator—my second mountain climb.

And, who was the principal at West Chicago Community High School District 94?

He was a somewhat raw and unknown thirty-three-year-old whirlwind of a school leader, Richard DuFour. I ended up directly in his path, sprinting and spinning along with his brilliance for the next thirty-seven years.

I loved my days at West Chicago, despite some incredible obstacles to success with students. West Chicago was filled with many injustices caused by a social structure divide of poverty and wealth, brown and white, love and neglect, low expectations and sometimes even lower expectations. Add to that three consecutive years of frozen teacher salaries; at times, the costs far outweighed the benefits. David Brooks describes the vocation mentality succinctly:

> Vocations invariably have testing periods—periods where the costs outweigh the benefits . . . At these moments, if you were driven by a career mentality you would quit. You're putting more into this thing than you are getting out. But a person who has found a vocation doesn't feel she has a choice. It would be a violation of her own nature.[35]

Hmm. Our profession, even though it is more than a career, even though it is our vocation, will have testing periods in which the costs of our vocation outweigh the benefits. And yet, we have no choice but to be who we really are.

West Chicago was filled with teachers who understood and viewed their work as their vocation, their contribution and calling in life. We banded together and shared the moral joy of our work with some incredible and diverse students, despite often very difficult conditions in their home lives and in the community.

For many of my teaching colleagues, this was a life fulfilled. I enjoyed their commitment to the school and the community. I admired their sense of family at home and the contribution they were making to the community as teachers and program leaders in our local community high school.

During my professional years at West Chicago, I also observed part of our faculty and staff that seemed numb to our obstacles, perhaps overwhelmed by them. They seemed joyless. Or worse, they seemed *soulless*. It seemed as if they wanted to deny joy to themselves and others.

They were not climbing either mountain. They were in a valley. I am not sure they were yet ready for the second mountain climb, but that did not stop me from wanting joy for them.

MY SOUL STORY

Once again, David Brooks provides some insight:

> The second-mountain people aren't averse to the pleasures of the world. They delight in a good glass of wine or a nice beach. But they have surpassed these pleasures in pursuit of moral joy, a feeling they have aligned their life toward an ultimate good. If they have to choose, they choose joy.[36]

My PLC colleague Mark Weichel, a school leader from the Omaha, Nebraska, area, describes his *vocation* in a unique way:

> This sounds super cheesy, but there have been times in my career as a teacher or administrator that I feel this little rush come over me that tells me I am doing the work that I was intended to do. Examples include times when I was working with an individual student through a tough time, supporting a teacher who poured his or her heart into a lesson for students, or [collaborating with] a group of teachers who were developing a new course and writing curriculum.[37]

Describe a *testing period* in your professional life so far as an educator. How did you respond, or how are you responding?

_____

_____

_____

_____

_____

_____

_____

_____

_____

_____

_____

_____

_____

_____

_____

_____

_____

_____

_____

_____

_____

_____

_____

_____

_____

_____

_____

_____

Reading the comments from Brooks and Weichel, I realized the second mountain part of me reveals these moments of joy in my professional experiences as a part of my soul story. I just feel at home when I teach.

Our thoughts (images and judgments), feelings (emotional responses), decisions (choices and character), physical actions (sleep, diet, and exercise), and relationships (personal and professional) all integrate into one whole to create our second mountain soul story, over time—a story that integrates each of these factors into forming the heart and soul of our lives.

I eventually realized the journey is not linear. There is a valley between the two mountains, and sometimes we can get stuck there too.

There is a second mountain secret, over time, however. The journey through a thriving professional second mountain soul story begins with understanding the role compassion plays as a headline in our professional life. And that secret is in the next chapter.

No Compassion, No Soul

S   O   U   L

When we practice loving kindness and compassion, we are the first ones to profit.

–Rumi

Suffering implies "conscious endurance of pain or distress."[38] The suffering of one should not be compared to the suffering of others. I do not claim that my suffering is any greater or less than your suffering. Suffering is part of the human condition. Our suffering is always personal.

Being teachers does not exempt us from suffering. There are many moments in our professional and personal life journeys, both hidden and public, that can cause suffering, difficulty, and conscious endurance. To suffer deeply means to be wounded at the soul story level of life.

Look around at the circumstances of your students or colleagues. Consider the daily barrage of local, state, and national news as well as world events. Suffering is indeed where we often catch sight of our soul story, or suffering is the place where it often finds us. And our soul story, it turns out, is revealed by our *response* to suffering.

Merriam-Webster defines *compassion* as "sympathetic consciousness of others' distress together with a desire to alleviate it."[39] To understand compassion is to understand the nature of your response to suffering by your students, colleagues, and community.

In an extensive review of the scientific literature about compassion, Jennifer Goetz and her colleagues at the University of California Berkeley, define *compassion* as "the feeling [emotional response] that arises in witnessing another's suffering, and that motivates a subsequent desire to help."[40] Compassion is different from empathy (a feeling and understanding component) because compassion results in *action*.

Think about a current

story of suffering by students or colleagues in your professional life. Which of the four responses to crisis best represents your current feelings or actions?

_____

_____

_____

_____

_____

_____

_____

_____

_____

_____

_____

_____

_____

_____

_____

_____

_____

_____

_____

_____

_____

_____

_____

_____

_____

There is an abundance of neuroscientific evidence that your response to a crisis of student suffering, such as the COVID-19 pandemic, involves your brain going through the following stages.

1. An awareness of suffering
2. Emotional involvement in the suffering
3. A wish to see relief for the suffering
4. A readiness to act or to help relieve the suffering[41]

The first two responses represent *empathy*—the *feeling* component. When you experience empathy, the pain center in your brain lights up. You are experiencing another's pain.

The second two responses represent *compassion*—the *action* component of wanting to relieve the other person's suffering. Now, a distinctly different area of the brain lights up—a *reward pathway* associated with your positive emotion.[42]

 # MY SOUL STORY

Think of it like this: empathy hurts, and compassion heals.

Also, you can think of it like this: compassion is so much more than kindness or politeness. Since compassion is a response to *relieve* another's pain or suffering, it is implicit that suffering is involved. Awareness of our students' suffering *should* cause us some pain.

Responding to the suffering of our students or colleagues is the essence of what it means to be a teacher. It is part of our joy. If you or I lack compassion, then we are out of touch with our soul story. We miss out on the healing aspect of compassion. Our soul story remains empty, and our vocation is diminished to a career endured. We fall short of our promise and potential to live fully.

Acts of compassion toward others are not just in our words. We reveal compassion in our nonverbal cues as well. Every lesson we teach and every interaction we have with our students, our students' parents, and our colleagues is also reflected in our facial expressions. Researchers at Harvard University, the University of

California, Riverside, and Stanford University studied the impact of nonverbal cues for helping elderly patients achieve positive health outcomes. They found that *leaning in*, *making direct eye contact*, *interacting with less personal distance*, and *smiling* have a significant association with positive patient outcomes. Likewise, lacking eye contact, making irritated facial expressions, keeping a distance, and looking away minimize positive patient outcomes.[43]

Which of these nonverbal behaviors would most likely be observed in your school, office, or classroom setting among you, your students, and your colleagues?

Consider this experiment. I come to your school, and I watch educators' and students' nonverbal cues and behaviors in the building *before* school starts each day for a week.

What evidence would exist that each educator demonstrates compassionate nonverbal behaviors toward others and her or his students?

MY SOUL STORY

A 2016 Pew Research Center study reveals that close to 35 percent of all Americans do not consider compassion for others to be among their core values.[44]

This indicates that at least one-third of your colleagues might not display compassionate verbal or nonverbal cues in response to the day-to-day struggles of students or colleagues.

As educators, however, we live by a different professional standard than our neighbors. We chose a social sector profession. We chose a *helping* profession, in the service of our communities.

We said we would act *in loco parentis*.

We joined a profession of *emotional* labor, and much like our friends in the health care industry, we agreed to alleviate the suffering around us. We become aware of the suffering that takes place inside and sometimes outside of our schools. We will not ignore it or abandon it.

If we come to work and lack compassion (in our verbal and nonverbal actions) for the suffering of our

What are the nonverbal cues you and your colleagues use to demonstrate daily compassion to others?

_____
_____
_____
_____
_____
_____
_____
_____
_____
_____
_____
_____
_____
_____
_____
_____
_____
_____
_____
_____
_____
_____
_____
_____
_____
_____
_____

${T}oo$ much compassion at work will burn you out. Do you agree with this statement? Why or why not?

———————————————
———————————————
———————————————
———————————————
———————————————
———————————————
———————————————
———————————————
———————————————
———————————————
———————————————
———————————————
———————————————
———————————————
———————————————
———————————————
———————————————
———————————————
———————————————
———————————————
———————————————
———————————————
———————————————
———————————————
———————————————

preK–12 students, then the school can quickly become a soulless institution and a culturally dead place. And then everyone suffers, especially the community.

Remember, the road to compassionate runs through empathy, and empathy begins by making a personal connection with your students and colleagues—seeing their pain, understanding their suffering, knowing their stories, and avoiding the malaise of dispassion.

Empathy is a one-way path coming toward us as we feed off the emotional cues and suffering of our students, colleagues, and parents. Compassion is a path that runs the other way—toward others as a responsive action to the pain or suffering we observe.

Compassion involves understanding our *shared* human condition, fragile and imperfect as it is. It is a willingness to extend understanding to others when they fail or make mistakes, a common, almost everyday occurrence as part of the learning process taking place in our classrooms and teacher team meetings.[45]

Instead of looking away or rolling our eyes, or blaming others for a student's or colleague's actions, we take a moment to reflect on how things might be difficult for them. By stepping out of our usual frame of reference and placing ourselves in their position, we start to see human beings who may be in some pain. "Compassion literally means 'to suffer with.'"[46]

Perhaps, then, it is reasonable to ask, "If I am compassionate every day, every school season, won't I suffer from burnout?"

MY SOUL STORY

To help inform the My Soul Story prompt, consider the following.

Burnout in our profession has three indicators: (1) emotional exhaustion, (2) a lack of personal accomplishment, and, get ready for it, (3) depersonalization. *Depersonalization* is the inability to make personal connections with your students and colleagues. Your nonverbal cues as well as your verbal cues, impatience, and complaints reveal this depersonalization. When depersonalization is combined with emotional exhaustion, it culminates in compassion fatigue—a literal running out of compassion for your students, colleagues, parents, and others in your professional life.[47] Your teaching life is no longer a calling, a vocation—rather, it moves toward the dispassion of becoming "just a job" to get you through each day.

A good friend and colleague of mine at Adlai E. Stevenson High School was usually a very compassionate school counselor. However, sixteen days into one school year, we discovered the school district had misplaced a student in several classes once previous school transcripts became available. The counselor refused to change the student's schedule and move him into the correct classes.

Depersonalization had settled into her professional life.

This student had been one of more than two hundred students seeking schedule changes over the past three weeks. He had become depersonalized to her, just another number in her workday. She was exhausted from start-of-the-year craziness. No compassion. No soul. Burnout was settling in, and it was only September.

Educators with low compassion are predisposed to becoming burned out. Thankfully, this guidance counselor was generally not low on compassion. It was what made her a great counselor. Yet she was also human and needed to regain her bearings after a rough start. We worked together on the issue, and she recovered quickly to experience another typically great year.

Know this: there is an inverse correlation between compassion and burnout. Yes! This means daily high compassion is associated with low burnout. And high burnout, in turn, is associated with low compassion.[48] They go in opposite directions!

This is good news indeed.

In *Compassionomics*, a remarkable book about compassion in the health care industry, doctors Stephen Trzeciak and Anthony Mazzarelli state:

> Under the same amount of stress, a determinant of who will or will not get burned out may be a person's compassion for others . . . Interventions to raise one's level of compassion could prevent burnout, or even counteract burnout in people who already have it.[49]

Could compassion, then, be an antidote for burnout? For health care providers, there is evidence that compassion is good for you. "Research shows that compassion for others can be a coping strategy to overcome personal distress and strengthen one's own resilience."[50]

Write about a situation in which you or your team members demonstrated compassion toward others at work. Did you or your team experience the sense of inner calm, personal achievement, and happiness described by Trzeciak and Mazzarelli?

_____

_____

_____

_____

_____

_____

_____

_____

_____

_____

_____

_____

_____

_____

_____

_____

_____

_____

_____

_____

_____

Trzeciak and Mazzarelli indicate that roughly 70 percent of people experience a good feeling when helping others in a meaningful way, along with the additional benefit of inner calmness and a feeling of self-worth. They add, "But perhaps the most interesting data is on human *happiness*. Neuroscientific research shows that the most potent activator of brain circuits involved in human happiness is actually . . . *compassion*."[51]

 # MY SOUL STORY

One caution: Do not confuse compassion with pity. *Pity* might seem to be an act of compassion, but it lacks humanity. Pity refers to feeling sorry for someone thought to be inferior or weaker than you. Pity is rooted in your sense of superiority over someone else. This sense of superiority implies a separation between *you* and *them*.[52]

Compassion, on the other hand, is quite different—when you have compassion, you do not consider the object of suffering to be weak or inferior, better than you, or worse than you in any way. Quoting Pema Chödrön, from her book *The Places That Scare You*:[53]

> Compassion is not a relationship between the healer and the wounded. It's a relationship between equals. Only when we know our own darkness well can we be present with the darkness of others. Compassion becomes real when we recognize our shared humanity.[54]

I read that last line from the Chödrön quote and thought how difficult yet vital it is to be able to see our most difficult students or colleagues as part of our *shared humanity*. As equals. And yet, this is exactly what our soul story calls us to do.

Being compassionate does not make us timid, weak, or tolerant of injustice, however. On a societal level, a compassionate response to injustice stems from our strong sense of moral outrage—a form of anger, but a constructive one (see chapter 11, page 83).

The soul story of our professional life often finds itself in our tough-minded compassion.

As I pointed out in *HEART!*[55], don't confuse love and compassion with softness. Being there for people is deeper than just wanting to relieve suffering. You must also be ready to warn, reprove, admonish, and hold a safety net of accountability as necessary. Sometimes compassion may also require honest reflection about destructive behaviors.

The word *compassion* often refers to compassion *toward* others—your loved ones, your students, your colleagues. Compassion also refers to *receiving* from others in your professional and personal life. Often compassion is *witnessed* between others.

There is also *self-compassion*. It is foundational to our soul story. *Self-compassion* is "compassion directed inward."[56] You extend compassion toward yourself when you are suffering, whether by your own mistakes and failures or by external circumstances you do not control. We examine the details and impact of self-compassion in chapter 13 (page 101).

A final thought as you leave this chapter: When you care deeply for your students and colleagues, your school can become a great place to work. As your students and colleagues witness your acts of compassion, specialized brain cells called *mirror neurons* help them to, in turn, become more likely to act with compassion themselves.[57] This reality is discussed further in chapter 24 (page 203).

Those observing your compassionate acts experience a distinct state called *moral elevation*. According to Sarina R. Saturn, assistant professor at Oregon State University's School of Psychological Science, "Moral elevation is triggered by compassionate behaviors. . . . Witnessing selfless compassion arouses a broader hope for humanity and induces a more generalized desire to help other people."[58]

Compassion is not a panacea, however. It is not a substitute for the constructs of high-quality teaching and learning. But, when you use them together, you become the type of teacher, and your school becomes the type of school, every parent would want for his or her child.

You and your team become part of a powerful and compassionate workplace, creating a culture of belonging, vulnerability, and validation—the kind of soul story school we will examine deeply in part 3 (page 121).

We close out part 1 of this book with the next chapter, The Soul Story Whisperers. Here we learn to listen to and sometimes search for the moral voice of our professional soul story guiding us along the way.

The Soul Story Whisperers

      O   U   L

I want to be remembered as someone who used herself and
anything she could touch to work for justice and freedom. . . .
I want to be remembered as one who tried.

–Dorothy Height

Our soul story—the pursuit of our moral good in order to create good in others—is part of our professional responsibility. We are in a profession in which we shape future generations today to honor and defend this good for the generations of tomorrow. Just as we have been the beneficiaries of the soul story whisperers in our lives along the way, we now, as educators, become benefactors for our students.

When needed, we act *in loco parentis*. When needed, we act with compassion. When needed, we work to erase social injustices in our school. We understand our second mountain climb and respond to the call of "What is my profession asking of me?" We respond by listening to the whispers of those we trust and becoming a soul story whisperer for those we teach and lead.

Consider the following soul story journey. As you read this story, look for the trusted voices that nudged this educator along in his professional life.

Imagine your grandparents are sharecroppers in Maryland, stuck inside a cycle of poverty in the 1930s and 1940s, and not that far removed from a generation of slavery. Your grandmother has a fifth-grade education, and your grandfather has a third-grade education. Ninety percent of their farming profits go to a White landowner.

Imagine your father, the son of those sharecroppers, wanting to go to college. It will be an opportunity to break out of their cycle of poverty. Now, imagine that White landowner telling your grandparents, "If you send your Black son to college, your 10 percent share of the profits will be lost. You will be kicked off the farm. You will be forced out of your home."

There is no need to imagine, as this story is true. Your father does go on to college, and your grandparents are forced out, as promised. Your father eventually becomes a reading teacher and then a principal of an all African American school during the time of school segregation.

Now, imagine you, the grandson of those sharecroppers, struggle to learn how to read, and there is talk of retention by a teacher, but your parents say *no*. Your father is a reading teacher. Both your mother and your father provide you with early experiences to eventually read at grade level and beyond. They become early soul whisperers in your young life.

You get a full scholarship to play basketball in college and decide on a speech and communications major. You graduate and go on to play one year of professional basketball overseas, and then, you injure your knee, eventually requiring two surgeries.

You return to the states; move to Arlington, Virginia; and need to earn money. You substitute teach in a local school. And then, a soul story whisperer appears in the form of a principal. "What do you really want to do with your life?" she asks. "You really should think about becoming a teacher. Come join our profession."[59]

But you have to *hear* that whisper. Your life is busy and full. So you stop, reflect, and finally realize your father had started to break the poverty cycle that had been part of his generational heritage by becoming a teacher. Could this teaching profession choice honor the legacy of your father? Something about teaching lights a fire inside of you. So, you listen. The affirmation of the whisperer provides the confidence you need to move forward.

You decide this is who you are. Teaching will become your place for contribution, so to speak. You go back to school at George Mason University and complete a teaching certification and master's degree in counseling, and secure a job as a physical education teacher and counselor in Arlington, Virginia, for fifteen years. You listen to the soul story whisperer.

Then one day, another whisperer comes along. While you are working as a school counselor, your principal says, "How about becoming a principal? You could lead an entire school!" You listen once again and follow this advice for your soul story journey. You go back to school to secure more credentials and land an assistant principal's job in Fairfax County, Virginia.

Soon after you arrive in Fairfax, principal Carolyn Miller takes you and other school team leaders to a retreat hosted by Rick and Becky DuFour. Without knowing it (sometimes whisperers don't even know they are sending a message), they, too, whisper to the heart of your soul story about the clarity and leadership you need to bring to your profession. And you respond to their teaching.

After you spend two years as an assistant principal at Lemon Road Elementary, Carolyn Miller tells you that you are ready, and you are hired as principal of your first school, Mount Eagle Elementary School. You are the third principal in four years. The school has hardworking, dedicated, and caring educators but lacks clarity in its mission and coherence. You change the structures and culture of your school in order to reach each child. You do not always win. But more good days start to pile up. Mount Eagle is a struggling Title I school, but within three years, it becomes a role model school, demonstrating significantly improved student achievement.

Your subsequent journey takes you to the opening of a new school—Mason Crest Elementary School, also in Fairfax County, Virginia. You are simultaneously close to and distant from the memories of your grandparents' sharecropper days. Those memories don't define you, but they do inspire your moral responsibility to create good in others.

You sense that you were born into the "right" family, as your parents provided you with the foundation to overcome your early reading struggles. Your grandparents' decisions in the 1940s changed the next generations for your family. And your passion comes from the fact that it should not matter what family a child is born into; he or she should have the same opportunities and endless possibilities as a child whose father is a reading teacher.

And yet, there is more.

There is a hunger inside your soul story that wants each and every day to matter. You commit every day of your professional life to equitable learning for each child. Your teaching and leading journey at Mason Crest results in your school, faculty, staff, and diverse student body receiving the first-ever DuFour Award for excellence. This prestigious national award represents a school's relentless pursuit of improved student achievement and adult engagement in the fulfillment of its professional work.

Mason Crest eventually earns an A+ rating from Niche.com, a search platform providing in-depth analyses of the quality of schools, partially for its achievement in the face of racial and economic diversity,

with 46 percent of its students being eligible for free or reduced lunch
services. Breaking out of the cycle of poverty for each child seems to
fit well with the *why* of your professional life.

If you follow the PLC at Work school life long enough, you will run
into the grandson of the sharecroppers in this story. He is one of our
most beloved and wise thought leaders at Solution Tree. His name is
Brian Butler. As with each of us, there is a lot more to Brian than his
résumé. Brian forged his life out of previous generations of slavery and
extreme poverty and built a soul story by listening to whispers from
trusted sources around him: *Pursue your moral good in order to create
good in others.* This is indeed a second mountain story.

Brian had to be willing to both *hear and respond* to his principal
when he was a young and raw substitute teacher. He did it again when
another principal challenged him to become a principal. When he
met and was hired by Carolyn Miller, he listened. When she introduced him to the PLC at Work process with Rick and Becky DuFour,
he listened again.

The best part of Brian's story is that it is not a unique story of listening to soul whisperers. You too have heard the important voices
of others in your soul story journey and listened as well. You most
likely have distinguished those whispers from the competing and
often loud, fast-paced voices of social media and other noise coming
at you every day.

Sometimes your soul story searches for and finds you through the
voices of others when you least expect it. You might ask, "How do I
listen to and become aware of the soul story whisperers in my life?" I
address that question more directly in chapter 21 (page 173). However,
part of the answer lies in first identifying trusted persons in your
professional life and then slowing down long enough to listen to
their wisdom.

Trusted persons in our professional and personal lives are first and
foremost persons with no agenda other than to contribute to our
growth and welfare. In our professional life, these persons are fully
present and give us a nudge without judgment, urgency, abuse, or solution. They know our story and care for us, well beyond our résumé.

They challenge us to a level of performance we did not think possible, for the essential purpose of creating a greater sphere of good
within us. The words of those we trust carry a greater weight during
our self-reflection. We weigh their advice carefully because they have
often demonstrated wisdom and a positive impact with us before.

MY SOUL STORY ♥

Brian took action on the advice from the whisperers in his life. And then one day, perhaps without realizing it, Brian became a soul story whisperer for others. He helped those in his professional life to contribute differently by asking them to consider growth roles as educators. Just as multiple principals and two very wise educators whispered *to* him, Brian gathered the strength, courage, and wisdom to become a whisperer to others.

This is exactly the promise and the hope of our soul story's moral imperative, when we search for it—that you and I become trusted sources of wisdom and knowledge for our students and our colleagues, with no other agenda than to help them learn and grow. We help them develop their self-efficacy, just as we model our learning, growth, and self-efficacy as teachers.

We see and feel the humanity of others. And we respond to it.

Becoming a soul story whisperer is not about your age or experience. It is about your willingness to see the positive potential in others that they often cannot see inside themselves and to obey your moral imperative to do the good expected from your professional life.

MY SOUL STORY ♥

It seems to me that this My Soul Story reflection is delicate. How do you overcome your own obstacles to a fully vibrant and fulfilled professional life, much less become a voice of reason for others? The chapters in part 2 and part 3 will help answer this question for you.

Thank goodness Brian listened to the soul story whisperers in his life.

May we all find the courage to seek stillness and listen to the voices of the trusted whisperers who appear for us along the way.

Who are the trusted soul story whisperers in your life? What is the best advice they have given to you recently?

_____

_____

_____

_____

_____

_____

_____

_____

Who needs you to gently whisper to them? Who needs you to engage or re-engage them in the work of our profession? Describe one to two actions you can take to become a more trusted voice in their lives.

_____

_____

_____

_____

_____

_____

_____

_____

_____

_____

The PLC Life Is a Seeking-Systems Life

S   O   U   L

Daniel M. Cable is an award-winning professor of organizational behavior at the London Business School and ranked as one of the twenty-five most influential management scholars in the world. In his 2018 book, *Alive at Work: The Neuroscience of Helping Your People Love What They Do*, Cable writes with clarity about the importance of activating our searching capabilities, or as he references them, our "seeking system."[60]

The seeking system pushes us to seek new hobbies and add new skills into our work life, just because they are of interest to us. "When we follow our seeking system, it releases dopamine—a neurotransmitter linked to motivation and pleasure—that makes us want to explore more."[61]

Cable goes on to say:

> Exploring, experimenting, learning: this is the way we're designed to live. And work, too. The problem is that our organizations weren't designed to take advantage of people's seeking systems. Thanks to the Industrial Revolution—when modern management was conceived—organizations were purposely designed to suppress our natural impulses to learn and explore.[62]

I believe this was the deep wisdom of Bob Eaker and Rick DuFour when they launched the process and culture of a professional learning community (PLC) in 1998. They knew that school life had become more like a dispassionate job: tedious and routine, with that stuck-in-a-rut, isolated feeling. As professionals, we seek a system that allows us to grow and explore.

The PLC life is a seeking-systems life.

Our brains are wired for the PLC process of growth and continuous learning throughout our lifetime of teaching. It is why I believe, as professional educators, we hunger for an era away from the controlled, top-down bureaucracy of many older school cultures and prefer the team-based freedom of a more loose-tight teaching and leading process. We enjoy opportunities at work to search, seek, and explore new solutions and improved strategies for teaching and learning, all in the service of eradicating the social injustices surrounding our school community and improved student learning.

More from Cable:

> Our evolutionary tendency to disengage from tedious activities isn't a bug in our mental makeup—it's a *feature*. It's our body's way of telling us that we were designed to do better things. *To keep exploring and learning.* This is our biology— it is part of our adaptive unconscious to know that our human potential is being wasted, that we are wasting away.[63]

Cable goes on to quote Jaak Panksepp, the late pioneer of affective neuroscience: "When the seeking systems are not active, human aspirations remain frozen in an endless winter of discontent."[64]

Panksepp nails it on the head, does he not? This is why we search for and locate our soul story as our professional life unfolds. Without it, we will get forever stuck in a season of discontent. Without it, we will never fulfill our potential as human beings, much less as educators.

According to Eddie S. Glaude Jr., chair of the Department of African American Studies at Princeton University, "What we put in and leave out of our stories tells us something about who we are."[65] We are responsible for every story in our professional journey, embracing the stories from our past and creating our new stories of the future.

We do not have the luxury of allowing a bad school season story to sit on our professional timeline. We cannot afford to waste our potential as teachers.

The lives of too many children and teenagers depend on us.

Part 1 was about searching and connecting to your soul story—*the pursuit of your moral good in order to create good in others.*

Any discussion of a school's quality is ultimately a discussion of the exploration of its community of adults. And yet, there are so many internal and external professional wellness, self-care obstacles we face during our soul story–seeking journey. In part 2, we work through those obstacles and learn how to use our soul story to overcome them—one day, one week, one school season at a time.

MY SOUL STORY ♥ ——————————————

Reflect on the seven
chapters of part 1 and the seeking-
systems ideas from this Final
Thoughts section. What are some
of your primary takeaways?

_____

_____

_____

_____

_____

_____

_____

_____

_____

_____

_____

_____

_____

_____

Include two to three
possible actions you can take to
better connect to your soul story.
Write these actions as *I will* . . .
statements, as you consider your
professional soul story progress
over time. Keep these statements
close at hand as you act on, connect to, and use your professional
soul story.

_____

_____

_____

_____

_____

_____

_____

_____

_____

_____

_____

_____

_____

_____

DEVELOPING YOUR
SOUL STORY

Essential Soul Story Question: Your soul story will overcome all obstacles. Are you using it?

> *Blaming your faults on your nature does not change the nature of your faults.*
>
> —Indian and English proverb

Your professional life thrives when you *use* your soul story *to overcome obstacles*.

In part 2 of this book, we examine many obstacles that can prevent us from achieving our soul story purpose: *fulfilling the promise of our professional life as a teacher and leader.* I use the words *we*, *us*, and *our* quite a bit, rather than *you* and *your*, because these obstacles are mine too. It feels more inclusive this way.

This O part of the book, *overcoming obstacles*, feels simultaneously messy and hopeful. In each chapter, we first examine an obstacle followed by suggestions and research for healthy responses to each obstacle.

Part 2 will feel a bit heavier than part 1. I encourage you to take your time reading and writing through these chapters. Many of the reviewers for this book asked me to remind readers that one paragraph after another contains a lot of information and deep ideas. No need to rush.

We begin part 2 with the obstacle of feeling lost and overwhelmed by the adversity and unexpected events of our work life. In chapter 8, we examine the idea of *falling up* as a potential solution to feeling lost and overwhelmed at times.

In chapter 9, we encounter the obstacle I call *living in the shallows*. We are often too hurried and too busy, with little time left for reflection. We live professionally on a superficial level. This chapter helps us discover five core values for living with greater depth toward professional wellness in our work life.

In chapters 10 and 11, we run into emotional intelligence obstacles and the subtle subtext of *Do our emotions control our daily responses in life, or do we control them?* We learn about the acronym *SASHET* and how we can use it to help us identify our positive and negative emotional states of being. An unhealthy reaction to anger with potential antagonism toward others can be challenging, so we dive into a full chapter about our soul story response to anger. Can we embrace, use, and overcome our moments of anger?

Much of our anger at either ourselves, or others, is directed by our need to be right. To be perfect. We see and feel our flaws and the flaws of others. Sometimes, we fail to see we are fully human. And as such, we can be difficult teachers and colleagues to be around. We fail to see that we are indeed good enough *for now*, as the title of chapter 12 indicates.

Chapters 13 and 14 help us learn to use self-compassion when facing professional life obstacles. We accept that sometimes through the trials of our more difficult school seasons, we find our way to greater growth, resulting in an improved and more positive connection to our work.

This part of the book may seem a bit challenging, as it forces us to recognize and control our weaknesses as we develop into our strengths.

Read slowly, and enjoy the road less hardened.

Lost and Overwhelmed

The child is in me still . . . and sometimes not so still.
—Fred Rogers

We have chosen a highly relational and intensively human profession. We work every day with students and adults who are not yet fully formed because we are each works in progress. Adversity, crises, and failure arise as obstacles. The daunting daily pace of our life and the often-haunting shadows of our childhood create surprises and challenges to us as we walk, run, and sprint through our professional life.

Our professional life is anything but certain. There are unexpected surgeries, job transfers, financial losses, personal losses of loved ones, sicknesses, promotions, achievements, pandemics, protests, and more. We adapt, we shift, we alter, and we *adjust*. We feel lost and overwhelmed at some point, in some moment during the school year.

We (you, I, our students, our colleagues) have many adversity stories—some that are known and some that remain unknown and buried somewhere.

First, there are *work-life* obstacles.

As I write this chapter, I am in my forty-seventh season as a teacher and leader. I have yet to have a school season completely adversity-free. Consider these real events from my past school seasons: One of my students receives a full ride to the University of Illinois and gets killed two weeks later in a snowmobile accident.

My boys' basketball team loses seven games in a row. Parents and fans are screaming and swearing at me during the games.

From the moment the day starts, I am running behind. I am five minutes late to my first class, every lesson is a half beat behind, and it shows. I have what feels like no control of

In what month are you reading this chapter? The time of year can impact your response. Write about two to three unexpected events (some you control and maybe some you don't) causing workplace adversity for you.

_____
_____
_____
_____
_____
_____
_____
_____
_____
_____
_____
_____
_____
_____
_____
_____
_____
_____
_____
_____
_____
_____
_____
_____
_____

my classes, and the not-so-well-planned lessons fizzle. The kids are antsy. Or is it me? After school, rain forces me to cancel practices and arrange rides home. On the way home, my car stalls (no kidding, it didn't like rain), and I have to get a tow and talk the driver into taking me home.

And then there are large-scale events such as starting a school year amid a pandemic health crisis.

Adversity indeed.

♥ **MY** SOUL STORY

Next, there are _home-life_ obstacles.

Consider this small sample of adversities at home over my past forty-seven school seasons: frozen water pipes, a flooded basement, my car crashing through the garage sending me to the hospital, getting hit by a car on my tractor while shoveling snow in the street, three kids (enough said), family sickness, family death, feeling alone, feeling sad, feeling angry, feeling I was letting everyone down and doing nothing well, fixing a bad bathroom with money we did not have, not knowing how the mortgage or Visa card would get paid, working extra jobs on Wednesdays and Saturdays to pay the mortgage, and experiencing a complete tear of my left knee's ACL while slipping on black ice (that I was too hurried to take the time to salt).

My moments are not for comparison. We each experience unique events (better or worse events) that knock us off balance. They are usually relative to the context of our life and the framework of change within our community at any moment in time.

Then there are _past life_ obstacles.

Can you remember your seventh-grade school year? Can you remember what it felt like to be twelve or thirteen years old and a seventh grader? Are the memories good or bad, or a mix of both?

Seventh grade was a really tough year for me. I was a lost and overwhelmed student. The summer before my seventh-grade year (1963), school district representatives came to my Aunt Dottie's house (see chapter 3, page 17). I had been living and going to school in the Rock Island School District for four years, but legally, I was still the ward of my father (who lived near Chicago) and not my aunt. I was illegally residing in her school district.

My aunt had two choices: (1) send me back to my father, who was my legal guardian, or (2) go to court and legally adopt me. My aunt wanted me to stay with her. My father wanted me to live with him. At age twelve, the choice was mine to make. In the end, I left the safety and security of my aunt's home and moved in with my father.

That summer of 1963, I joined my oldest sister, a graduating high school senior; my next-oldest sister, a junior; my brother, a freshman; and my stepbrother, also a seventh grader, along with my father; my stepmom, Connie; and a dog named Lady. To make room for me in their crowded three-bedroom, split-level house, they placed a makeshift curtain and bed in the basement. The transition to the madness of my father's house began.

MY SOUL STORY ♥

I don't pretend to think my seventh-grade story is unique. There are thousands of blended families across the United States, and many of them have much less than we had. We at least had shelter and the opportunity for a good education.

My dad and stepmom both worked two jobs. On weekends, they were a duo called Sweethearts of Song and played nightclubs across the Midwest. This, of course, left the five of us kids with a lot of unsupervised time. As the late joiner to this blended family, I found it tough to fit in, and I felt a gnawing sense of anxiety as seventh grade was about to begin.

Once school started, I played sports, studied at the school library, and used school as my escape. *In loco parentis.* This pattern of activity would continue through high school, as in many ways school was my parental refuge.

Consider some of the events in your current or past home life (which you feel you can share) that have caused you some adversity in the past.

_____

_____

_____

_____

_____

_____

_____

_____

_____

_____

_____

_____

_____

_____

_____

_____

_____

_____

_____

_____

_____

_____

_____

_____

I tucked my anxiety into a box, in the far recesses of my brain. And yet, as the school year moved along, the adversity of the change began to quietly creep into my young life.

On Sunday nights, I would sit in my makeshift basement room and become nervous and anxious. It felt stifling—almost like stage fright (I find it ironic that I became a public speaker).

How would I be ready for school on Monday? What if I was not prepared? What if I failed? I would freeze and often then fail to get my assignments done. It took everything my twelve-year-old brain had to overcome the dread from the cycle of another school week and the subsequent responsibilities of being a student. School was my refuge, and it was also my place of fear and anxiety. What a paradox.

In the end, it was my school counselor, Mrs. Schontze, and my stepmom, Connie, who rescued me. Mrs. Schontze helped me to not be afraid of new beginnings. Leaving the safety of that soul-filled home with my aunt and launching into the wacky world of reunion with my dad and siblings had left me with hidden doubt. My confidence was shattered.

I can still remember telling Mrs. Schontze how lost I felt. How I had made a bad decision to come live with my dad. I felt so alone, despite being in a house of seven. She listened and asked me if there was a family member I could trust.

I went to Connie about my extreme anxiety and about my fear of school every Sunday night. And the trust and the kindness she demonstrated toward me began a thirty-one-year friendship. For me, Connie was my middle school soul story nourisher.

MY SOUL STORY ♥

Think about your own middle school years. Can you recall moments of anxiety, when you felt lost or overwhelmed by the academic, social, or emotional expectations at school or at home? Who helped you during that time?

The obstacles and the adversity in our life path often run deep. With adversity comes pressure and then the fear of failing, not being prepared, not being loved or worthy, being distracted by the gauntlet of social media consuming us, or being less than we really are or want to be. We often feel lost, overwhelmed, and alone.

Our soul story can *overcome* the disquiet and adversity of our lives.

We use various mental maps to help us respond either positively or negatively to adversity when it comes along. A *mental map* is a "representation of the world or some part of it based on subjective perceptions."[66] Mental map responses to adversity in our lives generally follow one or two unhealthy negative pathways. One unhealthy pathway leads us to *further negative consequences*, creating a cycle of negative responses in which we are far worse off after the initial adverse event. Our unhealthy response causes us to create new conflicts and challenges and can leave us unprepared to respond positively to future adversity sure to lurk around the corner.

Another unhealthy mental map pathway is the circular path—a path for which the negative event creates no change. We essentially end up where we started without any growth. The event keeps us frozen in a way. We bury it for a while, but some adverse event will trigger our unhealthy and negative response once again.

Both of these pathways can cause us to feel even more lost and overwhelmed as we move through our professional life. But there is a third mental pathway to consider. This is the healthy response—a positive pathway of our soul story.

Best-selling author Shawn Achor describes it like this:

> [There is a third path] that leads us from failure or setback to a place where we are even stronger and more capable than before the fall. To be sure, finding that path in challenging times isn't easy. In a crisis, economic or otherwise, we tend to form incomplete mental maps, and ironically the path we have trouble seeing is often the most positive, productive one. In fact, when we feel helpless and hopeless, we stop believing such a path exists—so we don't even bother to look for it. But this is the very path we should be looking for, because [it] is the difference between those who are crippled by failure and those who rise above it.
>
> Study after study shows that if we are able to conceive of a failure as an opportunity for growth, we are all the more likely to experience that growth.[67]

Achor calls this third path *falling up*.

Think
about your latest bout with adverse events, and describe how you took or can take the third pathway of *falling up* as a positive approach to this past adverse event.

_____

_____

_____

_____

_____

_____

_____

_____

_____

_____

_____

_____

_____

_____

_____

_____

_____

_____

_____

_____

_____

 # MY SOUL STORY

A prime example I know of *falling up* in our profession belongs to my colleague, and Maryland school district leader Bill Barnes.

I met Bill in 2010 when my oldest daughter, Jessica (a talented mathematics teacher and school leader), approached me after a conference presentation and said, "Dad, I just saw the best presentation ever!" Thinking she might have been in my session, I took the bait and asked her who it was. Her reply, "Bill Barnes!"

I decided I better meet this guy.

At the 2019 national Mathematics in a PLC at Work conference, Bill shared his *falling-up* story—a story of extreme adversity from his childhood and how he overcame that adversity to become the incredible national educational leader, father, husband, and friend he is today. I asked Bill to share his story with you, and he agreed:

> There is a very interesting phenomenon when growing up as a child at risk. Some risk factors are invisible, while others are painfully present. For example, I grew up living in poverty, but I really didn't know it for most of my childhood. I spent my first five years living in a trailer park before bouncing around between friends and family for the next few years. Finally, we settled down in an 850-square-foot starter home. Throughout my childhood, I lived with or near people experiencing similar socioeconomic challenges, so my poverty was relative, even invisible. In fact, when I was given a used car for my sixteenth birthday (albeit, to help with a sixty-six-mile roundtrip commute to school), I even thought we might be rich.
>
> Though poverty remained an invisible risk factor for me, the presence of alcohol, abuse, and domestic violence was impossible to ignore.
>
> At some point early in my life, my father, a child of two alcoholics and the victim of traumatic physical and emotional abuse, succumbed to his demons. He began drinking heavily, often to the point of passing out. My father's fierce temper intensified when mixed with alcohol.

The abuse present in my home was usually emotional but sometimes physical. That abuse was directed toward my mother, my sister, and me. By the time I was eleven years old, I lived in a constant state of fear. I was withdrawing. But my mother, who was desperately trying to hold the family together, suffered the most. When my father stopped working altogether, she began working the night shift for the state government.

Even though my mom came home well after midnight, she would wake us at 6:00 a.m. for breakfast, handing us our school lunches with quick directions for preparing that night's dinner. She then managed the myriad of household tasks before heading off to work to start the cycle again. And she did all of this in a constant state of fear.

I share my story because it explains who I am, at my core. These experiences shaped me. They are present with me each and every day, and they are the primary reasons I am an educator.

First, at a very early age, when I was living in that trailer, I remember my mom, tears streaming down her face, leaning in to say, "Billy, you have to go to college. I'm not going to be much help describing what that will be like, but you need to know that I'll do everything I can to get you there." She followed with, "And, life is hard. To succeed, you are going to have to take risks. If you want to try something, don't worry about failing. I'll always be proud of you if you try.

"You do not want to go through life regretting missed opportunities. Say it with me, 'No regrets!'" I repeated, "No regrets." She told me that last bit over and over again throughout the years.

It is a major influence in my life today.

My second reason for choosing education became my teachers who provided safety, sanctuary, and hope. I believe I am a statistical anomaly. I shouldn't be in the position that I am in. I should have failed, or given up, or even quit along the way. But when I reflect upon my school-aged experiences, I can think of a series of teachers who went out of their way to show me kindness and open doors that otherwise might have remained closed.

At each turn, it seemed there was a teacher providing some opportunity that would lead to another opportunity, and then more opportunities, and so on. *No regrets!*

I wake up every day and drive to work thinking of ways to increase opportunities for our students. I know there are hundreds of students in our schools who are experiencing elements of my childhood *right now*. I want each one of those children to experience the life I have enjoyed.

Reflect on Bill's *falling-up* story. Who in your life needs you to help them *fall up* to the obstacles they are facing? What are the *I will*... commitments you can make to help a student or colleague (or even yourself) begin a *falling-up* journey?

_____

_____

_____

_____

_____

_____

_____

_____

_____

_____

_____

_____

_____

_____

_____

To that end, I have experienced a great deal of joy in my life. I am married to my best friend, Page, and we are proudly raising our teenage daughter, Abby. I give Abby lots of advice, because it is my job as her parent. I lost my mom to colon cancer when she was just fifty-three and emerging bravely from a life of fear. The advice I want Abby to hear most often is, "Life is hard. To succeed, you are going to have to take risks. If you want to try something, don't worry about failing. I'll always be proud of you if you try. You do not want to go through life regretting missed opportunities. Say it with me, Abby, 'No regrets!'"[68]

MY SOUL STORY

The first time I heard Bill's story, I had known Bill a few years by then, and I had no idea he had suffered such a difficult and abusive past. He recognizes it and has worked hard to understand it, but it does not define who he has chosen to become and his healthy daily responses as an educator.

The same should and can be true for us. To have an everlasting impact on the students we serve, we cannot get impatient, we cannot lose our temper, and we cannot get frustrated, no matter the adversity we face—past, present, or future. Our students and colleagues are counting on our healthy response to the adversity we face every school season. Our soul story is built on our healthy choice to use our pain and adversity as opportunities to *serve* our positive contributions today and tomorrow. May we remember why we chose this vocation, even on our worst days.

The journey is as important as whatever destination we hope for—and that story, our story as educators, finds its healing and laughter, its stillness and clarity, in the moments we realize we can't do it all without experiencing some stress and strain. At some point we say to ourselves, "Today, I am enough. And tomorrow, I will seek to be just a bit better."

It is in those moments we pull ourselves out of the shallows of our professional life and find deeper meaning in our work as a vocation.

The Shallows

S   ♡   U   L

The divided life is a wounded life, and the soul keeps calling us to heal the wound.

—Parker J. Palmer

When you operate from a soul story–connected depth in your professional life, you operate from a deep sense of self-*awareness*: "How do my actions impact others, and realistically, how am I contributing to a positive work culture each day?"

Yet, the professional life we live often conspires against our soul story development. We have a desperate need for our soul story to provide depth to our work life. Depth in our conversations, depth in our lesson plans, depth in our knowledge of our students' stories, and depth in our everyday interactions. Yet, depth is elusive, and the opposite of living with depth is living life superficially.

Living in the shallows.

The fast-paced, hurried, self-involved life drags us into the shallows every time. We don't have the time to deepen our relationships with family and friends, much less colleagues. Our soul story gets fragmented and divided, as our life becomes an "it's all about me" story. We lose sight of the second mountain.

We become too busy to plan for new and improved lessons and assessments. We lack the energy to spend time nurturing others. We feel that if one more thing gets added to our plate, we will crack for sure. We gradually take our family and friends closest to our inner circle for granted. We rationalize, "They understand how busy I am. They know I love them; do I need to pay attention to those relationships too?"

Has your shallow and hurried self ever caused you to think your teaching work life is merely a job and not satisfying your intended vocation? Why or why not?

_____

_____

_____

_____

_____

_____

_____

_____

Do you know anyone who thinks like that? What can you say or do to help that person reconnect to why he or she originally chose our profession?

_____

_____

_____

_____

_____

_____

_____

_____

_____

_____

When you operate from the shallows, you are disconnected from your soul story, and you become self-*obsessed*, too concerned with your own desires and interests, and unable to realize your negative impact on others. The shallow *self* reasons, "I might as well give up on contributing to or expecting much satisfaction from my professional life."

♥ MY SOUL STORY

I was thirty-five and in my thirteenth year of teaching when I accepted my fourth job in our profession at Adlai E. Stevenson High School District 125 in suburban Chicago. My professional life had moved from rural to urban and now to suburban communities. When I accepted the job offer, I was pretty sure I wouldn't stay long.

My plan was to stay three years at Stevenson and then move on to a more prestigious school district. A pretty selfish and ego-driven plan in a way, right? *I'll take the job because it will improve* myself. My *résumé*. My *plan for the future.* "This job is just a stepping-stone job," I said to my*self*.

The danger, of course, was that if I wasn't careful, that mindset would result in my not giving the best of my*self* to the job, because I wouldn't view it as worthy of my best effort. So, I would cheat my experiences with my students and colleagues. They would get the average me and not the best me that exists.

In the end, I stayed twenty-three more years and eventually served as district superintendent. So much for my *self*'s plans!

Something unexpected happened when I arrived. I fell in love with the place. Or, I should say I fell in love with the people. We had all types and flavors of teachers and leaders in our mathematics and science division of the high school and in our five K–8 feeder districts.

It wasn't long, however, until I noticed there were a lot of teachers and leaders operating from a soul story place of depth, and there were others who were disconnected from their professional soul story—operating in the shallows.

The Stevenson teachers and leaders living their daily professional lives from a place of depth were busy but not hurried. They were involved in the school through a myriad of activities *and* fully present when students, parents, or colleagues needed them. They would readily admit their work life was physically demanding but not soul story draining.

When you and I operate from a place of depth, we leave our egotistical tendencies at the door. We are able to see others—students and colleagues—and not be too self-absorbed and vacuous. When our work life is deep, we give our students and colleagues most of the credit, while also appreciating, with quiet confidence, our contribution. When our work life has its bumps, and we feel as if we are failing, we look in the mirror and ask, "How can I get better?"

Those teachers and school leaders were, for me, inspirational. I was able to witness some of the best teaching and learning of my young career. They pulled my*self*, and my efforts to serve them, to a deeper level. And they inspired me to give my best effort every day.

MY SOUL STORY ♥ ——————

Consider the following descriptions
for Person A and Person B. Choose and describe one colleague whose life resembles Person A and one whose life resembles Person B.

Also, decide which person's work-life state best describes your current work-life state: Person A's or Person B's. Provide some reasons for your choice.

Person A: *My work life*—I have a full schedule. A *lot* of activities. I am balancing many plates, including my team time, my family time, and some quiet reflective time, daily. My job is physically and emotionally demanding. I cannot do the job without the help of others.

Person B: *My work life*—I am preoccupied quite often. I am unable to be fully present due to the demands of my job. I feel physically and emotionally drained every day. If something unexpected happens in the next two weeks, I do not know what I will do. There are just so many demands on my time right now. I just don't have time to notice others.

They rarely played the blame game, and they kept their personal and professional lives balanced. They viewed their life balance more as a part of a positive *inner core* condition they were responsible for, and less as an outward condition that they were helpless toward, blameless for, or disconnected from, as in "It is someone else's fault I live a shallow life."

Unlike at my previous workplace, the number of teachers and leaders operating from a place of depth (Person A types—busy but not hurried) at Stevenson far outweighed the number of those disconnected from their professional soul story, operating on the edge of the shallows (Person B types—hurried and a bit out of control). It is no wonder Stevenson became the birthplace of the PLC process and a nationally recognized space for educating children at unprecedented levels of success. The majority of the faculty and staff operated at a level of depth navigating away from the shallows.

When we live our professional life in the shallows, everyone suffers. Shallow behaviors, living on the surface of our professional life, mask the truth below the surface. A colleague consistently shows up late to a required school duty. When a student arrives in the morning in need of help, this colleague acts as if it is an inconvenience.

Other symptoms of the shallows might include skipping required IEP meetings or recycling old lessons without much thought for improvement—lessons that are easier, more convenient, and faster, with less preparation time. Operating on the surface of his or her academic and pedagogical knowledge becomes the default method of teaching. No time for depth. Team meetings become no-show events.

Poor student performance is blamed on others—students, parents, or the previous years' teachers. When operating in the shallows, a colleague acts like a victim to professional struggles. He or she fails to use other teachers as valuable resources or for support because it is faster to do all the work alone, and it does not reveal his or her shallow life to others.

Burnout waits up ahead.

Don't be too quick to judge this colleague, though. The primary obstacle to living a less shallow, in-depth, fulfilled professional life is *us*. We are not that far from the drift to the shallows ourselves.

If we are not careful, we gradually replace the word *soul* with the word *self*. "My *soul* story" becomes "my *self* story." But they are not the same thing.

Our *soul story* is the place where we find our moral worth and become good in order to create good in others. We fulfill the promise of our professional life.

Our *self* story is the place where we start to lose our moral worth, become obsessed with ourselves, and neglect those in our professional life, and worse. We nimbly neglect those in our closest ring of influence—our family and friends.

Unfortunately, our everyday language applauds self-obsessed thinking: *Take care of my*self, *stand up for my*self, *be my*self, *express my*self. *Take a selfie with my*self. *Glorify my*self, *indulge my*self, and *satisfy my*self. My life trends toward shallow when my interests and thoughts go no further than my*self.*

A positive sense of self is, of course, healthy. But, what if your *self* is an obsessive, ego-driven disaster? What then?

In our profession, the shallow, obsessive self is dangerous.

What happens when one does damage, hurts, or abuses others? What happens when we are so hurried we cannot act with kindness; every child and colleague is an intrusion; and every request for our time is an inconvenience we meet with a sharp tone of rebuke because we are so harried, hurried, and irritated?

What happens when our *self* runs into a work-life hurried moment that is a disaster? What then?

In the opening epigraph to this chapter, Palmer provides a hint: "The divided life is a wounded life, and the soul keeps calling us to heal the wound."[69] To become a story of positive impact on others, our soul story seeks to cross the divide from a life in the shallows (ignoring the wound) to a life in the depths of who we are (healing the wound).

In my early days at Stevenson, my shallow life often haunted me. Sometimes the "it's all about me" monster would quietly stir inside me and rear its ugly head as a flawed and jealous me (more on this in chapter 12, page 91).

Sometimes my shallow self was just so tired, and I wanted to persevere, but I struggled to model the tenacity of *try, try again, and then try again. Never give up on anyone* is a tough mindset to adopt when your personal and professional life's pace is overwhelming.

Part of it was my ego: "I can do this by myself; I don't need help." My own shallow, self-obsessed behavior and expectations for perfection were destroying the hard work of others and not inspiring them. Yet, I so wanted to be inspirational.

Think about moments when your professional life has lacked depth. What do you do daily to stay fully present and really listen to your students and colleagues, as Katie does?

_____
_____
_____
_____
_____
_____
_____
_____
_____
_____
_____
_____
_____
_____
_____
_____
_____
_____
_____
_____
_____
_____
_____
_____
_____

I asked my colleague and health care clinician Katie Graves how she avoids the shallows at work and engages more deeply with her clients. She says:

> Staying present. It is easy to get lost in your own head and allow your thoughts to overtake your ability to be attentive and engaged with each person you encounter, whether that person is a patient (student), a coworker, or a family member. We are often so caught up in the results of our work, we miss the opportunity to be truly present with the person in front of [us], or even the space around [us]. Being fully present is essential to really listening, seeing, perceiving . . . and to working in communion to create something good and powerful. This type of depth is a truly healing response.[70]

MY SOUL STORY

∞

Our soul story can *overcome* the shallow life.

At Stevenson, we adopted a few governing core values—virtues designed to remind us to stay fully present with each other and our students. It did not mean we would win every day, but it did mean we could avoid the drift to our shallower selves.

We adopted these values, understanding the inherent busy-versus-hurried paradox residing in each one. These expectations would become part of a schoolwide culture of care that I consider part of the PLC at Work life.

Prepare for adversity.

Adversity is detailed in chapter 8 (page 59), but for our faculty, administration, and staff, this meant no more complaining because core adult and student behaviors were changing. Embrace change connected to the vision of our work. Come into the school year knowing the unexpected will happen. Accept the unexpected as part of our work-life routine, and respond in a healthy, respectful, positive, and supportive way. Be productively busy, ask for help, and ask a trusted colleague to let you know if you are becoming hurried.

Stop being selfish.

Share your technical knowledge for teaching and learning with others. Stop keeping your knowledge to your*self*. Get over your*self*. Commit to a cause greater than *you*. Think, "How are all the students in my grade level or course in this school, not just the students assigned to me, doing this year?" If you are an administrator, think, "How are we contributing to student learning in other school programs in the district, not just in my school or program? How can our school serve as a lighthouse for other schools?"

Leave your ego at the door.

When I arrived at Stevenson, I brought a big metal sign with me that I had above my classroom door at West Chicago. It was a sign I used during my basketball-coaching days. It looked like one of those street signs that might support your favorite sports team. I placed that sign right above my office door. It simply said, "Leave your ego at the door."

In my beginning days at Stevenson, I meant for the sign to be for my students and my colleagues as well. It took me a few years of maturity, but I eventually realized the sign was mostly for me. Yes, we should walk with confidence every day. Just make sure you temper it with humility of the *self*, with more passion for the cause of student learning than for the cause of your personal greatness.

Change what you can control.

We completely control our will and our choice for healthy responses to adversity. When you and I act like victims, we allow our heart and soul to be hijacked by others. Our will is within our*selves*. The will's fortitude and wisdom give us the ultimate strength, as in the strength to endure, contextualize, and derive meaning from the obstacles we cannot control and cannot simply overcome. "Will is the discipline of the heart and soul."[71]

Remember, we are in this together.

A soul story with depth lives in conscious awareness of the long-term picture of our careers as educators and not just the work of today. *This* school season does not guarantee a next season. Your soul story has depth when you are connected to others and solve the challenges in front of you *together*, as part 3, "U Is for Unifying" (page 121), will reveal. There is a nagging awareness that your colleagues in your next season may indeed be different. Each team picture, each season, has its own unique dynamic and energy and effort to help us avoid the shallows, together.

Examine these five
core values. Which resonates the most with you? In your daily work life, which of these core values is a strength? Explain.

_____

_____

_____

_____

_____

_____

Which of these five core
values presents the greatest challenge to you? Why?

_____

_____

_____

_____

_____

_____

What is one action you can
take in this school season to avoid the shallows and be more fully present every day?

_____

_____

_____

_____

_____

_____

_____

_____

 # MY SOUL STORY

Every year at Stevenson, I gathered our mathematics and science faculty at our open house night in September for a team picture. We were dressed in our best, and we would gather on some risers and snap the photo. This was before cell phones. No selfies, just a group photo that illustrated our emotion. Our humanity. Our togetherness. In all photos, there is always a story behind each smile, is there not?

What I did not fully appreciate in the first few years of this annual event was that those photos, posted on our office walls as reminders of our team of adults every year, would of course shift and change. Each school season had new faces, and other faces from the year before were no longer there. The photos reminded us that each school season of our lives is important, unique, and special.

Every school season will end, sometimes on our terms and sometimes not. There are no guarantees. The picture of the persons will change for your next school season. And yet, the picture of those persons in your current season is worth a thousand words of stories, and life, and hopefully depth and joy from the memories created during your professional journey, as we will discuss in detail in part 4 (page 185).

Our educational purpose is partially designed to make our school and community a better place to be and to live. Don't live the divided life, with one foot in the shallows and one foot in the deep end. The divided life will keep you from your soul story.

And for sure, don't let the shallows win. Stay out!

Head for the depth of your work and stay there. Seek to understand and then stay connected to healthy emotional responses in your professional life as you explore your emotional temperature next.

10

SASHET

S U L

*A person is essentially a collection of conscious experiences. Far
more than just bodies or just appetites, we are our experiences.
That is why we treasure the good ones.*

—Dallas Willard

During the early 1990s at Stevenson, the majority of the faculty and staff were
starting to rock the house. We shared a lot of positive experiences together. We were on fire
and working toward what would eventually become known as the PLC at Work process.
We were becoming a healthy school culture of academic and socially mature knowledge
workers pioneered by our principal and eventual superintendent Rick DuFour and his
colleague Bob Eaker, a professor from Tennessee.

Rick had several job offers to leave Stevenson and start the PLC at Work culture in other
school districts for more money and seemingly more prestige. The pressure on him was
immense, as the time to leave or stay was imminent. As he and I sat at a quiet breakfast
spot in Evanston, Illinois, on a Saturday morning, he had to make his choice. Monday
night was our school board meeting. The board needed a response. Would he stay or go?

I never forgot his answer:

> I can't leave Stevenson. It is not so much the place as it is the people. I love the
> commitment of our faculty and staff, community, and school board. Our *expe-*
> *riences together* to figure out how to educate students are unprecedented and
> life changing in many ways.[72]

And there it is.

We had created a healthy school culture of incredible, non-perfect people that was just
so very hard to leave. More money and more prestige do not supersede the value of a

Reflect on your current
school culture. Is it a healthy and
whole school culture? Is it the type
of culture that is just very hard to
leave? Indicate *yes* or *no*, and *why*
or *why not*.

_____
_____
_____
_____
_____
_____
_____
_____
_____
_____
_____
_____
_____
_____
_____
_____
_____
_____
_____
_____
_____
_____
_____
_____
_____
_____

healthy and whole (as in working for the greater good
of every student) school culture.

MY SOUL STORY

This did not mean our teachers and school leaders
were incapable of being overwhelmed by anger, fear,
and sadness. Sometimes our emotions got the best of
us. The weight of being *controlled* by our negative emotions was an obstacle at times.

Early in my career at Stevenson (about seven years
before that Saturday breakfast conversation with Rick),
I would walk our grounds in the morning to appreciate the cleanliness of our school buildings and the
alive vibe running throughout the school. It was my
way of centering myself at the beginning of each day.

I loved observing the life of our school and its healthy
and whole cultural pursuit. I often noticed a sense of
energy throughout and the positive emotions and influences exchanged between our students and our teachers.
I had this feeling our students wanted to actively participate within the walls of our school.

For several months, I observed the verbal interactions
and emotions displayed among our teachers, administrators, parents (either on the phone or in person), and
students in different areas of the school.

Some areas of the school felt very welcoming to me.
There was a positive emotional experience and healthy
responses and exchanges with our students. There was
a confidence and collaborative nature in the learning
progress of our students and faculty. There was a feeling
of joy. Our students seemed happy. The back-and-forth
banter was filled with humor and depth to our work
life, and no one seemed too rattled by the chaos and
noise that come as part of a school's culture.

Other areas of the school seemed edgy and empty
with an unwelcome, almost resentful feeling. In these
areas, it seemed like an intrusion on adult space when
students or other colleagues showed up for help. Our
students seemed almost scared to ask for help from
some of our teachers.

Some team meetings felt fast-paced, exciting, and energetic, with team members genuinely glad to be together and consistently kind to one another. Other team meetings felt boring, anxious, gloomy, and non-committal. Some conversations with parents felt sympathetic and kind, understanding and connected, and loving and optimistic, while others felt angry and resentful, agitated and anxious.

I had to wonder, what was the reason for this difference? How could our faculty, staff, and school leaders have created such a divergent culture and emotional embrace of our student and teacher experiences?

Some of our teachers and administrators displayed emotions of consideration and kindness, excitement and tenderness, and connectedness and sympathy. Other faculty and administrators often displayed negative emotions and consistently acted irritated and resentful of others, nervous and jittery, disengaged and dejected. Was it the school culture? The leadership? Their job? Their teacher team? Was it me?

MY SOUL STORY

Our overall academic content knowledge was pretty high, but for some of our adults, *relational* skills were pretty low. We had to acknowledge that the inconsistent display of negative emotions toward colleagues, students, and parents was an obstacle to our growth as a healthy professional culture.

On many mornings, I would face the dissatisfaction of a teacher or administrator as we were learning and growing into our relational health. I would witness teachers exasperated and yelling at parents on the phone or sometimes at our students or me. I observed one teacher put her fist through an overhead projector because she was so angry with her students. Other staff members would huddle up in small groups of two to three and gossip about others in our community— our students, students' parents, and each other. The negative emotions from these gossip whisperers had a bullying, blame-game, acting-like-a-victim effect.

Allowing our negative emotions to move us toward a lack of grace was a major obstacle we needed to overcome.

Consider the emotions displayed in your school among your students and their parents and your colleagues. In general, are these emotions positive or negative?

_____

_____

_____

_____

_____

_____

_____

_____

_____

_____

For the negative emotions— such as fear and anger—think about your behaviors and your colleagues' behaviors. Are your responses to anger or fear healthy or unhealthy?

_____

_____

_____

_____

_____

_____

_____

_____

_____

_____

We knew that in order to become a healthy and *whole* school culture, we could not stand divided *emotionally*.

Our soul story can *overcome* unhealthy emotional responses.

It has long been thought (and taught) there are roughly six categories of human emotions.[73] In 2017, however, University of California, Berkeley researchers Alan S. Cowen and Dacher Keltner suggested there are at least twenty-seven distinct dimensions of emotions intimately interconnected with each other, such as envy, joy, pride, and sadness. Our emotions are interconnected and do not act as separate clusters. We feel our emotions in varying states of interconnected experiences.[74]

Our emotions are "a conscious mental reaction (such as anger or fear) subjectively experienced as strong feeling usually directed toward a specific object and typically accompanied by physiological and behavioral changes in the body."[75]

Hmm. Slow that down and pull it apart. So emotion is:

- A mental response state
- With physiological changes
- Directed toward others or objects
- As feelings such as joy, sorrow, anger, or fear

Emotion is a state of feeling something. Got it.

A healthy and whole school culture reflects a *positive* state of feeling, and a *controlled* state of being. Our emotions do not get the best of us. We get the best from them.

So to check my emotional temperature, I ask, "How am I feeling today? Is my state of feeling positive or negative? And do those feelings (positive or negative) control my actions through unhealthy responses? Or do my actions keep my feelings under control in order to impact more positive daily experiences and healthy responses?"

These questions allow us to connect with our *emotional* intelligence.

John D. Mayer and Peter Salovey provided the original definition of *emotional intelligence* during the mid-1990s: "The ability to perceive emotions, to access and generate emotions so as to assist thought, to understand emotions and emotional knowledge, and to *reflectively regulate emotions* so as to promote emotional and intellectual growth."[76]

The italics in this quote are mine. So, we are to reflectively regulate our emotions? Every day? Yes.

MY SOUL STORY 💙

There is an interesting and effective acronym to help us examine our emotional state as we enter into each day.

Based on the research of David E. Carlson, author Anthony Mersino explored how we can leverage our emotional intelligence to help us meet our goals at work. Mersino used the acronym *SASHET*: **s**ad, **a**ngry, **s**cared, **h**appy, **e**xcited, **t**ender.[77]

The first three letters, *SAS*, reveal three *negative* emotions that provide daily data about the healthy and whole culture we contribute to and experience with others.

- **Sad:** Affected with or expressive of grief or unhappiness (Elements of sad include feeling down, grieved, dejected, depressed, or heartbroken.)
- **Angry:** Feeling or showing anger; a strong feeling of displeasure and usually of antagonism (Elements of angry include irritated, resentful, miffed, upset, mad, furious, or raging.)
- **Scared:** Thrown into or being in a state of fear, fright, or panic (Elements of scared include tense, nervous, anxious, frightened, or panic-stricken.)

The last three letters, *HET*, reveal three *positive* emotions that provide daily data about the healthy and whole culture we contribute to and experience with others.

- **Happy:** Enjoying or characterized by well-being and contentment (Elements of happy include optimistic, satisfied, contented, or fulfilled.)
- **Excited:** Having, showing, or characterized by a heightened state of energy, enthusiasm, eagerness, and so on (Elements of excited include antsy, bouncy, energetic, or ecstatic.)
- **Tender:** Showing care (Elements of tender include kind, sympathetic, warm hearted, or loving.)

Think about your daily display of emotions. Are they generally positive or negative? How do you personally become aware of, reflect on, and regulate your emotions each day in order to have a more positive impact on your students and colleagues?

In part 4, we focus on the H, E, and T positive emotions (happy, excited, and tender). In this chapter and the next, however, we focus on the obstacles presented through our S, A, and S negative emotions (sad, angry, and scared). When we live a life controlled by our negative emotions, we become frozen in our positive experiences with others. In many cases, we struggle to explain or identify why we are consistently negative in our experiences and our unhealthy interactions with others.

Thus, in our profession, we self-correct our daily negative impact on others as much as we can, because within any one week of the school year, we experience the negative SASHET emotions in some form or another. In most situations, a two-part self-reflection is necessary to overcome the obstacle of our negative emotions' becoming a bit out of whack.

First, ask yourself, "Which negative SASHET emotion or emotions am I feeling right now? Sad, angry, or scared?"

Second, ask, "*Why* am I feeling this way? What is happening in my work life right now, causing this negative emotional response? Why am I so mad every day at work? Why do I feel like I am failing this week? Why am I scared to share with my colleagues? Why do I gossip about others? Why do I act busy and ignore my students when they ask for help? Why do I get agitated so easily these days?"

MY SOUL STORY ♥

Part 1: Think about
your professional actions this past week contributing to your positive or negative impact on others. Which of the three negative SASHET emotions comes to mind when you ask, "Am I feeling sad, angry, or scared today?"

Pinpoint the emotion, and then ask yourself, "*Why* am I feeling this way?" Push hard on the *why*.

Part 2: List one or two
actions you can take to better control this negative emotion and offer a healthier response to it during your experiences with others. Write your actions as *I will* . . . statements.

There is a difference between *self*-care and *soul story* care. Self-care allows you to *become aware* of how your actions affect the many others in your professional life. It is your willingness to ask and answer the part 1 questions in the My Soul Story prompt.

Your soul story embraces your negative emotions without the judgment of good or bad, and identifies their existence. However, your soul story understands the need to commit to day-to-day actions to *do something* about your unhealthy responses to a negative emotion (the action commitments you wrote about in part 2 of the previous My Soul Story). Your action to write about what you are feeling—sad, angry, or scared—often diminishes the emotional intensity of the moment and allows you the space needed for a more healthy response to that emotion.

When you look back on the school seasons that stack up over time, it will be your soul story *actions* that become the essence of who you are; what your students and colleagues remember about you are the positive experiences they had with you along the way.

One caution: Despite your best efforts, certain negative emotional patterns re-emerge from time to time. It is in these moments that you may need to exercise a bit of self-compassion (see chapter 12, page 91).

It is your soul story that gives your life direction, strength, and harmony. That brings you, your team, and your school to a place that is healthy and whole. As educators, we declare, "We do not let negative, out-of-control emotions win the day in our school. We will pursue this wonderful alchemy of academic competence *and* emotional competence among the adults in our school. The school culture will reflect a process where our emotions no longer control us; we are in control of them."

As a teacher and professional, I know that my students deserve and *need* the best from me. As an administrator, I know that my teachers deserve the best from me every day. My family needs the best from me too. This can take its toll.

Dallas Willard reminds us of this reality:

> We live from our heart. . . . The human spirit is an inescapable, fundamental aspect of every human being; and it takes on whichever character it has from the experiences and the choices we have lived through or made in our past. A person is essentially a collection of conscious experiences. Far more than just bodies or just appetites, we are our experiences. That is why we treasure the good ones.[78]

Our students, colleagues, and families need us to make a positive emotional impact on them. We want them to have access to the best of us, and then treasure those good experiences with us.

So, I commit to time for reflecting (more on this in chapter 21, page 173), self-regulating my emotions, and then offering a healthy response to my negative emotions every day. I will insist on it from each of my colleagues too. And I will call them out (with grace) when they are not displaying healthy emotional intelligence in their work life.

I will help our school culture become not a place divided, but instead a healthy and whole emotional-wellness culture, recognizing, appreciating, and leaning into our diversity. A place of great experiences on most days. A place no one will want to leave.

Anger Never Wins

You will not be punished for your anger; you will be punished by your anger.

—Gautama Buddha

Anger is a difficult emotion to embrace *and* control.

Although it is human to become angry, anger is the most negative of all our emotions. I am not one to dwell on the negative for very long. Yet I know anger and our response to anger when misplaced, misdirected, or abused can leave a lifetime of regret.

A successful response to anger *needs* a connection to our soul story journey. The anger emotion is blind to our age, knowledge, or sophistication. It lingers in the shallows of our everyday work and life.

The emotion of *anger* is defined as "a strong feeling of displeasure and usually of antagonism."[79] It can be a challenging emotion for us all.

In A Note to Readers at the beginning of this book (page xi), I describe a time of suffering in my life—my final conversation with professional colleague and personal friend Becky DuFour in June 2018. If needed, take just a minute to reread that section before reading ahead.

In chapter 1 (page 7), I describe an event in September 2018 designed to heal and bring closure to that suffering. Next is a partial description of the three months in between, a story of anger, grief, compassion, suffering, and relationships.

I have a picture on my cell phone from June 20, 2018. I cannot delete it. Becky DuFour and I are with some colleagues on a stage. We are smiling with positive energy from our experiences after working for a few days with a group of incredible educators. It would be my last picture with Becky. This group picture-taking moment had become quite routine.

It was easy to take the picture for granted, as there is always a picture to take next time or next week, right?

During the summer months, our presentation team moves from one city to the next across the United States as we present our PLC at Work Institutes. Near the end of June 2018, we had two events simultaneously, which happens from time to time. I was at our PLC event in Santa Clara, California. Becky was in Atlanta, Georgia, leading our team at a school leadership event.

On June 26, Becky opened the conference with her usual terrific keynote address—her grace, calm, and infectious enthusiasm on display. During the morning breakout following her keynote address, Becky fainted. She fell off the stage and hit the floor hard. She was rushed to the hospital in critical condition. Her situation remained critical and did not improve over the next few weeks.

Over the weekend of July 7, her family, led by her daughter Hannah, had to make the compassionate and collaborative decision with her doctors to take Hannah's mom, and the grandma of her babies, off life support. It was Monday, July 9.

On the morning of July 10, I packed my bags and headed out the door to Rogers, Arkansas, for what would have been my next event with Becky. Before I left, my wife, Susan, and I sat at our kitchen table (isn't that where the most meaningful family and friend conversations often take place?), trying to make sense of it all, still in disbelief at the suddenness of the tragedy. We were aware it would be only a matter of days before Becky passed away.

That day, my connecting flight landed in Rogers at 9:48 p.m. My phone was blowing up with text and phone messages. I did not need to read or listen to them. I knew. I sat in the dark as the plane taxied to the gate, tears silently flowing down my face. I understood my sadness, but I was surprised at the depth of my *anger*.

I realized the moment was tapping into a series of family members' and friends' dying over the past two years. This mounting sense of loss had been building up as anger inside of me for quite some time. I missed them. And now, Becky. I called Susan once I got to the hotel, and we held onto a quiet conversation a little longer than normal.

The next morning, I was asked to lead our presentation team in prayer before we began our professional development event for the day. Praying before the event was not something we would normally, if ever, do. We are a team of many faiths and backgrounds, and our prayer was about connection to our more spiritual soul story, to our shared humanity and relational selves in a time of grief and the loss of someone we loved very deeply.

In that moment, life felt very fragile. It was a reminder that our days as professionals are finite.

During my first breakout session, I went off script (like we often do as teachers in a time of crisis) and shared my pain and a few stories, and then read from page 34 of *HEART!*[80], Becky's favorite poem by Marge Piercy: "To Be of Use."[81]

I asked group members to read and then respond to the poem's meaning for their professional lives. And then I explained what the poem had meant to Becky and why she had asked me to place the poem in *HEART!* I shared her favorite line from the poem: "The pitcher cries for water to carry, and a person for work that is real."[82]

I made it to our presenter lunch but could not go inside the room. I knew I was angry and hurt, and needed time to process—alone. Instead, I went outside and walked until the next session. I could not understand why people in the passing cars did not seem upset. "Don't you know what happened to my colleague and friend?" I wanted to shout out to every car. "Why isn't the world mourning today?"

I finished our afternoon sessions and did what I do on most summer days; I went for a run. This day on my schedule was supposed to be an easy three-mile run. I ended up running an angry, hard seven-mile run out in the country until I was exhausted, well out of the city, and racked with pain at the loss. More important, I was physically able to feel anger and hurt for Becky's daughter Hannah and son Matthew. I could not imagine the depth of their suffering on this day, and my soul hurt for them. Exhausted from my run, I bent over, hands on my knees, and screamed as loud as I could.

To the trees and the sky.

Over the next few months, the anger was still sitting inside of me as I closed myself off from my inner circle of friends, and only let Susan in. I processed my own grief and anger during my runs and my writing—alone. I knew that at times like this, relationships are important. But I also knew I needed to process by myself.

It was not until the fall, during Becky's celebration-of-life event, that I finally had the courage to spend time with my colleagues and exercise the selflessness needed to heal together.

How do you resolve your anger at work in the short term? What strategies do you use?

_____

_____

_____

_____

_____

_____

_____

_____

_____

How do you resolve your anger at work in the long term? What strategies do you use?

_____

_____

_____

_____

_____

_____

_____

_____

_____

And then, I finally wrote a letter to Hannah and Matthew, extending my compassion to them. I think it was at that point the healing of my anger finally began.

Anger is such a personal experience. My anger was resolved short-term through exercise. It was resolved long-term via compassion.

MY SOUL STORY

Your My Soul Story response is a reflection of your life as a mature professional. A soul story depressed by unresolved anger becomes an obstacle to a more fulfilled professional life. In our profession—a helping profession, no less—we are expected to not let anger win. Anger directed toward our students can never be abusive or hurtful. It would be a violation of our moral imperative and responsibility.

Our job is to partner *with* parents, *with* students, or *with* colleagues. Not *against* them. Remember the definition of *anger*? The emotion of anger is defined as "a strong feeling of displeasure and usually of antagonism."[83] If you allow it, your anger will place you in a highly negative state of energy directed at something or someone. Anger derails your *partnering with* others.

Anger begins to win.

As educators, we are to act professionally. Our profession expects us to always be the grown-up in the room. And the more cluttered our professional life, the more hurried our professional life; the more stressed out we are in daily life, the more likely we are to move quickly into the angry, judgmental, righteous phase of life. And then we become unapproachable.

Anger keeps winning.

When you and I are occupied by our first mountain climb—success, activity, money, lifestyle, reputation—we are living *externally*. The clutter and hurried days of our external life shrivel our professional soul story. The less time we spend analyzing our own anger triggers, the more we drift into anger moments that become embarrassing and public, and drag us into the shallows.

Anger has won.

My anger triggers have included losing my patience, thinking (or feeling) my opinion or effort didn't matter, witnessing socially unjust actions that harm or oppress children and adults, being made fun of by others, living through traumatic moments of loss, and experiencing threats to the shelter, financial health, or security of my family.

MY SOUL STORY 💜

Our soul story can *overcome* the anger in our lives.

Did you notice the italicized words in the second My Soul Story prompt? It provides a hint to overcoming your anger obstacles. Wharton School of the University of Pennsylvania professor and best-selling author Adam Grant suggests that in the face of an injustice, think of compassion toward the victim:

> Thinking about the perpetrator fuels anger and aggression. Shifting your attention to the victim makes you more empathetic, increasing the chances that you'll channel your anger in a constructive direction. Instead of trying to punish the people who caused harm, you'll be more likely to help the people who were harmed.[84]

What insight in that last line! In the face of an injustice, help the people being harmed rather than respond with anger to those causing the injustice. As you will see in part 3 (page 121), this is exactly the reason to stay connected, *together*, to our soul story pursuit.

A soul story that pursues happiness and belonging in its interactions with students, parents, and colleagues finds completeness and strength in its ability to *expect* anger, *embrace* anger, and *respond* to anger with grace and calm.

Anger is a valid and effective emotion when it leads to the *falling-up* response described in chapter 8 (page 59). Anger, resolved by a healthy response, can inspire meaningful action and change in school cultures and structures that foster inequities in learning for our minority and most marginalized students. Anger can

What are some hot buttons that trigger your anger at work? Write down an example.

_____

How can you choose to demonstrate *kindness and compassion* toward others when those hot-button situations start to arise?

_____

be used to finally open our eyes to the unseen, day-to-day suffering of our students.

Our healthy, short-term response to anger, such as staying calm and demonstrating kindness, is buoyed by an eventual response of compassion. As we develop a culture of compassion in our schools (see chapter 6, page 39), we start to dissipate the anger storm. We reclaim our value as educators. There is a reason not everyone can shoulder the stress and strain of our work.

The way we choose to respond to our anger ultimately reflects the daily values and virtues we claim to care about: *kindness, compassion, understanding, partnership,* and *awareness.*

You and I have a lot of power in the midst of our anger. The greatest power we have is to not let someone steal our inner joy. Kindness and compassion give to and serve the one who is being controlled by anger. But ultimately, they serve us too.

Kindness and compassion demonstrated toward others always win over anger. When we choose kindness amid our anger, it allows the conversation to turn positive and deeper. We begin to explore the real *why* behind our anger as we listen to one another and consider, "How do I communicate with you, and you with me, in a way that allows us to be aware of and understanding of our suffering?"

We are the professionals. We are the helpers. We ask, "How can I best serve this angry person in this moment?" The test of our professional soul story is that we give kindness when there is *no expectation of kindness in return.* The angry student, parent, or colleague may not yet be ready to return the kindness.

As I write this, that last paragraph feels to me like a big *request* of us. I am to return someone's anger toward me with kindness?

Yes.

I have always felt that kindness describes a type of love that takes the most ragged children (and some adults) who enter our path and creates value in them so they can eventually build value in others—forever. Is this not the purpose of our professional soul story journey?

We are to become better (good) versions of ourselves in order to create good in others.

Sometimes, the stress and strain of my professional life left me so worried about my own ailments, I could not lean into the anger of others. I could not get "big enough" to see past their anger or understand the issue from their point of view. I could only see the harm they were doing to others.

In hindsight, I either did not or could not find sufficient value in those people to demonstrate compassion toward them during their anger. Thus, I failed to connect the dots of how my actions and responses affected them, and vice versa.

Anger cannot win.

Controlling our anger is a *choice*. A tough choice. To identify with the experiences or lens of another person is also a choice. Passing judgment that someone does not deserve our compassion, and withholding it, is the worst choice we can make. It is for sure not a soul story choice.

There are many non-hurtful approaches we can take in response to our weekly personal anger moments. Some of us use humor (laughing quietly at ourselves), others use yoga, some sing, and others journal. I run.

Still others practice kindness.

Regardless of your choice (remaining calm, not letting anger win), it is important to accept anger as part of a normal emotional response, identify your triggers, and then respond in a way that de-escalates the situation.

To help you improve your anger response, you might consider taking the How Good Is Your Anger Management? test from MindTools (www.mindtools.com/pages/article/newTCS_88.htm) and immediately viewing the results.[85] The site also provides five key areas for improving your anger response. I scored a 69 when I took the test. I use my areas of strength and weakness to reflect on how I can improve on and personally nurture positive and healthy anger responses.

MY SOUL STORY

Our teaching profession is such a daunting, day-to-day second mountain climb. Emotions like anger and fear are natural in any walk of life. And yet, we have to be on our best game every day. Students are not the adults in the room. *We* are. Our profession is not for the weakhearted, that is for sure.

In the next chapter, I write about a colleague who was very angry with others in her life. What follows is

Take the anger management test at www.mindtools.com/pages/article/newTCS_88.htm. What did you learn about your anger response?

the rest of that story, so to speak. To know what got her to this point in her teaching and anger story, you will need to read the next chapter.

She left my office in anger. She was a younger teacher, only in the sixth season of her career. I was a more veteran teacher in my eighteenth season. She left with such a strong feeling of displeasure and antagonism toward me, she refused to talk to me for the last three months of the school year. Then in early July, this remarkable but angry teacher resigned. She did not tell me. She just left. And it hurt me. My last real conversation with her in March had not been pleasant. Since then, we had kept a safe distance.

Her anger had had a tight control on her workplace life, and it had damaged her relationship with not only me but also her colleagues. I felt a twinge of relief and guilt at the same time that summer. On one hand, I would not need to interact with her anger anymore (relief). On the other hand, I should have done *more* to help her (guilt). I should have had more compassion, more grace, more understanding, more kindness, more something.

I felt like I had failed a colleague and a friend.

I did not hear from her for five years. And then one day, I got an email. In it, she told me she had been angry with me for a long time. She told me I was right to have had that conversation with her. She told me I saved her marriage. She told me the words I used that morning were the exact words she had heard from her husband the night before. This had made her even angrier with me. She told me I had held the proverbial mirror up to her face, and what she saw was unbearable for a long time. She told me she had to leave. *They* had to leave. They needed a fresh start. And so, they did. She thanked me. We became distant friends, and I sent her a card of hope and joy when her first child was born.

Sometimes victories over our anger just take a little bit longer than we hope.

Kindness. Compassion. Understanding. Partnership. Awareness. Love. With these as our weapons in our anger battle, anger doesn't stand a chance.

Good Enough, *for Now*

S U L

None of us are perfect. We have biologies and pathologies that will inevitably trip us up.

—Ryan Holiday

This incredibly talented teacher sat in my office with a defensive posture. She did not like my using up her preparation time before school.

It was early March of her sixth school season. She was relatively young, a terrific teacher in so many ways, especially with her students, but not so much with her colleagues. I was concerned about her health and well-being. She affected the positive state of the work culture in our school building with a constant drumbeat of irritation and anger.

The cause? She possessed irrationally high expectations of herself and her colleagues. Her judgmental attitude toward the team's work and effort was defeating to others. She hated flaws discovered in herself and the flaws found in the daily work of her colleagues. She rarely celebrated achievements and positive accomplishments by the team as "good enough."

And, she did not accept my constructive criticism very well either. Working with her was like walking on eggshells. She would blow up at her colleagues and me, often without notice. She was acting counter to the school culture we were trying to create.

On my drive to school that morning, I had been distracted due to the meeting ahead. I had mulled over in my mind how to approach her. I knew it wouldn't go well. Yes, I was her boss, so to speak, in that I had more positional authority. But I was mostly her friend and colleague. I was more worried about the soul story of her life and well-being than about the latest disappointment and anger with her teammates and me.

Look Inward

Describe a time in your professional life when you had difficulty with constructive criticism. How did you eventually respond?

_____
_____
_____
_____
_____
_____
_____
_____
_____

Look Outward

Who in your professional life has a difficult time with constructive criticism? Have you tried to approach this person? What did you say, and how did it go?

_____
_____
_____
_____
_____
_____
_____
_____

The night before, I had decided to be direct with her. My general style with confrontation was to be more indirect. But I knew I needed to stop the eggshell walk. I needed to be a warm demander.

I settled for a direct hit to the issue and waited.

"None of us are perfect," I said to her.

The silence that followed fell heavily. My phone rang, and I ignored it. I finally added, "Your anger, your demand for perfection, your quick judgment of others, and your tone harm your colleagues and me. Despite your teaching talent, these issues have robbed you of joy and the joy of those around you."

Silence. Finally, I said, "How can I help?"

She made it clear to me that she did not need my help; she merely had high standards, and maybe I should be expecting more from her colleagues and myself. Also, her joy was none of my business. Our conversation digressed from there. I decided not to push the issue. I would take a more indirect approach.

For the next three months, I did what I could to help. I gently guided some of her team meetings, but the elephant in the room lingered. She and I did not have a meaningful conversation again. She needed space. I reluctantly gave it to her, determined to have the conversation again when the school season ended in June. She left the building on checkout day, before we could talk, and would not answer my follow-up calls the next week.

 # MY SOUL STORY

Her perfectionism was unhealthy, and her behavior took her to a life of discontent (see chapter 26, page 219, for more on joy in the workplace). She deserved so much more. The problem was not so much that she had perfectionist tendencies but that she could not recognize her perfectionism (and the anger that came with it) as an unhealthy response—a feeling that nothing is good enough, _ever_.

Looking in the mirror, I wondered, "What did I do to cause her misplaced anger? Did my holding up a mirror to her behaviors just make it worse? Could my tone or my criticism of her unhealthy perfectionism have been improved with more grace?"

There is a particular paradox to perfectionism in our professional life story.

On one hand, a healthy type of perfectionism is revealed when we expect ourselves and our colleagues to do well, and we treat failures as learning opportunities rather than indicators of inferiority. Healthy perfectionists are achievers with high standards of excellence. If we are healthy perfectionists, our aim for perfection causes us to feel inspired and content with our work life, not anxious and disappointed. We celebrate small victories one at a time.

On the other hand, the unhealthy form of perfectionism is revealed when we have an emotional desire to please or impress others because we're worried others will see us as less than perfect. We fear we will not be good enough. Somehow, we will not measure up to others' expectations.

If we are unhealthy perfectionists, our quirks and small mistakes can have such a toxic effect on us that although we desire success, we focus on avoiding failure. Our negative orientation is a constant grind on our inner circle of friends and family. We expect others' love and approval to be conditional on our having flawless expectations and performing perfectly. Which never happens. Never.

And if we do have an exceptionally flawless moment, it is a fleeting high. It will not last long before we are disappointed once more. In short, *perfectionism* is a "disposition to regard anything short of perfection as unacceptable."[86]

Hmm. So perfectionism is a state of mind we bring to work each day, in which we find the lack of a perfect performance *unacceptable*.

The unhealthy side of a perfectionist's mantra is to accept nothing short of a flawless performance or outcome. And to then feel disappointed. Seems like a bad recipe.

When failure to meet one's own impossibly high standards results in a feeling of personal worthlessness, being an unhealthy perfectionist can be self-defeating.

Unhealthy perfectionists worry about other people's standards. If they struggle, they procrastinate. "I'm not good enough" becomes the mantra of the unhealthy perfectionist.

Unhealthy perfectionism manifests itself at work in several ways. You are most likely self-critical much of the time. You label your work as failed unless it is flawless; you can always be a bit better and more fine-tuned. "I'm not good enough" can haunt you sometimes.

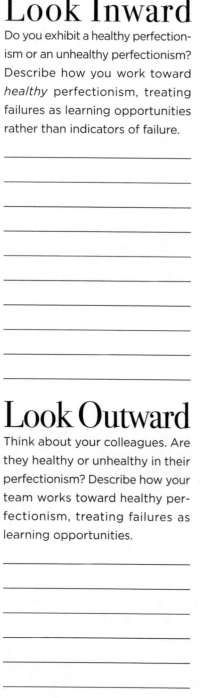

Look Inward

Do you exhibit a healthy perfectionism or an unhealthy perfectionism? Describe how you work toward *healthy* perfectionism, treating failures as learning opportunities rather than indicators of failure.

_____

_____

_____

_____

_____

_____

_____

_____

Look Outward

Think about your colleagues. Are they healthy or unhealthy in their perfectionism? Describe how your team works toward healthy perfectionism, treating failures as learning opportunities.

_____

_____

_____

_____

_____

_____

_____

_____

MY SOUL STORY

When I am writing, I am painfully aware of my deep flaws. I read books written by others and feel inept. I am clearly not as gifted, organized, or thoughtful. Other writers are so far ahead of whatever comes out of my brain. To some extent, we are all perfectionists. We want to do our best work. Yet our best work rarely happens on the first try.

Two closely related emotions can lead you right into the trap of perfectionism—(1) envy and (2) jealousy. Envy and jealousy can become an unhealthy comparison of yourself to others. Your soul story loses every time as soon as you start playing the comparison game.

Envy is a "painful or resentful awareness of an advantage enjoyed by another, joined with a desire to possess the same advantage."[87]

Jealousy is a "disposition, attitude, or feeling hostile toward a rival or one believed to enjoy an advantage."[88]

This is a first mountain problem.

Envy is an *awareness* you have an advantage over me. Jealousy is my *hostile attitude* toward you because I believe you have that advantage. "No one under the sway of envy or jealousy has a chance to think clearly or live peacefully. How could they? It is an endless loop of misery. We are envious of one person, while he or she, in turn, is envious of somebody else."[89]

Unhealthy perfectionism leads to envy during our first mountain climb. If I climb that first mountain by climbing over you, or through you, or shoving you down the mountain (so you don't have that advantage anymore), what have I gained?

Nothing.

The soul story journey of our professional life is empty if we only pursue the first mountain climb of "I'll accomplish more than you and be more perfect than you." Best-selling author Ryan Holiday describes that type of climb in his book *Ego Is the Enemy*:

> The farther you travel down the path of accomplishment, whatever it may be, the more often you meet other successful people who make

you feel insignificant. It doesn't matter how well you're doing; your ego and their accomplishments make you feel like nothing. . . . The only way you have value is if you're better than, have more than, *everyone everywhere.*[90]

You need to have more than, be better than, and be more perfect than everyone, everywhere? Well, good luck with that! And if that climb comes at the expense of and the oppression of others, then shame on you.

Thus, an unhealthy perfectionism hinders your relationship with others as you find yourself *passing comparative judgment* on those around you.

You are envious of their achievements and advantages they have over you. So you drag them down the first mountain of achievement instead of building them up or bringing them with you over to the second mountain of contribution. You can be difficult to please and jealous of what they have. Others may find you difficult to work with, challenging to collaborate with, or worse, hard to love.

MY SOUL STORY

Our soul story can *overcome* being less than perfect.

At the moment we become aware that our life is filled with flaws, we are on our way to a healthy form of perfection.

Productive perfectionists aim for high standards, of course, and expect those standards of others (just ask those who have to work with me). But if they miss, they try again. They admit to being human as a theme song. Not as an excuse, but as an understanding that learning and growing are at best iterative processes. Act. Reflect. Refine.

Then act to improve once more.

Productive or healthy perfectionism means understanding that our professional life is a series of rewrites. We fight the desire or the disposition to see only its flaws. We decide to let go and trust others to help us accept that our work life is one long, ongoing, formative learning experiment.

Look Inward

Do you exhibit behaviors of envy or jealousy at work? Do you pass judgment on and compare yourself to others? Why or why not?

_____

Look Outward

Think about your colleagues. Are workplace relationships hindered by envy or jealousy? Why or why not?

_____

"I am such a failure!" should not be a phrase you or I use because we tried something new that ultimately resulted in an imperfect process and outcome. Reserve that mantra for when you decide to not act or not try again to improve on the process and outcome of your work and effort.

If you decide not to make the next iteration better, then you have professionally failed your soul story pursuit. I have learned over the years to embrace my professional life as an ongoing iterative *learning process*.

Our soul story thrives when we have chosen to give the best of who we are in any given moment, and then find the strength to pick ourselves up when we fail (fall short of perfection) and try again to be a better version of ourselves. This cycle of learning and growing together is, by the way, *forever*.

My colleague and fellow author and presenter Regina Owens exemplifies how to use a healthy perfectionism to foster her professional impact. Here is her advice to us:

> If I am not winning the day, I am learning from it. Though this statement is positive, and one I aspire to live out loud, it has taken me a lifetime to embrace each experience in my life as existing to allow me to learn and enlighten my soul story.
>
> Each public moment of victory in my life was accompanied by many private moments of defeat. The defeat was not where I was conquered or captured by something or someone outside of me, but where I learned to boldly stand and humbly *be still* to defeat my fear, doubt, or unbelief. Each time I moved forward, I learned to listen and lead with love and authentic joy. I learned to be directed, disciplined, and determined to fulfill my purpose.
>
> I remember a lesson I learned early in my teaching career: my public [person] and private person needed to be the same. I learned that what I valued should serve my actions in the seemingly small (no one is looking) and the more obvious big (everyone is watching) moments in life. If I could act on my values in the quiet moments, the seemingly big and more public *self* moments would not pose much opposition.
>
> When I learned to live my virtues, there was no need to respond out of a scarcity mindset. There was no need to hoard and hold back my gifts and talents out of fear. There was no need to pursue perfection. The whole point of living is to be *perfected*.
>
> However, my perception of each and every event as an experience of faith or failure would determine if I would keep moving forward. A dear friend, a retired educator, always encouraged me to "keep your head down and keep moving." In other words, be humble and be brave—but keep learning and living.

For this to occur, you choose to change your perception from perfection to learning. It took me awhile to live and understand I am alive when I contribute to others, and I share the moments where I choose to conquer and overcome any fear of failure.

One of the most wonderful times of enlightenment for me occurred when I realized uplifting others was the best use of my gifts and talents. To be paralyzed by perfection simply meant I was choosing to fail—to stop—to quit—to give up—to give over what makes me feel alive.

That is my soul story.

Humanity needs us. We are beautifully connected. There are many people who have come before, who walk alongside us, and who will come after us. When we share those private moments of where we've overcome, when we live life out loud with grace—we win, and most importantly, we learn.[91]

MY SOUL STORY

Brené Brown is a research professor at the University of Houston Graduate College of Social Work. The author of several *New York Times* best-sellers, she writes about wholehearted living and how this comes from a place of worthiness:

> Wholehearted living is about engaging in our lives from a place of worthiness. . . . No matter what gets done and how much is left undone, *I am enough.* . . . Yes, I am imperfect and vulnerable and sometimes afraid, but that doesn't change the truth that I am also brave and worthy of love and belonging.[92]

Brown's thoughts are second mountain stuff (see chapter 5, page 31). We each have an imperfect story. The key to adversity resolution via your soul story is to find the peace that comes from knowing you and those you work with are enough.

As I was working on this chapter, Brown tweeted, "1. Don't look for confirmation that you don't belong or that you're not good enough. You'll always find it. 2. Remember you are more than enough. We need you."[93]

Take a moment to connect to Regina's story. What part of her soul story resonates most with you?

Take a moment to give yourself some credit. How are you designing a healthy response to your Health/Work/Play/Love dashboard this week?

_____
_____
_____
_____
_____
_____
_____
_____
_____
_____
_____
_____
_____
_____
_____
_____
_____
_____

As someone who has walked the perfectionism-contentment line my entire life, I have often thought deep contentment cannot become part of our life story through the *perceptions* we might have of the need to do perfect work and become perfect selves. The residue of more money, more time, more recognition, more power, more trophies, more likes on Instagram, or more followers on Twitter is a feeling of discontent. As Holiday reminds us, "You will never feel okay by way of external accomplishments. *Enough* comes from the inside."[94]

Enough comes from the inside. But what exactly does that mean?

New York Times best-selling authors Bill Burnett and Dave Evans have written about how to be a work-life designer by taking action, telling your story, and building your way forward. They provide insight into what it means to live within the trap and discontent of always needing *more* and how to ensure you don't fall into that trap as you balance health, work, play, and love expectations for your life.

> The real question is: How's it going, right now?
>
> A non-life designer, wallowing in the it's-not-good-enough end of the pool, vaguely malcontent with all they have, answers by saying, over and over again, "Not so good. Are we there yet?"
>
> If asked the same question, a life designer would say, "Life is good. Of course, I'm working on my gratitude and managing my Health/Work/Play/Love dashboard, and I'm always trying to make a more meaningful contribution at work, but I can honestly say that things are good and I'm pretty content with what I have. I have what I need, and that is good enough for now.[95]

 # MY SOUL STORY

The last few words from Burnett and Evans bring in a soul story truth for when we are teetering dangerously close to unhealthy perfectionism. We each say to ourselves:

I have what I need, and that is good enough, for now.

Good-enough teaching, good-enough grading, good-enough col-laborating, and good-enough effort today. Good-enough kindness and calm. Good enough in this job we have, for *today*. We will feel the contentment of our current effort.

Yet, there is a caveat. Tomorrow morning, we will seek to be better and to do better. As educators, we understand our student-centered profession demands we do not rest on our old knowledge. We will not settle for less than the continuous climb up our second mountain.

We will practice self-care and find time for reflection, remain bal-anced, be kind to ourselves, and practice gratitude.

In short, we will celebrate this day, as *we seek to soar* tomorrow.

The elements of self-care and self-compassion are next.

The Road Less Hardened

S   U   L

Instead of mercilessly judging and criticizing yourself for various inadequacies or shortcomings, self-compassion means you are kind and understanding when confronted with personal failings.

—Kristin Neff

Thus far in part 2, we have examined several challenging obstacles to our professional life. We have considered healthy versus unhealthy responses to overcome those obstacles as the school seasons of our teaching and learning life pull us forward. There are some days when my inner response to these obstacles sounds like this:

Feeling lost and overwhelmed? "Yep! Been there—how did you find me?"

Living in the shallows? "Yep! Got no time for depth! Who are you kidding?"

Got problems with SASHET? "Yep, got those too; I can't control *all* my emotions!"

Got anger? "YES! YES, I SAID!"

Got the perfection malady? "What did I do wrong? *Enough* already!"

MY SOUL STORY ♥

Reflect on the obstacles listed so far in part 2, "O Is for Overcoming." Which of these five chapters has the closest connection to your professional experiences in *this* school season?

How about being hard-hearted? Have you heard of that one? "Err, wait, what's that?"

Merriam-Webster considers *hard-hearted* a hyphenated adjective, as in *hard-hearted*, and defines it as "lacking in sympathetic understanding."[96] No matter which chapter and which obstacle you identified in the previous My Soul Story, each obstacle is part of being fully human. And each has the potential to lead you down a hardened professional road.

And it gets worse; the hardened and dried-up professional road is filled with "pothole synonyms," including compassion*less*, heart*less*, merci*less*, remorse*less*, ruth*less*, and more.

The hard-hearted road is a path with a lot *less* of the soul-seeking virtues our students and colleagues need. Worse yet, it has a lot less of the soul-seeking virtues we need from our*selves*. Less kindness. Less compassion. Less understanding. Less partnership. Less awareness. Less humor. Less love.

Can you imagine any child in the path of a teacher, support staff member, parent, school board member, counselor, dean, nurse, school social worker, psychologist, administrator, or custodian walking down a hard-hearted, hardened road? Just writing those synonyms was painful.

I paint this picture because it is a road you and I do not want to go down. The profession we chose suffers when we suffer a hardened heart.

"How does my slow drift down the hard-hearted road begin?" you might ask. It's as if amid the hurried and hassled aspects of our teaching life, we look up one morning, one season, somewhere along the journey, and ask, "When did I get onto *this* road? When did I become the kind of educator my colleagues are avoiding? When did I lose my sense of belonging and connectedness to my students and colleagues? And, why is no one else on this road with me?" The drift to the hardened road can happen to you and to me if we are not careful.

It's lonely on a hard-hearted road to nowhere.

None of us are immune from the danger of a slowly hardened heart for our work life. We think, "Someday I'll get around to helping others become better." But someday never comes, and then someday is gone. We think, "I am too hurried, too important, too lost, too angry, too sad, too scared of being rejected or hurt, or too flawed to get off of this 'I am a victim' of my circumstances hardened road."

We fail to see that what we are is—human.

All these obstacles—feeling lost and overwhelmed, living in the shallows, feeling emotionally disconnected from our professional life, living in fear and anger, and feeling we are not good enough—are *human* obstacles. Which means there is a soul story antidote. We can avoid this road throughout our career. No regrets needed. We can develop our *internal* good in order to fulfill our vocation: *creating good in others.*

Our soul story can *overcome* being hard-hearted.

How do you and I travel the road less hardened? The answer partially lies in expanding the compassion part of our soul story described in chapter 6 (page 39).

Recall that the word *compassion* often refers to our demonstrating compassion toward others—our loved ones, our students, our colleagues—both liked and disliked individuals. We also *receive* compassion from others—from those we consider to be our peers or our students—and by witnessing compassion between others.

As important, there is also *self*-compassion. It is foundational to our soul story. *Self-compassion* is simply "compassion directed inward."[97] You extend compassion toward your*self* when you experience suffering, whether by your own mistakes and failures or by external circumstances or oppression you do not control.

Do you remember the four stages that lead to compassion? There is neuroscientific evidence that in response to your own suffering, your brain goes through something like the following.[98]

1. An awareness of suffering
2. Emotional involvement in the suffering
3. A wish to see relief for the suffering
4. A readiness to act or to help relieve the suffering

Every lesson we teach, every interaction with our stakeholders—students, parents, and colleagues—reflects our behaviors toward *others* and our behaviors toward *ourselves.* Therefore, all our lessons and interactions reflect our empathy (the feeling or understanding of another's pain or suffering), our compassion (the action that flows from empathy), and our ability to demonstrate self-compassion.

In "Self-Compassion and Psychological Well-Being," published in *The Oxford Handbook of Compassion Science,* Kristin Neff and Christopher Germer detail much of the research on self-compassion and help to define it more clearly. "Self-compassion involves being touched by and open to one's own suffering, not avoiding or disconnecting from it, generating the desire to alleviate one's own suffering and to heal oneself with kindness."[99] Use this description of self-compassion to reflect on and respond to the My Soul Story prompt.

Do you currently take the time to practice self-compassion and improve your well-being by being kind to yourself? If yes, how? If no, why not?

_____
_____
_____
_____
_____
_____
_____
_____
_____
_____
_____
_____
_____
_____
_____
_____
_____
_____
_____

MY SOUL STORY

The link between self-compassion and personal well-being has largely been conducted using the Self-Compassion Scale test designed by Kristin Neff and described in detail in her 2011 book *Self-Compassion: The Proven Power of Being Kind to Yourself*.[100]

The test provides insight into six different categories for us to consider regarding our ability to use self-compassion as an obstacle destroyer: (1) self-kindness, (2) self-judgment, (3) common humanity, (4) isolation, (5) mindfulness, and (6) over-identification.

To find more information about Neff's self-compassion categories, visit Self-Compassion.org (https://self -compassion.org/test-how-self-compassionate-you-are), and take the online test. The test takes about ten minutes. Maybe share your results with a trusted colleague to assess your self-compassion progress with each other. I took the test online, and I scored a 4.12 overall (a high self-compassion score), which surprised me, as I can be pretty self-judgmental at times. My highest score was in self-kindness, so I guess I have that going for me!

Interestingly, self-compassion appears to facilitate a healthy coping response by moderating our reaction to negative events. According to Germer and Neff, individuals higher in self-compassion demonstrate "less extreme reactions, less negative emotions, more accepting thoughts, and a greater tendency to put their problems into perspective, while at the same time acknowledging their own responsibility."[101]

While at the same time acknowledging our responsibility.

Although self-compassion centers on the alleviation of suffering, it is not self-indulgent, it is not narcissistic, and it does not undermine motivation to improve. Instead, self-compassion expects you to act with a healthy relief response to your own suffering.

Recall my summer months after Becky DuFour passed away, as described in chapter 11 (page 83). I still showed up at every event and brought the best of myself to work every day. I stayed positive in my interactions with colleagues, students, and family members.

And I processed my anger and pain quietly during daily runs and through journaling about my suffering. I was responsibly self-compassionate.

Yet, I have not always won the self-compassion battle. Sometimes I was not even aware of my suffering. My busyness and my first mountain climb gave me an out: "I'll just achieve one more thing, win one more award, and I'll stay numb to my pain, as it is less destructive outwardly."

But not inwardly.

I understood that all humans are flawed and works in progress. I knew that everyone fails, makes mistakes, and engages in dysfunctional behavior. Yet, *I am in this alone* is a false narrative I would tell myself, especially early in my career: "I am not part of that common humanity." Self-compassion thrives in realizing that we are not alone in facing our obstacles.

Alleviating your suffering includes viewing your world as part of the larger human experience and being mindful of your pain and suffering. Try the following exercise as part of your soul story journaling for this book.

MY SOUL STORY 🩶

Consider a situation in which a colleague has had a really terrible teaching day. Write three statements you might say to your colleague going through that bad day.

Now, write three statements you would say to yourself if you were going through that same really bad teaching day.

There is usually a gap in the road between how others see you and how you see yourself. Think of it this way: When you are suffering, does your best friend know it? Do you tell your best friend about it?

What would your best friend say about you, to you? How is his or her narrative about your soul story different from the narrative running through your own head? Can you listen to and hear the validation of being human from the kindness of that friend?

That is the kindness you and I must speak from within when we are self-compassionate.

One caution: Being self-compassionate does not make us timid, weak, or tolerant of injustice. On a societal level, a truly self-compassionate response to injustice stems from our strong sense of moral outrage—a form of anger but a *constructive* one.

We serve the soul story of our professional life when we give ourselves a bit of tough-minded self-compassion and then use that compassion to erase social injustices experienced in our path every day.

The moment occurred on a midwinter Friday afternoon. I was about to meet with a teacher who had about ten years left to what had been a promising teaching career, a career recently faded into hopelessness, burnout, and anger. After three days of observation of his sixth-hour classroom, we were about to have his post-observation conference.

It had occurred to me that I needed to figure out how to approach the situation. In the aftermath of our discussion, how could we begin a journey down a road less hardened?

To some extent, he had lost his love for teaching. He was failing to love his students deeply. I had a right to be angry over his verbal treatment of students, his display of apathy and lack of preparation, and his somewhat cynical view of the administrators in the school. He was stealthily creating inequities in student learning at our school. And he wasn't very kind anymore.

His career, his vocation, was at a fork in the road. His life was going to be about either the road less hardened (teaching students with joy, gratitude, and grace) or the hard-hearted road (taking him down a road *without* joy, gratitude, and grace).

And the issue was urgent because he was suffering and so, in turn, were his students. My response to his failure and his future needed to be kind, tough, and grace filled. So I decided to walk with him down a different road, a deeper road.

I ignored my three days of observation notes and asked him to recall a time when he loved teaching. He talked about it for quite a while.

I then asked him to describe the moment he became aware that his love for students and for teaching his subject area had started to fade away. I listened.

Then, I asked him whether the hardened road was how he wanted to finish the final ten school seasons of his professional career. "It is a lonely walk," I said.

We agreed to use the weekend to create a plan of self-compassion and action for a different future. He would list five actions he could take, and so would I. On Monday, we would compare our lists and work together to rekindle the love of teaching that once existed. We collaborated on a plan for how he could become less hardened to his professional life, how he might be able to change the community's perception of him ("We don't want our children in his class"), and how he could win back the hearts of his students and their parents over time.

This is where the cyclical nature of the school year really helps. As the second semester and the following school year unfolded, his mostly new set of students had no direct institutional memory of him. They had heard he was a mean-spirited, grumpy teacher, but they were still new to him.

In the short term, we agreed to pair him up with the one colleague he could respect and listen to for guidance and help. In the long term, he spent the next four years of his professional life choosing "no regrets" decisions—laughing more, learning more, listening to his students, and appreciating their stories. He had chosen the road less hardened. He had chosen self-compassion and found in it glimpses of his own humanity. He would backslide from time to time, but it was better overall.

And then one September morning, he did not wake up. His chance to choose a "no regrets" life was over. His finite number of professional days was complete. His retirement day was not to come.

At his funeral, hundreds of students and parents were in attendance. All of them praised his humor, kindness, and love for students. He had left behind a more recent legacy of compassion toward himself and others. How awesome. How fearless. How courageous. He had chosen the road less hardened before it was too late.

In "The Secret Ailment," presidential advisor and educational author John Gardner describes those on the road less hardened:

> We have all seen men and women, even ones in fortunate circumstances with responsible positions, who seem to run out of steam in mid-career. One must be compassionate in assessing the reasons. Perhaps life just presented them with tougher problems than they could solve. Perhaps something

Sit with Gardner's thoughts. Whom do you know who has *forgotten what he or she is running for*? (Maybe it is you.) How can you help that person get back on the right road? The less-hardened road?

—————————————
—————————————
—————————————
—————————————
—————————————
—————————————
—————————————
—————————————
—————————————
—————————————
—————————————
—————————————
—————————————
—————————————
—————————————
—————————————
—————————————
—————————————
—————————————
—————————————
—————————————
—————————————

inflicted a major wound on their confidence and self-esteem.

Perhaps they were pulled down by the hidden resentments and grievances that grow in adult life, sometimes so luxuriantly that, like tangled vines, they immobilize the victim. We've all known such people—people who feel secretly defeated, maybe somewhat sour and cynical, or perhaps just vaguely dispirited. Or maybe they just ran so hard for so long that somewhere along the way they forgot what they were running for.[102]

The hardened road I think is best, for you and all who experience your life path, as a road not taken.

♥ MY SOUL STORY

In high school, I remember the first time I sang "The Road Not Taken" from the poem by Robert Frost. Music brings me to a rich place of emotion and healing.

Here is the last verse of Frost's "The Road Not Taken":[103]

> I shall be telling this with a sigh
> Somewhere ages and ages hence:
> Two roads diverged in a wood, and I—
> I took the one less traveled by,
> And that has made all the difference.

This last verse of Frost's poem has served as my reminder to live a path of kindness and compassion, caring and connection, and love and joy.

Which road should you choose?

Choose the road less hardened, indeed.

A Season of Obstacles

Goodness is the only investment that never fails.
—Henry David Thoreau

She was one of my best friends and a third-grade teacher. We played softball together on Friday nights. She struggled to be successful in the classroom. She was often late to meetings. Her principal didn't seem to help much, notice, or care that she was struggling. She didn't tell him how she resented his lack of support, because she was afraid of conflict. She was angry with her students for being imperfect, making mistakes, and not keeping up.

She gossiped with her friends and sometimes with me about her friends. I wondered what she might be saying about me to her other friends. She thought her problems were her job, her kids, and her age, but they were not. She showed up for a school field trip with alcohol on her breath. It numbed her to her pain. Her soul story was unraveling before her eyes. No one knew her real story of college alcoholism. It was hidden, even from me.

She sat in a season of obstacles to her professional soul story. She struggled to connect to the good that had resided deep within her soul in the past, the good that I knew existed inside my friend. She was not having a good present. Then, one of her teacher friends called and asked for my help.

At your next teacher meeting, look to the person on your left and to the person on your right. At that very moment, chances are one of the three of you is not having a very good present. Obstacles are acting to impede your progress and positive contribution to yourself and the others in your professional life.

Of the four states of well-being Loehr reveals, which one best describes your past school seasons compared to your current school season? Provide context for your story selection.

_____
_____
_____
_____
_____
_____
_____
_____
_____
_____

Do you work with anyone who is having a bad present this week? If so, how can you help him or her move toward a better present next week?

_____
_____
_____
_____
_____
_____
_____
_____
_____
_____

He or she (or maybe you) most likely is suffering from inward struggles. According to psychologist James Loehr Ágnes Hankiss), our ongoing soul story generally falls into one of four states of being, as it unfolds:[104]

- A good past has led to a good present (43 percent).
- A good past has led to a bad present (15 percent).
- A bad past has led to a good present (22 percent).
- A bad past has led to a bad present (20 percent).

Note that 35 percent of respondents indicate they are not presently experiencing a positive emotional year. They are not having a good present. But the word *they* makes the obstacles less personal. The word *they* is generally focused on someone else we work with, not us.

MY SOUL STORY

What about you and me?

Sometimes I did not have a good present for part of a day or a week. A few times, I might have had a bad present for a month, and once it was an entire school season. If I showed you a timeline of my professional career (we create a timeline in chapter 22, page 187), you would see many more positive moments than negative, but you would still see those negative moments and know that just like you, I experienced personal obstacles along the way.

Maybe they were obstacles of facing unexpected adversity, being overwhelmed, feeling afraid or angry over a recent experience, or having a sense of failure, grief, sadness, displacement, or intense change. Most of the time, my responses were hidden, but the obstacles were there nonetheless.

Yet, there is hope. Sometimes the obstacle can lead the way. You turn your adversity to your advantage. As Ryan Holiday reminds us, we can thrive and rally to every challenge we face and every obstacle that might cause suffering, and become better than if we never faced that challenge. The obstacle is indeed the way.[105]

Our seasons or moments of obstacles can often be the genesis for our soul story to find its footing. Our seasons of obstacles can become our bridge from a bad present to a good or at least better present—a professional life of fulfillment and contribution to our students, parents, colleagues, and community.

MY SOUL STORY ♥

∞

By my twenty-first school season, I was teaching one class a day (usually third period) and spent the rest of my time as a building administrator in charge of mathematics and science. I did not have a very good start to the 1993–1994 school season, only no one really knew it.

In February of the previous school season, my stepmom, Connie, had died. We had grown close over the years. It was a tough punch to my positive emotional state.

During the summer of 1993, my mentor, close colleague, and fellow textbook coauthor Lee Yunker's brain cancer resurfaced. He was fifty-three years old and regressed quickly. I was driving thirty miles to his home twice a week to see him as he began to lose speech and movement functions. He died in October, and I could not lift the cloud of sadness. It was a second punch to my positive emotional state.

And then my dad called me. He was living alone in Albuquerque, New Mexico, and I was working in suburban Chicago. Thankfully, we had mended the fences of my childhood many years before. He told me, "You need to come to Albuquerque. I need your help." That was November 1, his seventy-fifth birthday. He would not see his seventy-sixth. He was diagnosed with lung cancer and had four months to live. (A World War II vet, he smoked two packs a day to the end.) He made it to February 8. Punch number three. I was down for the count.

There were other obstacles too, and I felt as if I had nothing left in my emotional tank. My present was not good. I had no energy to get things done; no patience

Write about a time in your professional life story when it was a struggle to sustain a good present. (Others might not have known you were struggling.) How did you respond in order to get back to a more positive emotional state?

_____
_____
_____
_____
_____
_____
_____
_____
_____
_____
_____
_____
_____
_____
_____
_____
_____
_____
_____
_____
_____

with other people, including my family members; and no care or concern for deadlines.

How can we respond as we become aware of our drift toward a bad present? What do our seasons of obstacles (such as grief and sadness) teach us?

First, healing begins with awareness.

Second, healing resides within a spirit of gratitude (see chapter 26, page 219).

Third, healing is sustained through our actions of contribution.

These actions are essential elements in the fulfillment of our professional soul story.

To better understand how to effectively embrace obstacles in our professional path, consider the COVID-19 pandemic of 2020. It affected every human being in the United States and around the globe.

In 2020, COVID-19 impacted every educator both professionally and personally, regardless of job position or title. One minute we were digging deep into teaching and learning as we knew it, and the next minute we were told to go home. And stay home. And adjust.

Consider the raw data from January through December of 2020.[106]

- Total U.S. cases: 19,663,976
- Total world cases: 81,947,503
- Total U.S. deaths: 341,199
- Total world deaths: 1,808,041

This type of obstacle is not like the personal crisis of a torn ACL in your knee, in which you get the surgery, do the proper recovery, and go back to your normal life. This type of obstacle is paradigm shifting and life changing. The data represent too many soul stories lost and families impacted by this terrible virus.

Our classrooms and hallways became empty well before we were ready or finished. Without warning, we were suddenly idle or scrambling to meet the distance learning needs of our students. The 2019–2020 school season ended abruptly and was shocking to the system as we lost many of our normal end-of-year traditions.

The summer of 2020 and the start of the 2020–2021 school season were challenging, choppy, and uneven, with health concerns; child care issues; remote learning hurdles; and educational priorities colliding into a confluence of impossible, constantly-changing information and uncertain decisions. It was overwhelming for many school districts, educators, and community members. What was right? What was best for educating our children *and* maintaining their nutrition, health, and safety, as well as our personal safety?

The answer? *It depends.* This was very unsettling for a profession that thrives on advanced planning.

The obstacles in 2020 were paradigm shifting. The roughly 8:00 a.m.– 3:00 p.m., five-days-per-week normal school schedule with all students in a classroom, a schedule we all knew and understood, had become a nonviable, limited option.

Inequities were exposed more deeply than ever before, especially for our marginalized students and those experiencing poverty, homelessness, or lack of access to distance learning technology. We felt adrift despite our social media, Zoom, or other remote learning tools and other technological capabilities. COVID-19 created a redefined sense of our self and our work life.

Consider these words from my friend and colleague Lucy Van Scyoc of the Tulare Joint Union High School District in Tulare, California, in June 2020:

> What made this period of time so difficult for educators in our schools was the being forced to stop doing what is at the center of our profession. We thrive on the relationships and connections with our students and staff. Being forced to social distance, especially in an area like Tulare, where a lot of our students lack access to technology and Wi-Fi, made it difficult to continue nurturing relationships with our students.

> Communication with our students was difficult. The majority of our teachers have been able to connect with less than 50 percent of their students. This is heartbreaking, especially when we know that for many of our students, school is their safe place. These are the obstacles being created by COVID-19 that the adults in our schools must overcome.[107]

The coronavirus pandemic changed our world in 2020 and everything in it. Our personal and professional journeys were interrupted on a large scale most of us had not experienced, much less observed before. It included changes we did not anticipate or request. COVID-19, and its rapid and relentless impact, threw an obstacle of anxiety and uncertainty into our paths.

"Climb over this one!" it shouted at us. We did. But not without a struggle.

Yet, our soul story can be used to *overcome* a season of obstacles.

How did changes in your daily work life in 2020 help you become more *aware* of your students' needs and their struggles to learn within the community your school serves?

_____

_____

_____

_____

_____

_____

_____

_____

_____

_____

_____

_____

_____

_____

_____

_____

_____

_____

_____

_____

_____

_____

First, we become aware of how an obstacle affects us and our students, communities, and families.

From our educational perspective, we focus on the academic learning expectations of our grade-level or course-based standards while delivering on the promise of equity and access to the guaranteed and viable curriculum. We are also expected to address the students' social-emotional learning as we become more aware of various levels of student trauma that might affect it. Sometimes the obstacles can be more severe. The COVID-19 pandemic of 2020 caused adversity to the learning process for all stakeholders, including students, parents, staff, and teachers.

Consider this insight from my colleague and extraordinary school leader, Jasmine Kullar, from June 2020. She writes of her experience in the Cobb County School District in Marietta, Georgia:

> I can't begin to put into words the impact this has had on our district. As a professional, I am working through daily challenges through meeting after meeting, phone call after phone call—and as a mom, I am managing my own kids' learning while ensuring their needs are also met.
>
> My heart breaks when I think about those kids who do not have a support system at home—whose only out was being at school. These kiddos are at home and in increasingly abusive environments due to the pandemic. Yes, as educators, we teach, but so many of us do so much more than that. The pandemic became this massive obstacle in providing our usual face-to-face in the nonacademic support of schools. As a result, so many kids are struggling right now—as educators, we feel so helpless sitting in our homes.[108]

♥ MY SOUL STORY

In 2020, we had to instantly reframe our circumstances. We became hyperaware of our students' backgrounds, home lives, and surroundings. We faced the COVID-19 pandemic by building our *awareness* of the many health risks, the dangerous impact of physical distancing as social beings, and the expectations of learning in a remote environment.

Second, we find places to demonstrate our professional gratitude. Demonstrating gratitude was especially needed in 2020, despite losing many of the routines we knew so well.

Before the pandemic, it was easy to slip into taking love and friendships, hugs and handshakes, high fives and hellos, and music and the arts for granted. Not now. Maybe never. In that 2020 season of suffering and obstacles, we learned to appreciate the gifts of time, work, and friendship our loved ones have to offer, especially when those gifts are taken away.

The COVID-19 pandemic illuminated the larger reality of our professional lives—the reality of living and dying and of caring and being cared for increased our dependence on one another.

David Levine, a freelance health and wellness writer, cites the work of Richard Davidson, professor of psychology and psychiatry at the University of Wisconsin–Madison and founder and director of its Center for Healthy Minds, regarding a positive outcome of the social distancing stressors of 2020:

> We can't think of ourselves as an isolated island. Nature simply does not honor those distinctions. This is an opportunity to expand the boundaries of what we consider our in-group. This is what the pandemic is illustrating. . . . It can, I think, help us navigate the uncertainty we are all facing. . . . It is not to deny or minimize or diminish the uncertainty and real suffering going on. But it can be beneficial in helping people get through their everyday life.[109]

MY SOUL STORY ♥

If we are not the beacons of light in the world, who will be? How great would it be if our revised school schedules, curriculum, and student groupings are used to eventually soften the lines across our diversity, expand the boundaries of our in-group, and unite the dignity and humanity of every student and adult in our school community?

Third, healing is sustained through our actions of contribution. In 2020, we learned to contribute to the learning and growth of our students in new ways.

HOW are schedules, structures, and technology shifting and being used to create a more inclusive culture across the diversity spectrum within your school?

_____

_____

_____

_____

_____

_____

_____

_____

_____

_____

_____

_____

_____

_____

_____

_____

_____

_____

_____

_____

_____

_____

_____

_____

Reflect on the COVID-19
pandemic as an obstacle in your professional life in 2020. What have you learned? How did your teaching behaviors to support student learning change to create an "awe family" response?

_____

_____

_____

_____

_____

_____

_____

_____

_____

If you were not yet teaching
in 2020, reflect on this question from the student perspective: How did your best teachers respond to the change?

_____

_____

_____

_____

_____

_____

_____

_____

_____

_____

An initial part of facing and overcoming COVID-19 was based on our willingness to yield to the expectations of social distancing, the wearing of masks, and the creation of effective and engaging remote lessons despite the obstacles. Those fundamental acts *contributed to the benefit of others* in our professional and personal lives.

According to Neff and Germer, neuroscientific evidence supports that observing generosity toward others improves our well-being. This, in turn, causes a distinct emotional state called *moral elevation*. Neff and Germer write, "Simply observing this compassionate sensitivity to suffering coupled with selfless actions to alleviate the suffering is enough to cause profound psychological and physiological experiences in the witness."[110]

Moral elevation is known as part of the *awe family* of emotional states. In 2020, the COVID-19 pandemic obstacle needed an *awe family* response. The *awe family* facilitates "the integration of vast and unexpected experiences into a person's understanding of the world."[111]

Responding to the COVID-19 crisis resulted in the reveal of several personal soul story highlights by educators in the United States and globally. My colleagues at Elk Grove High School in Illinois, led by Principal Paul Kelly, delivered meals to the community and to students' homes during the crisis.

In a time of unusual and uncertain plans, we went deep to make personal contributions (large or small) to others. We pushed to find new remote learning solutions while prioritizing our health and the health and safety of our students and colleagues. We remained radically optimistic about our humanity during an unprecedented crisis moment of unknowns.

 # MY SOUL STORY

We may not have won the "good present" moment *every day* in 2020. Some days were most likely overwhelming. Crisis will do that to us. Yet, we did the best we could in 2020 to stay in a good present and let the obstacle show us the way forward with our students and colleagues.

∞

Back to my third-grade teacher friend, whose story opened this chapter (page 109). I was able to connect her to a place and a colleague to walk with her into an alcohol recovery program. As she was able to face her obstacles without shame (via self-compassion and a few trusted friends), her life as a mom, a teacher, and a friend began to reconnect her with her soul story. She took action to make choices for a professional story of contribution and purpose, a story of mostly better days—days of a good present from a bad past. She knows she did not overcome her obstacles alone.

In my tough 1993–1994 school year, my third-hour students saved me from my personal place of sorrow. Those high school seniors have passed their twenty-fifth high school reunion. A photo of that class sits in my bookcase at home. Frozen in time. In the photo, we are outside under a tree, and I am in the front helping three students hold a student horizontally across our arms as he rests with his head on his hands. Like most of the class, I am laughing with him.

I hope those students can feel how much they gave to me that year. They made me laugh, at times they drove me a bit crazy, and above all else, they reminded me time and again of my humanity. Without knowing it, they helped me overcome the pain of a difficult season. They reminded me of my passion for teaching and the joy I could find in the journey, even during tough times.

I bet your students have brought you back to laughter and a deeper connection to your soul story on more than one occasion too. Locate that good present. If you are there, do what you can to stay there. If not, recruit a friend or colleague to help you get there. Our profession needs you and me to be there. It is part of the rest of our story, yet untold.

And by the way, bring someone with you, maybe a few someones. We are not meant to overcome our obstacles and move through this professional journey alone. Our soul story thrives in community with others and pulls us toward a better present today and a great present tomorrow.

The PLC Life Is a Corrosion-Free Life

S   ♡   U   L

During my early research review for this book, I came across a jarring phrase. I wrote it down in a notebook and started writing about its meaning and connection to my personal and professional journey. It caused me to stop and ask whether hatred ever has a place in our professional and moral path. The phrase?

Hatred corrodes the container it is carried in.

Former Wyoming senator Alan Simpson used the phrase at the funeral of George H. W. Bush in December 2018.[112] An online search revealed the phrase as a possible rephrasing of the Chinese proverb: "Hatred corrodes the vessel in which it is stored."[113]

Reflections about my teaching and leading life caused me to think, "What if I am that container? Does my being overwhelmed at times corrode my container? Does my sometimes hurried, shallow, or out-of-control life corrode my container? Have my ego and envy, anger and fear, jealousy and insecurity caused me to corrode my container? Did my first mountain climb cause me to corrode my container through an occasional indifference to others?"

If I allow these obstacles of part 2 to thrive within me, then I am not just losing contact with my soul story; I am destroying the container that carries my very essence as a person and as an educator.

It is why I cannot accept any form of hatred. Nor should you. The antidote to the obstacles we have examined in part 2 is a professional soul story response of contribution and compassion, unity and belonging, and love and care, including responsible and accountable behavior; it is not a response of hatred and division. How can we be in touch with our soul story if we hate others? Divide ourselves from others? There is no room in the PLC life for hate in our hearts.

But beware. Hate is perhaps our last and greatest obstacle. Hate doesn't just corrode our container and corrupt our professional spirit; hate sometimes corrodes others' containers as we idly stand by and watch. In that sense, we are complicit in allowing a culture of hate to fester in others.

Whatever you do, please take a stand *together* against any actions that tolerate implicit or explicit forms of hate and oppression. Do it with love and urgency, but take that stand. How can a book about the moral imperative of using our soul story to *create good in others* not encourage educators to take a stand against oppression and hate?

In the words of Martin Luther King Jr.: "Hatred paralyzes life; love releases it. Hatred confuses life; love harmonizes it. Hatred darkens life; love illuminates it."[114]

As teachers in a profession of helpers, we have a lot of power to stand together in the fight against hatred. A PLC culture expects us to eradicate all forms of hatred and division within our school community. We are to do the best we can to help our students live *corrosion-free*. That alone makes our professional soul story pursuit, and the obstacles we work hard to overcome, worth the struggle every single day.

And, as you will discover in part 3 of this book, it is a challenge best met and nurtured in community with others.

MY SOUL STORY ♥

Reflect on the seven chapters in part 2 and the views on hatred in this Final Thoughts section. What are some of the obstacles that connected most for you? Was it avoiding the shallows and living more deeply, or healthy responses to your negative emotions, including anger and perfection? Perhaps it is the need for daily self-compassion, or accepting the positive response needed to recover from the constant stress of the COVID-19 pandemic of 2020.

Include two to three possible actions you can take to better connect to your soul story over time. Write your reflections as *I will*... statements, and keep these statements close at hand as you measure the progress of your professional soul story.

PART 3

DEVELOPING YOUR
SOUL STORY

U

Is for Unifying

Essential Soul Story Question: Your soul story thrives in community. Are you developing it?

A growing body of evidence suggests that the single greatest driver of both achievement and well-being is understanding how your daily efforts enhance the lives of others. The defining features of a meaningful life are "connecting and contributing to something beyond the self."

—Tom Rath

Your professional life thrives when you *develop* your soul story *in community with others.*

Part 3, "U Is for Unifying," is about the collective-care *culture* we lead, create, and design in our school through community with others. Our soul story falls far short—empty and incomplete—without community, meaningful relationships, and belonging to a culture that values our contribution to others.

In chapter 15, we discover that our unity lifts us up and collectively hauls us up the second mountain climb. Our soul story expects us to lead the community climb forward, and our unity allows us to achieve a life of meaning and well-being far beyond what we could possibly achieve on our own. It is in the unity of our community with one another that we are able to overcome so many of the obstacles described in part 2 and erase potential student learning inequities caused by our isolation.

Yet, community and relationships come with their own challenges too. They require a willingness to pursue intimacy, create an inclusive culture of belonging, become vulnerable as we learn to trust others, and, above all, establish a culture of validation.

Chapters 16–20 provide a series of challenges as we take our daily work *beyond*—out of the shallows and into a more fulfilling soul story depth.

In chapter 16, we search *beyond* the bricks of our school community walls to determine how to create a *school culture* of belonging for every student. We search to find the soul story of our school.

In chapter 17, we move *beyond* our shallow attempts to become a *teacher team community* in search of a collaborative intimacy with our work life.

Then we move into our *systemwide community* culture *beyond* a genial and shallow collegiality and into the deep, soul-filled work of vulnerability in chapter 18.

Chapter 19 moves the cultural lens back to our *classroom community* and begs for a soul-filled search well *beyond* tolerance for the diversity, words, and actions of our students toward a much deeper sense of validation for each child or teenager.

In chapter 20, we expand our second mountain soul story climb (see chapter 5, page 31) by understanding how our school does not work in isolation from its extended local community. We act as an organism of interdependence, working beyond our school community as part of an extended community.

Chapter 21 concludes part 3 with a nod to taking care of ourselves. Living a balanced quietude life. The quietude life is similar to, but more complex in routine than, my call for a balanced Quadrant II life in *HEART!*[115] How does our need for solitude and silence balance with our need for community as part of our unified work life?

Here we go!

E Pluribus Unum:
Thriving in Community

S   O   L

*We are caught in an inescapable network of mutuality, tied in a
single garment of destiny. Whatever affects one directly affects
all indirectly.*

—Martin Luther King Jr.

Have you had a chance to be part of opening a new school building during your professional journey? I have. Only once. During my third season of teaching.

It is an exciting time. Everything is new and fresh. You can see, touch, and smell the fresh paint, new desks and materials, new technology and room spaces, shining hallways and floors, and new library, cafeteria, and gym. Maybe you have your own classroom to decorate and inspire others.

Now imagine you are part of a team designated to design a seal or symbol for the school with a school motto. Think of the motto as a short expression representing a singular and crystal-clear core value for all who enter your hallways and classrooms. Your team must both design the artwork for the seal and determine the motto itself with the caveat that the motto must be less than eight words total.

On July 4, 1776, a congressional committee was charged with creating a motto and designing a seal for the newly established United States of America. On August 20, 1776, that committee submitted a Great Seal design with the motto *e pluribus unum*. Although the original Great Seal design was not selected, several iterations and a few years later, the original motto survived. In 1782, the Great Seal, whose design included a bald eagle and a few other symbols, was approved by Congress with that original motto: *e pluribus unum*.[116]

Does your school have a motto? If yes, what is it?

_____

_____

_____

_____

_____

Do you have a school seal or emblem? If so, describe it or take a picture of it.

_____

_____

_____

_____

Write about the history or story of your school seal and motto. If you don't know it, ask around to find out.

_____

_____

_____

_____

_____

_____

_____

_____

_____

_____

_____

_____

_____

MY SOUL STORY

E pluribus unum is Latin for "out of many, one."[117] A simple motto, yet complicated in its meaning. The motto suggests a core value of coming together every day, season in and season out, for one core purpose: *many uniting into one.*

We come to our place of work, our school, to work *together* and unite as one. We fight injustices and unite as one. We overcome our obstacles and unite as one. We erase inequities in student learning and unite as one. We solve our complex problems together and unite as one.

So, we unite as one. We become a community. Yet, what exactly *is* community?

The word *community* signifies "a unified body of individuals," such as "a body of persons of common and especially professional interests scattered through a larger society."[118]

Breaking down the word *community* further, *com-* means to be "with, together, jointly."[119] *Unity* indicates "a totality of related parts" or "an entity that is a complex or systematic whole."[120]

More than just a unified body of individuals, our community also becomes a *professional* community of related parts. As professionals, we embrace our obligation toward positive moral standards and follow a professional learning community soul story motto that indicates this ideal: *We will be interdependent. We will all depend on each other.*

Easy to say and very hard to do.

Advancing the values of working interdependently with colleagues has benefits. Consider the findings of the multigenerational, eighty-year-old Harvard Grant Study on adult development and aging begun in 1938:

> "The surprising finding is that our relationships and how happy we are in our relationships has a powerful influence on our health," said Robert Waldinger, director of the study, a psychiatrist at Massachusetts General Hospital and a professor of psychiatry at Harvard Medical School. "Taking care of your body is important,

but tending to your relationships is a form of self-care too."

Close relationships, more than money or fame, are what keep people happy throughout their lives, the study revealed. Those ties protect people from life's discontents, help to delay mental and physical decline, and are better predictors of long and happy lives than social class, IQ, or even genes.[121]

The Harvard Grant Study makes it clear our unity and our individuality do more than just coexist together; they *thrive* together. As the researchers point out in the study, "Embracing community helps us live longer, and happier."[122] We are happier in our personal and our professional lives when we work together and build bonds of family and positive relationships at work. As we walk, run, jump over, and sometimes crawl our way through obstacles during the school year, our professional soul story *thrives* in community, in working together.

MY SOUL STORY

A soul story *community* culture is not shallow.

It is not a culture where the motto is "We will be nice to each other so we can avoid conflict." It is not a culture of comparison: "I am better than you," or "I am worse than you." It is not a culture in which people think, "I will climb over you and through you as I claw my way to isolation and do my own thing."

Happiness becomes a shallow and incomplete goal when your happiness, your climb, comes at the expense of others. How did Martin Luther King Jr. state it in the epigraph to this chapter?

"We are caught in an inescapable network of mutuality, tied in a single garment of destiny. Whatever affects one directly affects all indirectly."[123]

Your selfishness, my selfishness, has an impact on others whether we know it or not. We are caught in an inescapable network of mutuality. We walk into our school building, and our actions of love or hate, indifference or commitment, neglect or intimacy affect everyone else in that building directly *and* indirectly.

We will all depend on each *other.* Does your own unique team or school motto align with any of these words?

_____
_____
_____
_____
_____
_____
_____
_____
_____
_____

Think about your professional community. Write one sentence that describes evidence you work together as a community of related parts.

Write an example of interdependence with a colleague that you can share with others.

_____
_____
_____
_____
_____
_____
_____
_____
_____
_____

Describe a decision
a colleague recently made that
directly or indirectly affected you.

_____
_____
_____
_____
_____
_____
_____
_____
_____
_____

Now describe a decision you
recently made that directly or indirectly affected your colleagues.

_____
_____
_____
_____
_____
_____
_____
_____
_____
_____

Let that sink in for a moment. You, I, and our actions or inactions each day are not insignificant.

MY SOUL STORY

A soul story *community* culture is deep.

Our professional life and our school life thrive as we participate in a culture of contribution and cooperation. As you read in chapter 5 (page 31), our choice of this profession is best served when we understand that choice as our *vocation*. Our soul story wants us, as teachers and leaders, to dig deep down into our moral purpose every time we become aware of any student or adult actions of social injustice that demand our active and *collective*—mutually defined—response.

In our second mountain climb, we are tethered together because it is a treacherous climb. If I fall, you will catch me. If you fall, I will catch you. Every year, our team will learn to climb higher, more treacherous paths because we become *interdependent*. We value a culture of belonging, vulnerability, emotional intimacy, and validation (the topics of the next four chapters). And we pursue this collaborative culture, because it helps us to root out any systemic and invisible social injustices that may exist in our school and community.

My esteemed colleague and best-selling author Anthony Muhammad has dedicated his life to transforming school cultures. He writes with great clarity about the trap of a school culture built on our collective failure to root out the social injustices surrounding our professional life. He refers to this failure as *functional hypocrisy*. Here are his words:

> Every human being wants to be successful. This unspoken agreement is a part of the ties that bind us together as educators. Our mission statements express hopes like *success for all*, *lifelong learners*, and *reaching his or her full potential*. It is difficult to logically and ethically argue against the assumption that every human being yearns to be fulfilled and successful, and that schools play a major role in this hunger in human nature. It would also be naïve to believe that just because we know something, we act upon it.

Schools are a microcosm of society at large. The American Declaration of Independence stated that "all men are created equal" at the same time slavery was legal, Native Americans were being killed and pushed off their land, and women were not given basic human rights. How can people articulate one humane purpose yet live in another reality?

I call this functional hypocrisy.

People love to live in a world of idealism theoretically but benefit from privilege practically. It is like hedging a bet where I am the winner, no matter the outcome. Schools have towed this line for over a century. Declaring the lofty goal of egalitarianism (success for all), but living the benefit of meritocracy (success for the privileged) practically. If educators are to embrace their SOUL, this duplicitous reality has to be acknowledged, deconstructed, and replaced with an environment that welcomes and promotes the success of any student who enrolls in that school.[124]

Thus, the first step in resolving a problem *together* is acknowledging that the problem exists.

MY SOUL STORY

Recall the first line of part 3's epigraph from Tom Rath (page 121): "A growing body of evidence suggests the single greatest driver of both achievement and well-being is understanding how your daily efforts *enhance the lives of others.*"[125]

After reading Rath's comment, I thought *we exist to enhance others' lives* would be a great motto, and only six words! Our collective soul story helps us build a culture that enhances the lives of *all* others by helping us define and then honor a set of positive core values that do not shift or change much over time. Core values are not words put on paper as a matter of convenience. We unite around them. We defend them. We live them and take action on them.

We make it clear to all newcomers, "This is a great place to work and to live your profession. We are a great mountain to climb. But it is not a great mountain for everyone." We add, "We work to become aware of our

Take a moment to reflect on Anthony Muhammad's comments. Identify your awareness of any current practice or routine that might reveal a form of *functional hypocrisy* in your school.

_____

_____

_____

_____

_____

_____

_____

_____

_____

_____

_____

_____

_____

_____

_____

_____

_____

_____

_____

_____

_____

_____

_____

_____

_____

Ask several colleagues to describe in one sentence what they *do* for a living. Then ask them what they are *doing* each day at work to enhance the lives of others. Write their comments.

_____

_____

_____

_____

_____

_____

_____

_____

_____

_____

_____

_____

Then ask yourself these same questions!

_____

_____

_____

_____

_____

_____

_____

_____

_____

_____

_____

_____

_____

_____

_____

functional hypocrisy, and then we act to eradicate the inequity revealed. We live our core values.

"If you choose to climb our school mountain, you will be tethered to others, and you will be expected to contribute to the climb and to support the growth of others, who will in turn climb ahead of you and then lift you up and ahead. You are expected to inspire and support others, and they will do the same for you.

"To do so, we work, live, and act on four core cultural values: belonging, vulnerability, intimacy, and validation. If you enter through our doors, these are the values we will expect you to represent every day. These core values call you to respect and care for *all* others: our students *and* our colleagues. Will you join our team?"

Culture doesn't expose what we *do* for a living—you might be a third-grade teacher, the technology coordinator, the dean in charge of student discipline, a counselor, and so on.

Rather, culture asks, "What are we *doing* for a living?" We energize the work of our colleagues; we search for inequities in our school routines and practices; we inspire students to learn each day; we collaborate with colleagues on essential standards and assessments; we create new ideas for lessons others can use; we validate the work of others. These are just a few soul story examples that embody how our collective work connects to core values that promote the good of others.

MY SOUL STORY

There is one final caveat about community unity and the cultural value of interdependence as you and your colleagues climb the second mountain together and expand your impact on school culture.

The bundle cannot lose the individual flower.

In the U.S. Great Seal described at the beginning of this chapter (page 123), the bald eagle carries an olive branch in its right talon and a bundle of thirteen arrows in its left talon. It wears a shield of thirteen red and white stripes, with a constellation of thirteen stars above. These were symbols of unity for the thirteen original states forming the new union of the United States.

In the original seal proposed in 1776, the motto *e pluribis unum* ("out of many, one") was based on a drawing of a hand holding a bundle of flowers. The essential element of this drawing was the intentional image of a bundle of flowers appearing as if they are in unity with one another, yet, each flower can still be individually "seen."[126] You and I cannot lose our strength as individuals for the sake of the team. Our individual contributions to the team during the second mountain climb are unique to us. Thus, in the best professional learning communities, there is a subtle professional wellness balance between your own self-care and the collective care of your team.

In chapter 17, you will examine the strengths and constraints of intimacy within the collaborative nature of your professional life. First, however, we explore a precursor to intimacy as we begin with the soul story of your school, which is, above all else, a story of deep belonging. And that story is next.

Beyond Bricks and Mortar: Belonging

S   O      L

A nation's culture resides in the hearts and in the soul of its people.

—Mahatma Gandhi

I close my eyes, and I can see, feel, hear, and smell a very solitary moment from the past.

I am standing in the gym, known as the Fieldhouse, at West Chicago Community High School District 94. It is 11:00 p.m. on a wintry Saturday night in February. I am at center court, smack dab on top of our Wildcat logo. All the lights are out, and I am alone.

I can see the lights of the red exit signs above all the doors as I circle the logo and look up at the shadows of still-open bleachers and the residue of streamers, wrappers, and signs discarded all around. By Sunday night, all the mess will be cleaned, the bleachers will be put away, and the bricks and mortar of the Fieldhouse would stand silent once again.

And in that moment of stillness, in that moment of winter quiet, it occurred to me that the facility itself, the empty gym I was standing in, was just that. Empty. Soulless. It was just a building. The hallowed memories of events with those walls spoke to me in a way, but the bricks and mortar in that moment seemed so quiet, so empty. Yet, I felt so deeply connected to that very space. So emotionally close.

Just ninety minutes before this moment of solitude, the building had been on fire; it had been rocking. The soul of that building had been revealed in the soul of its people. It was in every person in that gym. It was in every heart pounding and cheering from both sides of the court. It was in the wild roller coaster of emotions from players and fans. The building had reverberated from the hearts and souls, the very essence of the people from

Stand in your classroom or area of the school where you spend most of your time—your center court, so to speak. Make sure the space is empty of other people. Turn in a full circle, and take it all in. Now, write down two to three of your best memories so far in this space.

_____

_____

_____

_____

_____

_____

_____

_____

_____

_____

_____

_____

_____

_____

_____

_____

_____

_____

_____

_____

_____

our community, and how we belonged together, interwoven and blended into that event in time.

In that moment of stillness, I was very aware that the memories created inside that building would be inside me forever. Time seemed, just briefly, to stand still and let me hold onto something I was privileged to be part of and did not want to let go.

While I was standing on center court, in the silence and the quiet, I knew there would be a day down the road when I would come back to that very place and feel the strength of those memories. I didn't want to let go of the people, the experiences, and the inclusion that made me feel as if I belonged. Selfishly, I needed a quiet moment with my own thoughts, my own gratefulness; I had belonged to something special.

In the stillness of that moment, I felt pain too. Sadness. Grief. The pain surprised me. The pain wasn't from the result of the game (we had won); the pain came from feeling and knowing I would no longer belong to or be part of the West Chicago community. I was letting go of a community I had grown to love. I had not yet told the players on my team, but I knew that would be my last time coaching in that gym.

MY SOUL STORY

Those memories you can feel in that empty classroom or office space are memories of the children and adults who have passed through your life. They are memories of _connection_.

How then does the soul story of your school—_the intentional actions to nurture a culture of learning and good in order to create good in others_—reveal itself to you and the community? One word.

Belonging.

Belonging is such a loaded word. You are in or you are out. You are included or you are excluded. You are part of a class, an activity, or a teacher team or you are not. You identify with the school mascot ("I am a Wildcat") or you don't. You connect with your students or you don't. Your school and the people within it create a soul-filled place of belonging or they don't.

An understanding of the neuroscientific evidence regarding belonging informs a painful reality. A school culture that accepts actions revealing a lack of belonging cues is a very dangerous culture.

> Studies by Naomi Eisenberger at UCLA find that being excluded activates our pain system, suggesting that being excluded is a threat to our very survival. When we're excluded from a meeting, when we don't get invited to key events, or when our ideas are ignored, we feel the pain in the same areas of the brain where we experience physical pain.
>
> The pain of rejection or humiliation is just as real as the pain of a stubbed toe. Whilst social pain may "feel" different (just as the pain of a stubbed toe feels different to stomach cramps), the networks processing it in the brain are the same.
>
> In that context, social exclusion is not simply a misfortune; it's painful for someone. We tend to think of the pain of exclusion as somehow less impactful than physical pain. But the research suggests we should be more concerned about the potential pain generated by excluding others, especially when this is done inadvertently without the opportunity for amends.[127]

The Belonging Project at Stanford is a collegewide, multidimensional effort to promote emotional health and personal well-being through a connection within the communities of Stanford University's campus. The project looks closely at students who feel disconnected and distressed because they are not part of a larger community. It references this evidence as *thwarted belongingness*. The project also looks at specific activities and actions that develop a sense of belonging by connecting students to "those who share their distinct life experiences, interests, or goals."[128]

Thwarted belongingness—what a powerful and painful phrase.

MY SOUL STORY ♥

Consider the studies at UCLA, the pain of exclusion, and the phrase *thwarted belongingness*.

Describe a time in your life when you have personally suffered from exclusion or *thwarted belongingness*.

Identify the students or colleagues in your school who (either intentionally or unintentionally) have suffered exclusion within the school culture. How did you respond?

In this chapter we ask, "What is the soul story of our *school*?" The soul story of your school reveals your collective moral goodness and your coming together for the common purpose of student and adult learning. You either create a culture of *belonging* or tear away at its fabric.

The soul story of your school is found in your collective actions to create a place of belonging for students, and reveals a place (bricks and mortar) where *none* of the groups of persons (adults and children) in your school are marginalized or excluded.

You rely on common values that hold the community together and simultaneously recognize and celebrate diversity. Through shared values of belonging, your school community rises above the norms of selfishness, indifference, and elitism that often result from the "it's all about me" mindset.

Unsurprisingly, a culture of belonging is a prerequisite for learning. It is not a "nice-to-have" option for learning. Educational research affirms school norms of belonging help bridge the achievement gap and provide support for an improved academic learning environment.[129] Norms of belonging include a focus on students working in social situations and the development of student self-efficacy (confidence and belief they can do the work assigned) through a culture of formative learning processes.

Thus, at the heart of a soulful professional learning community is the bonding and binding together around norms of belonging. The end result is the creation of a bridge to understanding other cultures, connecting with a world we often don't see or know— a world of difference far beyond ourselves as the adult teachers and leaders in the school— an honoring of our diversity; a diversity that is visible and invisible, spoken and unspoken.

MY SOUL STORY ♥

Write two to three specific actions you *commit to* each day to create a more inclusive and safe place of belonging for your students and colleagues.

Then share these actions with your colleagues and reflect on your thoughts about what was discussed.

In his book *The Culture Code: The Secrets of Highly Successful Groups*, Daniel Coyle[130] indicates that culture is not something you and I *are* as much as it is something we *do*. Much as having empathy is different from acting on that empathy through compassion (see chapter 6, page 39), there is a difference between being *aware* of a culture of belonging and *acting* on that awareness.

Coyle provides a road map to actions that nurture belonging. Think of these as belonging cues within your school culture. If they are present, you are most likely well on your way to a *belonging and inclusive* soul story in your school.[131] As you examine the following seven belonging cues, reflect on your daily actions for developing a belonging culture in your school. Take special note of the belonging cues you view as a personal strength.

Over-communicate your listening.

As educators, we often fail to listen to our students and colleagues. Say a student shows up at your desk for help before school. Do you stop everything you are doing—no phones, no distractions, no computers, no projects—to listen and engage the student in conversation? We send students a belonging cue when we listen to what they say and don't give in to the distractions of our computers, watches, or other sources of social media interruption.

Coyle describes the belonging cue of authentic listening in such a way that it requires we ignore distractions and fully engage in listening to students or colleagues: "When I visited the successful [belonging] cultures, I kept seeing the same expression on the faces of listeners. . . . The only sound they made was a steady stream of affirmations—*yes, uh-huh, gotcha*. . . . Relatedly, it's important to avoid interruptions. . . . Interruptions shatter the smooth interactions at the core of belonging."[132]

Spotlight your fallibility.

It takes great strength to admit you do not have all the answers and to say to others, "Show me how this idea advances our work together."

Coyle provides some necessary guidance on this belonging cue: "We have a natural tendency to try to hide our weaknesses and appear competent. . . . Instead, you should open up, show you make mistakes, and invite input with simple phrases like 'This is just my two cents.' 'Of course, I could be wrong here.' 'What am I missing?' 'What do you think?'"[133]

Coyle further indicates that when we ask for help from our students or colleagues, we spark a "How can I help?" belonging cue in the listener. The listener feels more connected to us because he or she shares in and belongs to the solution.

My elementary school colleagues from Kildeer Countryside School District 96 in Illinois provided clarity for me on this belonging cue. They indicated that belonging is a core value for every school in their district. By admitting they "know what they don't know" and being willing to be vulnerable with each other, they create a belonging cue that fallibility is an acceptable part of a culture of vulnerability (more on this in chapter 18, page 151), which in turn impacts belonging.

Overdo thank-yous.

One phrase from Coyle says it all: "When you enter highly successful cultures, the number of thank-yous you hear seems slightly over the top."[134]

During my early years of teaching at rural Stillman Valley (see chapter 5, page 31), the idea of excessive thank-yous first began to creep into my teaching life. I thought of them not as belonging cues per se, but rather as ways of encouraging a spirit of perseverance and effort in my students.

Although thank-yous often appeared in my verbal remarks, they mostly were in my written responses and feedback. I wanted my students to know I had high expectations for them *and* I believed they could reach them. After every piece of grading feedback, I would simply write, "Thank you," with an exclamation point and a smiley face.

I used some of my bus driver money to purchase *I love math* pencils with smiley faces and thank-you words on them. But I did not just give those out randomly; students had to earn those precious gems through effort and proficiency.

Coyle indicates thank-yous are "more than just expressions of gratitude; they're crucial cues for belonging that generate a contagious connection and safety."[135] When we say thank you, we are showing other people we value their contribution.

Make sure everyone has a voice.

As Coyle indicates, making sure everyone has a voice is "easy to talk about but hard to accomplish."[136]

Borrowing from Coyle's idea, complete the following My Soul Story prompt as it applies to your specific job or role in school. Think about the students or adults you work with daily and how well you know and understand *their* voices. Ask a variety of students or colleagues that represent the diversity spectrum in your school.

MY SOUL STORY ♥

Pick up trash.

This is a second mountain belonging cue. We create a culture of belonging when we seek ways to serve others at school. No matter what our job positions or titles are, no job is too big for you or me.

My coaching colleague at Stillman Valley, Reg Murray, taught me that no job is too big or too small. "Serve others. Pick up the #@&* trash, Tim," he would say to me. Reg was a colorful guy. He didn't necessarily mean the actual trash (although that might have been the case sometimes); he meant it as a metaphor for not thinking I was too big for any tasks I would ask anyone else to do.

Coyle calls this mindset *muscular humility*: "a mindset of seeking simple ways to serve the group."[137] Bottom line, if you have muscular humility, there is no routine task in your school you wouldn't do, *even if no one were looking*. That is the mark of an educator who serves.

Capitalize on threshold moments.

Moments of arrival to a group present themselves as moments ripe for belonging cues. And in our profession, we often miss them.

Think about your last job change. Perhaps you took a job at a different school or district. Maybe you made a job change from a school to a district-office position, such as instructional coach. Or perhaps you made a job change within your school or from teacher to counselor.

Coyle indicates, "The successful groups I visited paid attention to moments of arrival. They would pause, take time, and acknowledge the presence of the new person, marking the moment as special. *We are together now*."[138]

Now I understand why my mentor, Rick DuFour, was so insistent we make the threshold moment of arrivals to Stevenson something special for each teacher. If you joined the Stevenson family to work in any educational role, especially as a teacher, the following is what your first day would look like.

Ask these questions of each person you interview, and write down their responses.

1. What do you most like about our school?
2. What do you like least about our school?
3. What would you change about your school if you were *in my shoes*?
4. Whom do you need to thank?

For each question, write one summary sentence about the voice of those you work with (your students or colleagues).

Consider asking these questions at your next all-school meeting, at your next team meeting, or in your class.

_____

_____

_____

_____

_____

_____

_____

_____

_____

_____

_____

_____

_____

_____

_____

Write about your first day in a new job. Describe various cues that let you know you belonged, marking the moment as special. If there were no belonging cues, what could have been done differently?

_____
_____
_____
_____
_____
_____
_____
_____
_____
_____
_____
_____
_____
_____
_____
_____
_____
_____
_____
_____
_____
_____

Before your first day, your direct supervisor contacts you via email, social media, and text. Your mentor teacher (who is also a collaborative team member) calls you to answer any logistical questions before your arrival. When you arrive at your desk, there are a variety of goodies waiting for you, including Stevenson sports gear (in your size), flowers, a "welcome to the school" card, an agenda for the day, and various supplies as needed for the year.

A special welcoming luncheon barbeque is set up for all new faculty and staff. Your mentor teacher is there with you, and photos are taken to be used in a "welcome to the Stevenson family" video.

♥ MY SOUL STORY

We view these moments of arrival as important for our students as well. There are special sessions all transfer students attend throughout the year, along with their assigned student mentor. We view student arrival days as an important opportunity to let our new students know they belong in their new school (unlike my unceremonious arrival to my third-grade class in 1958 ["Go sit over there"] described in chapter 3, page 17).

Embrace fun.

I am glad Coyle includes this in his list of belonging cues. It is fundamental to a school culture. Learning deeply is hard work. Making sure everyone has a voice that is integrated and heard is hard work. Measuring what really matters, as a team, is hard work. Creating focused priorities is hard work. Treating each other with warmth and kindness is hard work. However, as my physics colleague Jim McGrath would say, "Physics to be learned must be phun."[139]

When there is laughter (not sarcasm and bullying) and enjoyment in the learning journey, it sparks a connection to our content for teaching. Learning and laughter are not mutually exclusive. We can work hard *and* have fun along the way. Happiness at work is best when merged with a culture of high expectations, hard work, and high levels of support.

MY SOUL STORY ♥ ———

Of these seven belonging cues, which is your greatest strength within your school's belonging culture?

_____
_____
_____
_____

_____
_____

Which cue is a great strength of all the adults within your school's belonging culture?

_____
_____
_____
_____

_____
_____

If you could start to improve just one of these belonging cues in your school culture, which one would it be, and what action would you take to improve it? What action would _all_ the adults in your school need to take?

_____
_____
_____
_____
_____

_____
_____
_____
_____
_____
_____

While a school's culture and soul story are built with a foundation of belonging, a _team's_ collective-care soul story finds its depth in denying neglect and embracing _intimacy._ That cultural soul story challenge is next.

Beyond Collaboration: Intimacy

S   O   ♡   L

Covenantal relationships . . . induce freedom, not paralysis. A covenantal relationship rests on shared commitment to ideas, to issues, to values, to goals.

—Max De Pree

It was late on a Thursday night in July, the end of day two at a summer PLC at Work Institute, as I walked through the bridge from one tower of the Omni Atlanta Hotel to the other tower. The connecting elevators also required a floor change, and as I walked down a now very quiet corridor, I could see a team of about fifteen educators sitting in a circle, some on sofas and chairs and some on the floor.

They had their binders out and were in small groups, listening and talking with animated voices about their plans for the following school year. They had come together as a guiding coalition team from their school district.

As I watched them from afar, I could not tell their job titles or descriptions, but what *was* clear to me was that they had a feeling of intimacy with their work. The work really mattered to them.

I felt a twinge of envy.

The sheer force of their sharing and energy at the end of a long day indicated these tired and dedicated professionals were "all in" as a team. I thought to myself, "That is the best way to live your work life: not with a toe in the shallow water, but with a leap into the deep end with friends who help each other." These educators were exhibiting a type of

Describe two specific actions you have taken in the past month to make a meaningful contribution to your closest colleagues, your students, and other members of your school.

If you have not taken any actions of contribution to others, ask yourself, "Why not?" If knowing the actions would benefit you and the receiver, what is holding you back?

_____

_____

_____

_____

_____

_____

_____

_____

_____

_____

_____

_____

_____

_____

_____

_____

_____

_____

_____

_____

intimacy rare in our profession, and in my experience, only displayed by the best of school teams.

I missed that type of interaction with my own colleagues. I missed the sheer joy we would feel as our creative ideas merged into future action. I missed the deep conversations about how we could tweak and twist our work into improved learning for every student.

The sharing and the vulnerability among this group of educators were palpable. I decided not to interrupt their work. It would have been selfish on my part. But oh, how I missed that feeling and unity that come with team _intimacy_—a type of warm friendship that develops over time with colleagues.

And there it is. That was the root of my envy.

On a July evening in Atlanta, a team of educators working in that quiet lobby space were doing so much more than collaborating. Their quest to find the _soul story of their team_ was on the far right of a continuum between neglect and intimacy.

Lucky them. And fortunate for their students and parents too.

I couldn't help but wonder _why_ they were engaged in such deep relationships and contributions with one another. Were they aware that one of the greatest drivers of both achievement _and_ their emotional well-being was the idea of _contributing to something and someone far beyond the self_?

Tom Rath writes:

> Knowing that we're making meaningful contributions to others' lives leads not only to improved work outcomes but also to enhanced health and well-being. Even small acts of generosity trigger changes in our brains that make us happier. . . . Energy is created that measurably benefits the giver, the receiver, and the whole organization.[140]

 # MY SOUL STORY

Consider Rath's wisdom regarding our work as professionals and the energy and engagement displayed by the teachers and leaders I observed at the

Omni Atlanta. After completing the My Soul Story, think about your colleagues' contributions as well.

Do you have a favorite book, one that you go back to time and again for professional wisdom and insight, at this stage of your career? I have had many, but in my sixteenth season as an educator, I came across a small paperback by a gifted writer named Max De Pree of Herman Miller furniture fame. Written in 1989, *Leadership Is an Art* has been dog-eared, flea-bitten, marked on, and dragged around in my backpack over the years.[141]

The opening epigraph in this chapter is from that book: "Covenantal relationships . . . induce freedom, not paralysis. A covenantal relationship rests on shared commitment to ideas, to issues, to values, to goals."[142]

De Pree's use of the phrase *covenantal relationship* seemed a bit outdated to me for that era in education, much less today. We don't really speak of our professional relationships as covenantal. And yet, that is exactly what deep relationships are. Covenants are the agreements that *bind* you and your team members together and enable you to meet your students' needs by meeting each other's needs.

Covenants are more than merely *participation* in team collaboration. Collaboration occurs when you agree to work together as a group. Yet, that collaboration can often be neglectful and shallow. In educational parlance, it is called *PLC lite*[143], in a derogatory sort of way.

Covenants represent something deeper, actions that are more intimate and less neglectful. You pursue a type of professional *closeness*. Closeness requires making an enemy of the superficial or shallow life described in chapter 9 (page 67).

Closeness requires a complete rejection of the freedom to neglect others. Closeness is a personal choice to honor the covenants of your team.

Covenants are positive agreements that allow for your voice to be heard and flourish. Covenants are manifested through more serious agreements or promises made by your colleagues and collaborative team members, week in and week out, to fulfill your greater purpose— the improved and proficient learning of every child *and* every adult in your school.

When you and I make a covenant together, I expect you to honor your part of the agreement with your actions. And you expect the same from me. This covenant is a norm we will honor, even when we disagree. As you will read in the next chapter (page 151), there is a vulnerable quality to covenantal relationships.

Reflect on the phrase
covenantal relationship. What does that phrase mean to you?

_____

_____

_____

_____

_____

_____

_____

_____

_____

_____

How well does the idea of
professional closeness with colleagues describe your current workplace culture?

_____

_____

_____

_____

_____

_____

_____

_____

_____

_____

_____

_____

In turn, covenantal relationships give our work deeper meaning and fulfillment. They nurture the unity of our team. They expose the *soul story of our team*—our team's contributions to climb that second mountain of contribution to others, tethered together, revealing a shared wisdom surrounding our daily work life.

MY SOUL STORY

Scott Carr, a Missouri educational leader and trusted colleague, speaks to the positive and deeper meaning guided by the work of your team:

> We are not asking team members to give up their identity; rather we are asking them to commit to the right work and do no harm as part of their identity. All our decisions are driven by a positive moral compass to simply do what we know is right for the benefit of student learning.[144]

How then do we build intimacy and interdependence into our second mountain collaborative efforts?

We begin by asking, "What will be our impact? What does our profession expect from us?" We ask over and over, "Are we working on the right things?" We become more aware of our students' diverse needs, and we take responsibility to stay positively charged every day. And we do this while responding to change, conflict, and adversity that almost always come to the surface.

I asked colleague, friend, renowned education writer, and speaker Mike Mattos how collaborative teams move beyond neglectful collaboration (whether the neglect is benign or intentional) and toward closeness and intimacy for the purpose of improved student learning. Here is what Mike had to say:

> Teaching is a deeply personal profession. When done well, it continually challenges our mind, body, and spirit. When educators work collaboratively to ensure their students learn, the burdens and benefits of teaching are multiplied. True collaboration requires members to share successes and struggles, and invest in each other's professional and personal growth. It would be naïve to think this level of co-laboring is achieved without developing trust and professional intimacy between teammates.

Most teams do not develop this level of professional intimacy, because most schools do not expect or require their teacher teams to dig deeply into the essential elements of focused collaboration for improving their practice. Most teams settle for regular meetings to coordinate their individual efforts.

Critiquing each other's instructional practices, challenging assumptions, and holding each other accountable difficult. Likewise, sharing your struggles and strengths requires a willingness to be vulnerable, honest, and reflective—all outcomes that are hard to achieve with colleagues that have not developed a significant level of professional intimacy.

Educators are most willing to invest themselves deeply when the purpose is viewed as profoundly important, and when they enter the relationship fully aware of the potential risks and rewards.

Mission represents the fundamental purpose of the organization—to ensure every student learns at high levels. Achieving this outcome requires a collaborative effort and resonates with why most educators joined the profession in the first place.

Vision paints a picture of what the school—and the educators within it—must become to achieve their mission. This step provides clarity on the level of collaboration—and hence, the level of intimacy—that must be developed to ensure learning for every adult and child.

With agreement on the organization's mission and vision, the staff then define the specific *values*—actions and behaviors—that each member must develop and demonstrate to achieve these outcomes. These agreements create a culture of trust and intimacy.

And finally, achieving these outcomes will not happen overnight. So the school must establish clear and measurable *goals* to begin their journey and track their progress.

When educators approach their job collaboratively, they are going to share the obstacles and rewards of the work. When teammates fail to create covenantal relationships, the challenges seem exponentially greater, while the benefits seem divided and diminished.

But when educators fully commit to the right work and honor the commitments that develop trust and professional intimacy, each educator has the best opportunity to fully engage their soul story.[145]

As a professional, think of intimacy with your team as the opposite of neglecting your team. Think of intimacy as *actions* of personal responsibility you and every member of your team can take to advance the collaborative work of the team. These are actions you care enough about to ensure your voice is heard and you listen to the voices of others. You are *not* neglectful of others. You honor the agreements made with your colleagues.

Reflect on Mike's advice, and then rate *your* current efforts to move beyond neglectful collaboration and toward a more intentional team and professional collaboration and intimacy for improved student learning.

MY SOUL STORY 🩶

Use a forced ranking scale of 1, 5, or 10 to grade your progress toward helping your team be less neglectful and more intimate in their collaboration.

(1 means you don't think about the factor very often; 5 means you intentionally think about it; and 10 means you think about it *and* act on it.)

Write your rankings on the lines provided, and then explain your rankings in the following spaces.

____ 1. **Impact:** I will take responsibility to understand the nature of my impact on my relationships with my colleagues and students. I will ask, "How can I listen better?"

__ 2. **Honor:** I will take responsibility to honor the work-related agreements of my colleagues. I will ask, "Are we doing the right things?"

____ 3. **Awareness:** I will take responsibility to be aware of and understand the emotional lives of my students and colleagues. I will ask, "What does each person need?"

____ 4. **Engagement:** I will take responsibility to be fully engaged each day with my students and colleagues. I will ask, "How do I get and stay charged?"

____ 5. **Balance:** I will take responsibility to understand that I own my destiny and impact and do not place blame for my efforts on others. I will ask, "How do I embed my uniqueness into the agreements of the team?"

Take a closer look at your intimacy rankings for the first four actions. These four actions are part of the community and belonging actions described in chapters 15 and 16 (pages 123 and 131). Also notice they each start with the same five words: *I will take responsibility to.* They reflect personal actions that support Rath's opening epigraph for part 3 (page 121):

> A growing body of evidence suggests that the single greatest driver of both achievement and well-being is understanding how your daily efforts enhance the lives of others.
>
> Scientists have determined that we as human beings are innately other-directed. . . . The defining features of a meaningful life are "connecting and contributing to something beyond the self."[146]

Rath is describing our human need and responsibility to both feel included and make sure others are included. We possess a fundamental drive to form and maintain lasting, positive relationships with other people. Thus, being intimate with our work is part of our story of community, inclusion, and belonging. It is a story of intimacy with our colleagues as part of our work life.

There is something so energizing, intoxicating, and incredibly deep about overcoming obstacles we face at work and achieving levels of student learning previously unheard of, knowing we did it because of our collaborative efforts. We climbed that mountain of learning, *together*.

And yet, there is a caveat. Intimacy, community, and inclusion do not mean you and I sacrifice our uniqueness and our diversity for our team's sake. In our professional lives, we have two contradictory needs: belonging *and* individuality. Review action 5 in the previous My Soul Story. Note that we also must seek to get the balance of our input and team agreements just right.

Yes, balance.

"How do I embed my uniqueness into the agreements of the team?" you may ask.

In one research study across 250 global organizations, *inclusion* references both uniqueness and belongingness, with a slight edge to belongingness.[147] *Inclusion* means we honor the covenantal relationships with our colleagues by belonging to the team *and* maintaining the unique and distinct qualities we bring to the team.

Feeling included is necessary to form and maintain lasting, positive relationships with our colleagues. To be included, feel like we belong, find our unity, and become more intimate with our work mean we balance our relational covenants by embracing the uniqueness and the talents of each team member.[148]

Write about how you
maintain your uniqueness while
simultaneously honoring agreed-
on actions of your team.

_____
_____
_____
_____
_____
_____
_____
_____
_____
_____
_____

What advice do you give
to new teachers on your team?

_____
_____
_____
_____
_____
_____
_____
_____
_____
_____
_____

MY SOUL STORY

Is the struggle for a collaborative soul story of unity, belonging, and intimacy worth the daily effort? Yes.

Without our collective and collaborative soul story (the team pursues its moral good in order to create good in others), we get disconnected from our work. We begin to feel as if we don't belong. Without it, we drift toward an endless stream of mediocrity and dullness.

With it, we find our niche, our place of belonging. It would be proper to say that by choosing to invest time in one another, by creating and developing materials together, by participating in ongoing discussions about lesson design, and by maximizing our strengths to benefit the team, we _learn to belong_.

By arguing, cajoling each other, convincing each other of our _unique_ positions, and refusing to let each other quit the hard race of our daily work, and by finding our common ground, searching for potential inequities caused by the wide variance in how we might teach our curriculum, and erasing social injustices _together_, we experience belonging and intimacy in our work life.

So, why is the cultural pursuit of team intimacy so hard to achieve?

You might be tempted to ask, "Doesn't our team take away my freedom?" No. Our team _feeds_ our freedom, our passion, and the sacred nature of our work.

Consider the difference between _freedom from_ (external constraints) and _freedom for_ (internal constraints).

Freedom _from_ is freedom from _external restraints_. This is a freedom from interference or restrictions by your team agreements. These restrictions are imposed by other people, perhaps those on your team. This is the type of freedom from a source of control. Our mindset becomes, "No one can tell us what to do."[149]

Yet, according to _Merriam-Webster_, a _professional_ is "characterized by or conforming to the technical or ethical standards of a profession" while "exhibiting a courteous, conscientious, and generally businesslike manner in the workplace."[150]

Thus, as *professionals*, we do not have the freedom to do bad stuff or rest on our old knowledge. We have a moral imperative and responsibility to *do no harm*. We don't have the freedom to make decisions that do not improve student learning. Thus freedom *from* does indeed have restraints and boundaries.

Susan Moore Johnson, with the Harvard Graduate School of Education, addresses what happens when we choose to work in isolation and fail to honor an ethical standard of working together: "The more that teachers—even the best among them—keep to themselves, the more the content and quality of instruction varies from classroom to classroom. . . . Students are very likely to get an uneven and incoherent education."[151]

The inequity monster creeps in.

In a *Kappan* interview about her 2019 book *Where Teachers Thrive*, Johnson describes professional, culture-care working conditions that attract teachers and enable teachers to continuously improve their craft: "In well-organized schools, teachers constantly work with and learn from each other. Those schools are designed to build the collective capacity of all teachers to ensure that students receive consistently good or great instruction."[152]

Thus, as educational professionals, we do have *external* constraints on our freedom. This is a key aspect of your teams' professional intimacy, with the caveat that your unique and informed voice is heard and included within those constraints.

We have our uniqueness, and we should make many of our own decisions and create lots of new ideas and experiments for improving student learning. Yet, we do so within the constraints of the relational agreements for effective routines and practices made with our team members and other colleagues.

Our internal decision to honor the team agreements is a type of freedom *for*.

Freedom *for* is the internal freedom needed *for choosing* a life of contribution to the team. You and I have the *freedom for* making a difference. It is our inward choice (freedom to make that choice) toward our behavior *for* the good. To be positively free is to be our own master, acting rationally and choosing *responsibly* to be in line with the best interests of our students and their learning.[153]

While reviewing this chapter, author, school leader, and trusted colleague Chris Jakicic mentioned to me, "The following list is insanely practical. Make sure the reader doesn't miss this list!"[154]

Look Outward

How do you communicate with a team member who is neglecting the decisions of the team?

What can you do in the next month to help that team member understand the difference between freedom *from* those decisions and freedom *for choosing to contribute to those decisions*?

_____

_____

_____

_____

_____

_____

_____

_____

_____

Look Inward

What can you do to improve your commitment to the team agreements and decisions? What can you do to improve your contributions to the team?

_____

_____

_____

_____

_____

_____

So, let's follow her advice. Consider these team meeting strategies and suggestions for balancing freedom *from* team constraints with freedom *for* team contribution.

- Make it safe to speak up at team meetings.
- Prod yourself to speak up if you tend to be quiet.
- Slow down the voices of those who want to talk first.
- Advocate your position, and then ask for suggestions to improve it.
- Confront any ego-driven person in the group.
- Sharpen the focus of the team purpose— *improved student learning*.
- Brainstorm new ideas for improved student learning, and experiment *together*.
- Commit to the team decision, even if you disagree.

Are these strategies part of your current team norms for unity in your professional work-life decisions?

MY SOUL STORY

As you share with colleagues the various aspects of your day-to-day work, you find your freedom because you *choose* to honor your alliances with them. You become part of a team that embodies your unique voice, ensures that voice is heard, and integrates your voice into a new whole that benefits all students.

These are the benefits of deep belonging, of knowing the joy of contributing to your work life with others. Maybe you will experience the intimacy of that school team in the Omni Atlanta Hotel sometime in your lifetime of work.

Imagine the barriers to positive student performance you could then break through and the places of inequity you could erase, *together*. What a professional life it would be.

Only there is one problem. A culture of vulnerability is required to maximize your progress toward unity. We tackle that schoolwide and districtwide culture-care hurdle next.

Beyond Collegiality: Vulnerability

> *In my research I've found that building a culture of trust is*
> *what makes a meaningful difference. Employees in high-trust*
> *organizations . . . collaborate better with their colleagues,*
> *and stay with their employers longer. . . . They also suffer less*
> *chronic stress and are happier with their lives.*
>
> —Paul J. Zak

As we have discovered thus far, our professional lives thrive when we work in the unity of community with others, create a culture of belonging, and nurture our desire to become more intimate with our professional work, teaching, and leading. Becoming part of a dynamic soul story school and team requires a willingness to spread a culture of *vulnerability* across the school system as part of the soul story of the school or district.

Like you, over the years, I have developed a variety of professional and collegial friendships. Those relationships gradually become more vulnerable, which then leads to increased trust.

One of those trusted friendships is with my colleague and well-known educational leader Aaron Hansen. Having Aaron as a reviewer for the manuscript of this book, I knew I would get honest feedback from him, both supportive and constructive in its criticism. In one part of his review, Aaron wrote to me:

> The story [from chapter 11, page 83] about your anger and losing Becky is tender. I really appreciated the vulnerability of your sharing because we are friends and Becky was a friend. I think that every person has loss followed by anger. And it often doesn't have anything to do with life in the school. I think giving teachers a place to acknowledge that it's okay for them to have some time to process loss without being perfect is an important permission you're giving them through

Consider your three
to four closest professional friends.
Now think of the word *vulnerability*. What are your immediate
reactions to the word? Are they
positive or negative feelings and
responses?

Thinking of those close professional friends, describe two ongoing
actions you take to be vulnerable
with them.

_____
_____
_____
_____
_____
_____
_____
_____
_____
_____
_____
_____
_____
_____
_____
_____
_____
_____
_____
_____
_____

your example. I hope it's also giving educators empathy to recognize that others may go
through some stretches where they are not at
their absolute best while they process the hurt
that usually lies beneath anger.[155]

Why share Aaron's message? I suppose, in part, to
let you see the human side of all we do. I am taking a
risk when I tell you that part of my anger story. I am
taking a risk when I share with you my imperfections
and not-so-great moments. As you will see, I am, in
essence, taking the first step in the *vulnerability loop*.

MY SOUL STORY

But, I am getting ahead of myself a bit.

What exactly is vulnerability? Following is some
insight from *Merriam-Webster*:

Vulnerable is ultimately derived from the Latin
noun *vulnus* ("wound"). "Vulnus" led to the
Latin verb *vulnerare*, meaning "to wound," and
then to the Late Latin adjective *vulnerabilis*,
which became "vulnerable" in English in the
early 1600s. "Vulnerable" originally meant
"capable of being physically wounded" or
"having the power to wound" but since the late
1600s, it has also been used figuratively to suggest a defenselessness against non-physical
attacks. In other words, someone (or something) can be vulnerable to criticism or failure
as well as to literal wounding.[156]

You might wonder why none of us are sprinting to
stand in the "let's be more vulnerable" line! Consider a
quick summary of the *Merriam-Webster* quote. It suggests that if we are vulnerable, we are defenseless against
verbal attacks, and we are capable of being wounded.

It seems to me that all the soul story obstacles of part 2
are rolled into one word: *wounded.*

Wounded by being criticized, wounded by not being
good enough, wounded by failing, wounded by falling short of goals, or wounded by being too angry, too
scared, or too open to being hurt.

"Why would we want to be vulnerable?" we ask. Is
vulnerability as a system wide, school wide cultural
value all that important?

Yes, from a soul story point of view.

From a *thriving* professional learning, culture-care point of view, there are plenty of reasons. First, consider this question: Based on your professional experiences, which comes first, vulnerability or trust?

MY SOUL STORY ♥

The neuroscience of trust affirms that vulnerability is a precursor to trust.[157] Vulnerability creates and strengthens a trust culture throughout your school system. Vulnerability becomes more than an aspirational value (we hope for it) of the culture; it is a core value (we live it) of the culture.

Paul J. Zak is the founding director of the Center for Neuroeconomics Studies and a professor of economics, psychology, and management at Claremont Graduate University. He indicates one of the primary methods for building *systems* trust is to show vulnerability throughout all levels of the organization:

> Leaders in high-trust workplaces [think school systems] ask for help from colleagues instead of just telling them to do things. My research team has found that this stimulates oxytocin production in others, increasing their trust and cooperation. Asking for help is a sign of a secure leader [teacher, educator]—one who engages everyone to reach goals. Jim Whitehurst, CEO of open-source software maker Red Hat, has said, "I found that being very open about the things I did not know actually had the opposite effect than I would have thought. It helped me build credibility." Asking for help is effective because it taps into the natural human impulse to cooperate with others.[158]

A great example of systems trust built through a culture of vulnerability across all school buildings can be found at the nationally recognized Kildeer Countryside School District 96 (preK–8) in Buffalo Grove, Illinois. In a Zoom meeting with fifteen participants, I asked the district leadership team members, led by Superintendent Julie Schmidt, about intentional actions that nurture a healthy soul story culture throughout their school district.

Does being vulnerable with your colleagues build trust? Or does trust build into and shape a culture of vulnerability? What is your intuitive guess? Which comes first? Explain your thinking.

"How do their teachers and leaders create a culture of sustained and systemic vulnerability?" I wondered. The following summarizes the thoughts that poured out of their exchanges with me and with each other during our one-hour Zoom meeting:

> We see ourselves as *learning* leaders. We are not afraid to ask questions or ask for help. Let's try to see if others can help us with better solutions. There is a vulnerability we display by being clear to others *we know what we don't know*. We view that mantra as a strength and not a weakness for anyone working in our schools. We do have high expectations for performance, but our system is designed to be horizontal where good ideas and actions can emerge from anywhere.
>
> We model for our staff this sense of vulnerability, and in turn, expect it back from them. None of us are too big. None of us know everything. We are all learners together. We have a saying in D96: *learning has no boundaries*. We want to view our work as (1) it is never done, and (2) you are not alone.
>
> Above all else, as teachers in our district, one core value drives all the rest of our work. All of it. We have chosen a relentless commitment to the social-emotional learning and development of our students first, closely followed by their academic knowledge and learning. The same priority holds true for our adults too. We are never done learning.[159]

District 96's system wide vulnerability response reveals an interesting core value: all adults in the system will be students, *forever.* As the district leadership team members told me, "We are all learners together. We have a saying in D96: *learning has no boundaries.*"[160]

Think about that for a minute. In this profession, you and I will be students forever? Yes.

Think back to chapter 15 (page 123) and your thoughts on a unifying school motto and seal; *learning has no boundaries* would be a great team, school, and district motto. I wonder what the seal might look like. Art teachers reading this, jump right in!

Learning never ends, then?

Exactly.

You and I are students for life. We temper our quiet confidence (some might say *arrogance*) with humility because we realize that despite all we know, there is still so much more we don't know. Yet, because we pursue forever learning, we should become just confident *enough*.

So, vulnerability is our willingness to be confident *and* seek help from others. The best school cultures of vulnerability move far beyond the oftentimes one-way nature of collegiality.

We develop a culture of vulnerability when the giver ("I'll signal my vulnerability to you") and the receiver ("You will either accept or reject my request for help") interact. Our back-and-forth communication signals our vulnerability to one another, and we, in turn, build a more trusting relationship beyond collegiality.

Coyle refers to this back-and-forth process as the *vulnerability loop* and references Harvard professor of organizational behavior Jeff Polzer when he states, "Vulnerability is less about the sender than the receiver. 'The second person is the key.'"[161]

Coyle provides brief descriptors of the vulnerability loop "steps."[162] The following is my adaptation of his five steps with my comments in italics.

1. **I send out a signal of vulnerability to you:** *I am not sure how to use this e-learning tool. Can you help me?*
2. **You detect my signal of vulnerability:** *Hmm. Tim needs help from me?*
3. **You respond by signaling your vulnerability:** *I have had this same problem in the past. Let me help.*
4. **I detect your signal:** *This has been hard for you as well.*
5. **A norm is established; closeness and trust increase:** *Wow! We both have weaknesses. We can help each other.*

And the vulnerability loop process begins again as trust is developed. Now, practice with a colleague.

MY SOUL STORY ♥

Coyle states, "Exchanges of vulnerability, which we naturally tend to avoid, are the pathway through which trusting cooperation is built."[163]

Educators and authors, Mona Toncheff and Sarah Schuhl, are passionate for their work yet humble in spirit. They describe what it can be like to experience deep professional and, ultimately, personal closeness through mutual vulnerability.

Our paths first crossed in the 2013–2014 school year. How do we know that? Because that is

Choose a work-related topic and a colleague who will be your partner through the five steps of the vulnerability loop. Decide who will go first, and then demonstrate a mutual vulnerability loop on the topic using the five steps. Finally, reflect on and write about your experience.

_____

_____

_____

_____

_____

_____

_____

_____

_____

_____

_____

_____

_____

_____

_____

_____

_____

_____

_____

_____

_____

_____

the first year in our shared "Mona and Sarah" digital folder that houses our work, new ideas, and bank of resources we used that school year and every year since.

Having never met in person, we were part of a team of mathematics consultants working at two different schools with the Jefferson County Public Schools in Louisville, Kentucky. Sarah was new to the team and took the first vulnerability step by sharing her PowerPoint and plan for the first meeting at her school, asking our team for feedback. Mona quickly took the second vulnerability step and responded, sharing some additional ideas to grow teacher learning. The school visits went well, and after meeting in person, we began sharing more ideas and trusting one another.

It started with a simple PowerPoint presentation, and we have shared highs and lows of our professional careers, shared family concerns and celebrations, and become lifelong friends. We often say we cannot imagine doing our jobs without having each other as colleagues and friends. And, through it all, we keep learning and having fun![164]

Close relationship research by Harry Reis and colleagues finds that being responsive to the *other person's vulnerability* is important for the sustained quality of a relationship.[165] Their research supports the vulnerability loop suggested by Coyle and demonstrated by the professionals in District 96, and personally represented in the sharing and trusting relationship described by Mona and Sarah.

A team, school, and district soul story and culture of care are built on the very core of who we are and why we are in this profession—the improved and proficient learning of every student entrusted to us, *in loco parentis*.

Yet, something else Coyle mentions strikes me as significant to our soul story: "The idea of vulnerability loops is useful because it helps illuminate connections between seemingly disparate worlds."[166] The idea of illuminating our connections across diverse cultures feels like another great school motto to me.

Our school and district culture is nourished and lives daily within our soul story experiences across all types of personalities; a diversity of thought; and differences in how we look, what we wear, and what we believe, coming together within a culture of belonging, intimacy, and vulnerability. A school culture of high academic expectations thrives and soars when we live these core soul story values of unity each day.

This is the type of place I want to work.

Beyond Tolerance: Validation

S   O   ♡   L

What sculpture is to a block of marble, education is to the human soul.

–Joseph Addison

James Tyree was the sculptor, and I was the fourteen-year-old block of marble (or perhaps some lesser block of stone). Tyree, you see, was my cross-country and track coach.

I had a friend down the street who talked me into trying out for the cross-country team. It was the summer before high school, and I had some prior evidence of not exactly being a terrific athletic talent.

Awkward and a bit gangly, I immediately took to the *idea* of running. It was like an escape from everything going on at home. I showed up at the first practice wearing an old pair of basketball sneakers and long pants. I did not know running cross country meant running three *miles* or more each day.

For the first two weeks, I wanted to quit every day. But there was something about Coach Tyree that made me want to show up for practice in that hot Chicago summer. He had this intense "you can do it" vibe with every member of the team, which I can best describe as *validation.*

Validation is a "process of recognizing, establishing, and confirming the worthiness or legitimacy of"[167] our students as persons. Validating relationships in our profession show up in many forms, such as teacher to student, or coach to athlete, or sponsor to club members. Sometimes those relationships can be soft, and sometimes they can be tough.

As August ended and school started, Coach Tyree pulled me aside and told me I had made the team (little did I know everyone makes the freshman and sophomore team), which immediately improved my confidence *and* my performance. His validating action of seeking me out for a one-to-one conversation (I remember being a bit scared of him) indirectly told me I was worthy of being on his team. At that time, he did not know my backstory, my home life, or my two middle school years of being cut during basketball tryouts.

In practice, I remember him dropping back to my group of runners (I was rarely in the lead group) and running alongside me, as I was huffing my way through our fartlek run and inwardly complaining. He looked at me and yelled, "Kanold, it isn't supposed to be easy! Running is hard work! Let's go!" He was right. It was challenging work. *Stop complaining and suck it up* was his real message.

But he also said, "Let's go!" His subtle message was that he would be in it with me. Although it might not seem like it, this too was validating. He believed I could become a decent runner with enough practice long before I did. Moreover, he would help me get there.

In September, we went to a place called Schiller Park in Itasca, Illinois. The great thing about Schiller Park was that the race ended at the top of a hill. Imagine three hundred runners across a one-hundred-yard field, funneling into a space about twenty yards wide at the four-hundred-yard mark, running all out for two or three miles, and then running up a steep hill to the finish. It really was quite challenging. On that day, I finished 137th, and I remember thinking that it was the first time in my life I had some worth as an athlete.

I lay on the ground gasping for air, pretty sure I would not make it back to the team bus. And there was the shadow of Coach Tyree. "Way to go, Kanold. You broke the top 150! Not bad!"

Know this: no one in my family was there or even knew much about my running. There were no athletes among my family members. A few wondered why I would participate in such a painful activity. My minor celebrations of progress were always with Coach Tyree.

By early November, I was running with the top seven out of twenty-three or so runners on the team. Our final race for the year was a major event at Schiller Park with top athletes from schools around the area. It had snowed the previous day and was snowing the morning of the meet. Temps were in the low thirties.

We used shoes that had these really small cleats in them, like tiny spikes. My right shoe's spikes cut me during every race, including this one, because I run pigeon-toed (still to this day, my right foot points inward when it lands and occasionally hits my left ankle). It was one of my many limitations as a runner. And then came the hill. I made it through the finish line and fell into the snow and collapsed for a while.

I had come a long way from that first hot August day, wearing sneakers and throwing up in a field. All those conditions, all those challenges. All the training. I was 162nd that day. I had finished what I had started.

Coach Tyree hugged me and thanked me for not giving up. In a moment of exhaustion, I felt a strange joy. That morning, coach and teacher James Tyree was able to look past my limitations and validate my efforts, improvement, and confidence as a fourteen-year-old freshman, at a time when my family life was in chaos. He acted *in loco parentis*.

It was only years later, when I was teaching and coaching at Stillman Valley, that I was able to understand his level of validation to my life as a runner and as a person. You see, I wasn't his best runner, not even close. I was at best a C- or D-level runner. I might have been an A student in algebra 1, but not in cross country. But that did not matter to Coach Tyree. I was *his* runner. Therefore, I had value. Validation is an action (spoken or otherwise) you and I take *toward* others.

After my freshman year, I moved to a different high school and never spoke to Coach Tyree again. Unsurprisingly, I discovered in preparing for this book that he had made the Illinois Track and Cross Country Hall of Fame in 1990, having had respected, championship-caliber teams during a thirty-year career.

MY SOUL STORY

Part 3 of this book has been about unity. There is unity in our school relationships, unity in our belonging, unity through intimacy with our work, and unity through a culture of mutual vulnerability (and the building of trust).

These elements of unity come together to reveal the heart and soul of our classroom life and the heart and soul of our co-curricular (student athletics and activities) life. The soul story of our professional life moves us far beyond our standards for academic learning and pulls us to places for inspiring student effort to learn and lean into such knowledge.

Describe a time from your K–12 years when you clearly remember a teacher, coach, or school co-curricular sponsor who validated your talent, effort, diversity, or emotions throughout a specific grade level, course, or student activity.

Teaching, as our *vocation*, unfolds our second mountain soul story of contribution far beyond the subject-matter content we teach. To achieve successful teaching of that content, we plan for and provide validating relationships with our students: validation of their diversity; validation of their efficacy and their effort; validation of their emotions, especially their fears; and validation of their mostly temporary, yet maddening, complaints about life.

Neuroscientist and Northwestern University professor Martha Burns writes about brain research on the effects of teaching. Burns writes:

> Serotonin is associated with a feeling of well-being and is a powerful modulator of neuroplasticity. As teachers, we are very familiar with the importance of enhancing students' *sense of trust and confidence* in the educational process, which can help increase serotonin levels in a positive way.[168]

The italics in the Burns quote are mine, and here's why. A sense of classroom trust and student self-efficacy (students' *belief* in their capability to do the work you ask them to do) is nurtured via a culture of belonging and vulnerability, and *thrives* within a validating culture. High-energy feedback in the form of high expectations for the class and the belief each student can meet those expectations through formative learning is a soul story pursuit.

The essential feedback message to our students sounds like this: *I am giving you these comments because I have very high expectations for you and this class, and I know you can reach them.* It is a three-part message:

1. *This class is special.* We have high expectations for the performance of this class. What we are doing here is important.
2. *You* are part of this class.
3. *I believe you can reach these high standards.* It will take effort and reflective, repeated practice, but you can do it. I am not giving up on you, *ever.*

Jon Saphier is the founder and president of Research for Better Teaching and a deep thinker about the messages we send to our students designed to improve their efforts to learn. He states:

> The ability to do something competently—anything— mathematics, racecar driving, dancing, public speaking—is primarily determined by effective effort and your belief that you can get proficient at it. "Smart is something you can get." The bell curve of ability is wrong. Even what we call "intelligence" is malleable. Thus our work as educators, in fact, a major part of it for some students, is to . . . give students belief, confidence, tools, and desire.[169]

One of the best classroom sculptors of students' belief, confidence, tools, and desire is my colleague and outstanding North Carolina middle school teacher Bill Ferriter. Bill is a "tempered radical," as he states in his blog, The Tempered Radical (https://blog.william ferriter.com), and he has a knack for creating dynamic learning opportunities that validate the work and effort of his students.

When I asked Bill about his soul story legacy as a teacher, he said, "What drives me are the students I can't quite reach. I want to be able to point to kids whose lives are different (hopefully better) because of our effort to learn *together*."[170] I then asked Bill to expand on his professional commitment to a classroom culture of validation. This is what Bill had to say:

> A few years back, my principal asked about my end-of-grade test scores. "Bill, your results are some of the best in the school," she said. "How do you do it?"
>
> I think she was expecting me to describe a strategy for teaching science that others could easily replicate.
>
> But the truth is much simpler than that. "I care about the kids," I told her. "And they *know* it."
>
> What does "caring about kids" mean? For me, it means making sure that every student feels recognized in my room. More importantly, I want every student to believe that he or she is worthy of recognition. Finally, I want to convince every student that he or she is a capable, competent learner. If students believe in their own abilities, they are far more likely to lean in when the intellectual going gets tough.
>
> That's validation.
>
> What's heartbreaking is that by eighth grade, many students have given up on themselves.
>
> After years of being defined by the letters and numbers that we use to rate their performances, C and D students don't always see themselves as worthy of recognition. Recognition goes to the students who are on the stage during honors assemblies— not to the kids who struggle with task after task, year after year. That realization—"No matter how hard I try, I'm never going to be good enough to meet my teacher's expectations"— causes struggling students to quit trying. You'd quit too if you spent years working at a task without ever earning the highest marks.
>
> So how do we make sure every learner feels validation, including those students who haven't experienced a lot of success in our classrooms?
>
> For me, the answer is to end most lessons by asking students to share wonder questions in class. "Turn to a partner and

Write a few sentences about your connection to Bill's words of wisdom about the role validation plays in our professional lives. Then provide an example of validation in your classroom or school culture.

share something that you are wondering about right now," I'll say. I hope those conversations will reinforce the notion that curiosity—a trait that kids of all ages share but that gets pushed aside in too many classrooms—is cool. "The most successful people are willing to wonder," I'll nudge.

After a minute or two, I'll ask a few students to share their wonderings with the rest of the class. Each time a student shares a wonder question, I validate his or her thinking in front of his or her peers. "What a *great* question!" I'll say excitedly. "I never thought about that before." Or, "That's what I was wondering, too. So glad we are thinking about the same things."

There's nothing special here, right? I'm responding the way teachers *should* respond to ideas offered by the kids in their classrooms.

But for students who rarely have their thinking publicly validated, these moments mean *everything*. They serve as constant reminders that every student has thoughts worth sharing. More importantly, they serve as constant reminders that my classroom is a place where every student can make contributions worth celebrating. That's validation too. And it's a strategy any teacher can replicate right now.[171]

Bill's words cut through the fog of validation for me. He just slices our work down to its most basic purpose with a vision of rare clarity about who he is as a teacher.

MY SOUL STORY

In chapter 7 (page 47), we examined soul story whisperers in our lives—the people who come along and, if we are willing to listen, whisper to us, "You should do this, you can do this, and you must do this. It is your vocation."

Validation is like that, but I believe it is much deeper and more sustained. It is our attempt to let those we teach and lead know they are worthy of our daily time and energy and understanding. For the short period he was in my life, James Tyree provided validation and a sense of worthiness at a time when I was struggling. He made a big impact on my life.

Al Foster was like that too. Only Al Foster chose to be more of a validating sculptor for an extended period of time. Al was my high school honors geometry teacher.

Al knew my family life was a bit messed up.

Al knew I could go to college, despite financial constraints. So I went to college.

I went to the teaching university where Al went to college.

Al was a mathematics education major, so I was a mathematics education major.

Al had a dry wit and a weird sense of humor; I just settled on humor.

Al taught me how to teach. I modeled my lessons after his style of student engagement.

Al called me when I was thinking of leaving the profession: "Kanold, you need to interview for that job at West Chicago; and if they offer it to you, say *yes*!"

So, I said *yes*.

Al was a mathematics textbook author. I became a mathematics textbook author. (Al helped to make it happen.)

Al was a public speaker at state and national meetings. So, I became one too.

Al talked about serious topics. My first message was "Trigonometry, Calculus, and the Calculator: A love triangle!" (I thought it was funny!)

Al jumped into my professional life from time to time without judgment, especially since we were different in our personalities and perspectives. He offered only validation, despite our differences. I decided to do the same for others. To this day, it is my way of honoring Al.

Al was more than a soul story whisperer. Al was a sculptor.

And so are you.

We are educational sculptors. And our students are so much more than mere blocks of marble. They are the heart and soul of our work life. Our students are why we decided to climb this second mountain.

Some students pass through our lives, and you and I ask, "Did we make a difference?"

And like Coach Tyree, you may never know. Your impact seems short. Other students pass through and, for whatever reason, you keep on sculpting. Your impact lasts longer term. And sometimes there is

Think about the sculptors of your professional life. Name them. Write about them. If they are still alive, thank them.

_____

_____

_____

_____

_____

_____

_____

_____

_____

_____

Now, *you* be the sculptor. Who are some of the more diverse students in your life?

Who needs you to intentionally validate, value, and inspire confidence in their learning? Don't wait to get started.

_____

_____

_____

_____

_____

_____

_____

more permanence to your validation. Al Foster decided to come along for the ride of my entire life journey.

So, who are the sculptors of your professional life?

MY SOUL STORY

Until now, I have danced around a key word in the chapter title—*tolerance*.

If *tolerance* is "sympathy or indulgence for beliefs or practices differing from or conflicting with one's own,"[172] then validation is an action beyond mere awareness of those differences.

Becoming a soul story–whispering sculptor is not about your age or experience. It is about your willingness to see the positive potential in others that they cannot see inside themselves. And then you choose to follow the moral imperative to become a more trusted voice who inspires belief, confidence, and a desire to do the good of validating *all* the others in your professional life.

In the end, my stories about Coach Tyree and Teacher Foster are not unique to me. Coach Tyree's and Teacher Foster's professional roads and second mountain climbs are filled with life-changing sculpting of students and adults just like you and me.

And so is yours.

As you climb the second mountain, occasionally look down and enjoy the view. See all the students and colleagues who have been the beneficiaries of your hard work and commitment to the good. Take time out to quietly declare, "Today I am a sculptor."

20

Beyond School: Community Engagement

S   O   ♡   L

*If all human beings yearn for success, why are some students not
successful? . . . A healthy school culture recognizes and embraces
the flaws of the environment and agrees to work together to
change that reality.*

           —Anthony Muhammad

After I signed my first teaching contract in the district office of Meridian
Community School District 223 in the aforementioned Stillman Valley, Illinois (see
chapter 5, page 31), I walked out to my beat-up Volkswagen Beetle, asked some students
to push me down the hill, popped the clutch (you might need to look up that phrase),
and started my career as a teacher. With my school district map in hand, I began my
drive around the community.

It occurred to me that maybe I should explore the extended community I was about
to serve in four months. What was the town of Stillman Valley like, as well as the various farms and businesses served by the district? I knew I was joining a *school community*
and wondered about the nature of the businesses and the residences of my new *extended
community* served by the school district.

I drove around town looking at the homes and churches. Off Main Street, there was
a bank, a gas station, a deli, and two bars. I headed west on Route 72 and saw a mobile
home park to the north, where I would eventually live with a fellow science teacher, and
then north to where the district bordered the impressive Rock River along Route 2. I drove
through the community of Byron, a school community archrival as I would soon discover.

Consider your current school or district boundaries. Do you know about them? Use a boundary map to reflect on the community your school or district serves. What do you notice?

_____
_____
_____
_____
_____
_____
_____
_____
_____
_____
_____
_____
_____
_____
_____
_____
_____
_____
_____
_____
_____
_____
_____
_____
_____

I completed my community tour heading east on Route 72 to Davis Junction and Monroe Center, where I would eventually make some great friends and play softball several nights a week. I thought it ironic I had spent so much time hanging out on Higgins Road, also known as Route 72, in Chicago over my high school and college summers. It was the very same Route 72 that ran through my new village community.

I knew nothing about farming and the agricultural community at the time. But I would learn how to drive a tractor and more. I learned to respect the hard work of the farming community and the Midwest wholesomeness of the families trusting me to educate their children.

I would learn quickly that my professional life, my work life at school, was not isolated but rather _interdependent_ with the extended community surrounding the school. Take a look at any community on Google Maps, and you will see a local school district (or two) overlays that community.

MY SOUL STORY

Sometimes our school districts serve several communities. During my twenty-two years at Stevenson, in the Chicago suburb of Lincolnshire, our district boundaries were extensive. We served seventeen distinct townships and municipalities, with a wide variety of suburban and rural communities and identities.

In general, our schools and school districts are expected to serve and respond to the ever-changing nature of the extended community. We move in concert with one another. This interdependence with our extended community and stakeholders is a fundamental law of nature.

We cultivate a sense of responsibility and sincere concern for the welfare of those in our extended community—parents, businesses, and other governmental agencies—in turn, they do the same for our school community. The pulse and tempo of the greater community are reflected in and influenced by the school community, and vice versa. The symbiotic nature of our connection to the community has never been more apparent than during the COVID-19 pandemic.

Gareth Morgan is a professor emeritus of organization studies and a distinguished research professor at York University in Toronto. One of his landmark research studies, *Images of Organization*, describes various ways organizations, including school organizations, might be better understood.[173] In one chapter, Morgan describes an organization as an *organism*, or as part of our biology in a way.[174]

He explains that an organization cannot afford to act independently from its environment. Every action our school takes affects the environment we live in. The actions and beliefs of our community impact and affect our school. And in turn, our school's actions deeply impact the extended community as well.[175]

Morgan's work causes us to ask, "Do our schools and our many programs respond to the changing nature of the greater community we serve, and perhaps influence that community? How can we adapt to a changing environment within our greater community? How can we achieve a good fit and create trust with our greater community?"

The answer partially lies in ruthlessly eliminating any hypocrisy within our school culture. *Hypocrisy* is a "feigning to be what one is not or to believe what one does not believe. It is a personal behavior that contradicts what you claim to believe or feel."[176] *Hypocrisy* then is an issue of integrity and undermines how the school both leads and responds to the greater community it serves.

When the school community does not act in a way that contributes to the growth and well-being of every student, then separation begins. Isolation of the school from the extended community sets in.

To offset isolating our classrooms and our school from our community, our actions need to speak louder than our words.

When I first arrived at Adlai E. Stevenson High School, we claimed to our extended community of seventeen townships that we were a college preparatory institution. These were our *words*. They are egalitarian, are they not? This claim meant *all* our students deserved an equal opportunity to and access to levels of success that would allow them some type of postsecondary educational experience.

Our actions and data revealed, however, that only 50 percent of our students went to two- or four-year college institutions, including trade schools. In truth, we should have declared, "We are a great college preparatory institution for *half* our students."

The question became, How can we be more internally focused as a school district and better adapt our actions to meet the needs and expectations of the extended community?

How do we avoid the dangers of *functional hypocrisy* and move from the awareness Anthony Muhammad wrote about in chapter 15 (page 123) *to action*? Here is what Anthony says:

> Neuroscientists agree that human beings are not wired to naturally accept culpability, and that the brain protects itself from blame by processing unpleasant revelations through the amygdala—fight or flight response. It is not uncommon for people confronted with their own personal privilege to deny the privilege or seek evidence that exonerates them personally or vilifies others for underachieving. Denial or victim shaming will not bring us together.
>
> The likelihood of success in the American public school system is higher for students who speak English, come from middle- to upper-income-bracket households, embrace auditory and visual learning, embrace the dominance of Europeans in all areas of curriculum, and have parents who advocate for special opportunities and educational access. Students who do not share these personal experiences or characteristics are generally discarded in the system and are victims of blame or denial by the very educators who claimed their mission was *learning for all*.
>
> *Functional hypocrisy* is a very difficult obstacle to overcome.
>
> It means rethinking what it means to be successful and questioning almost everything we know about achievement and distinction. If all human beings yearn for success, why are some students not successful? Is it because of some inherent flaw in the student or some inherent flaw in the culture of the system that serves the students? A healthy school culture recognizes and embraces the flaws of the environment and agrees to work together to change that reality.
>
> If we truly believe that all students are destined for success, then are we willing to change our pedagogy, curriculum, assessment, learning resources, norms, and behaviors to respond to the needs of those students?
>
> Student learning does not improve because of change of beliefs alone; it improves because *action* follows that affirms those egalitarian beliefs. I have witnessed many schools willing to talk the talk of equity and universal achievement, but not very many willing to walk the walk.
>
> Change is tough, but necessary, and the ability to witness the growth and development of a child is highly fulfilling because an educator was willing to endure the discomfort of change.[177]

MY SOUL STORY ♥

One of my takeaways from Anthony's wisdom is this question: *If all human beings yearn for success, why are some students not successful?*

The discomfort of changing the current reality is the whole point of our soul story pursuit. *Denial or victim shaming will not bring us together* with the community we serve.

In normal times, it is possible, yet far from ideal, to operate as a school community in isolation, with minimal connection to the extended community. However, in 2020, any form of isolation from knowing more about our extended communities collapsed.

In 2020, the COVID-19 pandemic made ignoring the needs of our extended community all but impossible. Remote learning delivered us directly (via Zoom or otherwise) into the homes of the community and brought disturbing awareness of inequity and variability of access to learning environments from home to home (if there was a home). There was a stunning reawakening to the community's needs and the support necessary to provide many families access to shelter, food, child care, broadband, and other basic human needs.

Our students became much more than a seat to fill, a paper to grade, and a statistic of performance. They became more *real*.

As Pope Francis declared in April 2020:

> This crisis is affecting us all, rich and poor alike, and putting a spotlight on hypocrisy. . . . This is a time to be converted from this kind of functional hypocrisy. It's a time for integrity. Either we are coherent with our beliefs, or we lose everything.[178]

Whoa. Did you read his last sentence? As professionals, we are *either coherent with our beliefs, or we lose everything.* Coherence with our beliefs acts as the fundamental foundation to our personal and professional integrity.

My colleague Jenn Deinhart provided a great example of the power of integrity during the early days of

After reading Anthony's ideas about actions to eliminate functional hypocrisy in your school culture, write down two to three inequity practices or routines in your school that you and your colleagues need to address.

_____

_____

_____

_____

_____

_____

_____

Highlight one action you, your team, or your school should take to walk the walk of an egalitarian (all students are equal and deserve equal rights and opportunities) school culture.

_____

_____

_____

_____

_____

_____

_____

the COVID-19 pandemic in 2020. Jenn is a mathematics instructional coach at Rose Hill Elementary, part of Fairfax County Public Schools in Virginia. Her work life had been a maddening, fast-paced time of anxiety, as she helped her teachers cope with the stress of online planning, new learning, and revised engagement with the extended community.

Jenn wrote the following in response to a prompt about life as an educational professional during the late spring of 2020:

> COVID-19 presents so many different obstacles. Some people, like my immunocompromised mother, are in complete isolation, and her technology skills make it harder for her to connect.
>
> Others, like my brother, are at home with three kids under five years old. He wakes up by 3:30 a.m. most mornings just to get his online lessons prepped or assignments graded. And he feels like he is not doing right by anyone.
>
> My other brother is in constant fear of losing his business. His bar was last open on March 16, he has liquidated everything he could, and he waits each day for the loans to come through.
>
> My dad is considered essential; he has to go to work. We anguish over this reality, as he is seventy-two years old. Retirement isn't an option, as he owns the business and he feels responsible for the well-being of every individual he employs and each of their families.
>
> None of these scenarios are tragic, as [my family and I] are all still able and healthy. But as educators, I feel like it is our responsibility to understand that everyone is experiencing COVID-19 very differently. Our ability to be flexible, give families viable options for distance learning, and continue to support the emotional well-being of the students we miss so much is contributing to the greater good.
>
> In this pandemic, we are taking turns being the teammate with a more positive outlook. We help each other recognize how much we have learned in a short amount of time to be able to provide hope, love, and learning for our kids under these circumstances.
>
> We aren't on the front lines like the health care workers. We aren't risking our lives out there as part of the essential workforce; but instead, we are the behind-the-scenes care and will continue to be. Educators have been and will be providing so much more than academic support into next school year.
>
> I think it is important to recognize that we will be forever changed by this pandemic.[179]

We will be forever changed by this pandemic.

Her words spoke to me. As teaching professionals, we live with integrity and connection to the students in our school community by adapting to the changing community we serve and in which they live.

MY SOUL STORY 🩶

Our soul story pursuit creates unity within our school community and with our extended community at large. We model our moral and intellectual qualities, such as good judgment, best effort, respect, kindness, honesty, service, integrity, and citizenship. These virtues are modeled, upheld, and practiced in every part of our school's life for the benefit of the extended community.

By ensuring our words, actions, and celebrations model positive behaviors for contributing to the greater good of our soul story, we refuse a mindset of "How good do we *have to be* for the community we serve to leave us alone, let us operate in isolation, and live our functional hypocrisy?"

MY SOUL STORY 🩶

Instead, we earn the trust and respect of our extended community—every day, every school season, year in and year out—when we ask, "How good *can we be?*" We not only engage with the people in our extended community, we pull them forward, serving as a lighthouse of excellence for them and their children.

This is the professional soul story life we seek.

How did your connection to children, teenagers, and parents in your community change due to the COVID-19 pandemic in 2020?

_____

_____

_____

_____

_____

_____

_____

_____

_____

_____

_____

Describe how the actions of the adults in your *school community* are aligned to and validate the messages your school gives to the *extended community*.

_____

_____

_____

_____

_____

_____

_____

_____

_____

_____

_____

21

The Quietude Quest

S   O   ♥   L

> *To be steady while the world spins around you. To act without*
> *frenzy. To hear only what needs to be heard. To process*
> *quietude—exterior and interior—on command.*
>
> —Ryan Holiday

Do you participate in a book club? Or perhaps a professional book study? Whether a book-of-the-month event or a yearlong study with your professional friends, there is an expected reflection that takes place in solitude (as you prepare) and in public (as you share with others).

Being still is an almost impossible expectation in this mad-dash social media world we live in. Being still feels empty when you are a doer. Being still is hard to do when your life is busy. Being still is completely neglected and impossible when living the hurried life discussed in chapter 9 (page 67). Yet, being still is essential to our daily well-being, our soul story development, and the artistic and creative nature of our profession.

Take a look again at Holiday's words from the epigraph for this chapter: "To be steady while the world spins around you. To act without frenzy. To hear only what needs to be heard. To process quietude—exterior and interior—on command."[180]

Holiday's last sentence provides direction to his readers. Why should we get still? Oh yes, to *process quietude*. What does that mean? It turns out *quietude* means "repose, as in a quiet state of rest" with synonyms of *serenity* or *solitude* and *stillness*.[181]

Most times there is no time for quietude, much less during a crisis in our lives. No time for a routine of solitude, silence, and reflection. We are too busy *doing*, engaged in the many tasks that swallow up our days. There is no time to rest our brains, we think, as we

Do you currently place some quietude time into your daily life? If not, why not? If yes, describe your routine.

—————————————
—————————————
—————————————
—————————————
—————————————
—————————————
—————————————
—————————————
—————————————
—————————————
—————————————
—————————————
—————————————
—————————————
—————————————
—————————————
—————————————
—————————————
—————————————
—————————————
—————————————
—————————————
—————————————
—————————————

balance the demands of work, family, and friends. And yet, that faulty thinking severs us from our soul story.

MY SOUL STORY

Thus far, you have read through twenty chapters about seeking and searching for the deeper soul story of our work life. Together, we have examined numerous obstacles to a more complete professional life. We have considered how to overcome those obstacles via healthy responses to our emotions. I have asked you to strengthen your soul story development in community and unity with one another, reaching out to create cultures of belonging, intimacy, vulnerability, and validation.

It is true we are in a profession of emotional labor. We contribute to creating good in others. Yet, at what cost to our professional wellness, our personal health and well-being?

Don't we need *some* time alone? Away from the noise, the relentless daily pace, and the never-ending conversations? The constant inputs from everywhere? The constant pressure of deadlines? Time away from the *fast, faster, fastest* model of our work design?

Yes, we do.

Sometimes, our second mountain climb just needs a routine of quiet, of solitude, of silence and reflection. Stillness is hard work because it feels so foreign, so empty. Yet, the benefits abound.

We often discover elements of our soul story when we intentionally embrace daily moments to quiet the noise and become maddeningly still. Holiday illustrates this notion of stillness across a wide spectrum of thought when he states:

> The Buddhist word for it was *upekkha*. The Muslims spoke of *aslama*. The Hebrews, *hishtavut*. The second book of the Bhagavad Gita, the epic poem of the warrior Arjuna, speaks of *samatvam*, an "evenness of mind—a peace that is ever the same." The Greeks, *euthymia* and *hesychia*. The Epicureans, *ataraxia*. The Christians, *aequanimitas*.
>
> In English: *stillness*.[182]

The stillness we seek, the quietude, begins with intentional solitude. I think we intuitively know this, but as the seasons of our professional career unpack, it gets increasingly more complicated to find the time. My best years for solitude were my first six years of teaching at Stillman Valley.

It was an era of chalk, and every night after practice ended (I coached sports throughout the years), I would practice my lessons over and over in my classroom to make sure I was ready for the next day. I was in solitude for sure—no one around except a custodian I often tracked down to let me out of the building.

These sessions would take me about two hours to practice at the board. I would occasionally sit in a student desk and stare at the board in order to see and feel the lesson from the student's point of view. I loved the quiet. No one was disrupting the creative-thinking process. I was in my twenties and did not yet have family responsibilities.

Some of my friends asked me if I felt alone during those planning sessions. They asked if I felt *lonely*. I never did. I saw the solitude and the quiet as a benefit to learning *on my own*. Those practice lessons were *focused*!

Sherry Turkle is an MIT professor and founding director of the MIT Initiative on Technology and Self. In "Connected, but Alone?" a TED Talk reflection about her book *Alone Together: Why We Expect More From Technology and Less From Each Other*,[183] Turkle says:

> How do you get from connection to isolation? You end up isolated if you don't cultivate the capacity for solitude, the ability to be separate, to gather yourself. Solitude is where you find yourself so that you can reach out to other people and form real attachments. When we don't have the capacity for solitude, we turn to other people in order to feel less anxious or in order to feel alive. When this happens, we're not able to appreciate who they are. It's as though we're using them as spare parts to support our fragile sense of self.[184]

In her studies, Turkle seems to verify the door to belonging, intimacy, vulnerability, validation of others, and participation in successful relationships is *purposeful* solitude, with an embraced silence (especially from our technologies).

Holiday verifies solitude as necessary to reduce the daily noise from our lives and bring greater clarity to our work-life relationships:

> It is difficult to think clearly in rooms filled with other people. It is difficult to understand yourself if you are never by yourself.
>
> Sometimes you have to disconnect in order to better connect with yourself and with the people you serve and love.[185]

Write down your immediate reaction (in this moment of your professional life) to the advice from Turkle and Holiday and the importance of daily solitude.

———————————————
———————————————
———————————————
———————————————
———————————————
———————————————
———————————————
———————————————
———————————————

How can you improve your routines of silence and reflection each day? Describe a new commitment to quiet time. Consider sharing this idea with a trusted colleague as you learn together.

———————————————
———————————————
———————————————
———————————————
———————————————
———————————————
———————————————
———————————————
———————————————

Much of our professional soul story requires deep and meaningful conversations, connections, and commitments with others. And yet, both Turkle and Holiday remind us that to participate in unified relationships with others, without losing ourselves in the process, requires moments of solitude.

Take some time to reflect on your intentional efforts to place moments of solitude into your daily life.

MY SOUL STORY

Would you agree with the following sentence?

As educators, we are artists.

I never thought of myself as much of an artist. My students would verify that my hand-drawn mathematics diagrams were mostly indecipherable. The fine arts are an enjoyable part of my life but not necessarily something I'm a participant in.

Yet, an *artist* is "one who professes and practices an imaginative art."[186] We do this in every lesson, every day! We create lessons; we create strategies for student engagement; and in 2020 during the COVID-19 pandemic, for example, we created lessons and used e-learning tools and video lessons at a breakneck pace. We are artists, and teaching is our canvas.

Looking back at my early Stillman Valley teaching days, in the silence and solitude of my classroom, and with no internet, cell phone, or online sources to add to my lesson creation, I would sit in the silence and create on a blank canvas. In my case, it was my blackboard. Today, the canvas is a digital tool, including words, pictures, and video combinations.

In those intentional moments of solitude, late in each day, I would get quiet enough to deeply listen to my students' questions and concerns from the lessons of that day. I would process and reflect on my impact as a teacher and listen to my inner voice on what I needed to improve for tomorrow.

No noise, no distractions, just paying attention to *what I hear in the silence.* Listening is an active and not a passive process. It was in the quiet moments of my Stillman Valley days that I would get still enough to process all my conversations and connections with others.

Holiday describes the Kamppi Chapel in Helsinki, Finland, a church of silence of sorts. He says, "You walk in and there is just silence. . . . The kind of silence that lets you really start *hearing*."[188] So, we cultivate silence. We develop a routine in our day that relentlessly eliminates the hurry and the noise around us. And we *listen*. The Kamppi Chapel may be the exception, but usually this type of listening requires solitude as well.

I have a routine every morning that I call "coffee with the coach," in which I sit in the dark and the quiet. It is a deep moment of stillness for me before anyone else in the house is up. I follow the same general thinking and listening pattern each day:

"Which of the SASHET emotions am I experiencing this week? Why? Who in my family or among my trusted colleagues has spoken to me lately, and how have I responded? Who are the soul story whisperers in my life whom I trust, and am I listening? Which of my family members, friends, and colleagues are on my mind? Why do I care so much about what others think? How can I be more thoughtful about reaching out and connecting with them before this week is over?"

As often as possible, I sit outside and listen to these questions. I try to empty my mind of what is ahead for the day. I know our brains actively internalize and evaluate information during times of silence. I am aware there is neuroscientific evidence that when our brains experience silence—no noise, no conversations, no social media distractions—new neurons are firing away like crazy.[188]

Solitude and silence required. Literally.

Without a planned voluntary routine for solitude, you will not find silence in your day. Without a commitment to be completely silent, listen to your thoughts, and regulate your emotions positively, solitude is empty. The silence and solitude pair walk hand in hand.

MY SOUL STORY 💜

What is your routine to give yourself the gift of silence each day? Consider sharing this routine with your colleagues and encouraging them to create their own routines.

My biggest problem with daily moments of quiet, solitude, and silence or quietude is that after these moments, I often can't remember the thoughts that kept drifting in and out of my head during them. Good stuff sometimes too! Especially when the solitude may be in a place that sparks my silence into deep thought and reflection about how life is rolling along. This is where some type of notebook or journal that allows you to write out or see your thoughts might be helpful.

I have kept journals my entire professional life. I always keep one small notebook in which I write out random thoughts, creative ideas, and reflections on my work and my family, good or bad. Sometimes I do this in moments of silence and sometimes in moments of craziness, when the thought or observation just hits me. Sometimes I use voice notes on my smartphone. I know a good idea will be gone from my brain in a heartbeat if I don't write it down or voice it immediately.

Writing in my notebook helps me be more active during my quiet time, my solitude time. Jack London provided such advice for young writers back in 1903:

> Keep a notebook. Travel with it, eat with it, sleep with it. Slap into it every stray thought that flutters up into your brain. Cheap paper is less perishable than gray matter, and lead pencil markings endure longer than memory.[189]

I like his words: *every stray thought that flutters up into your brain*. What a visual!

MY SOUL STORY ♥

How do you currently record and keep track of your reflections and the *thoughts that flutter up into your brain on a weekly basis*? How do you use your reflections to impact your daily work life?

Our quietude notes are not for someone else to read. They are not blogs, tweets, or Instagram or Facebook posts. They are not for our children. They are for us, the writer of the notes. Holiday says:

> Journals aren't for the reader. They are for the writer. To slow the mind down. To wage peace with oneself. . . . Where am I standing in my own way? What's the smallest step I can take toward a big thing today? Why am I so worked up about this? What blessings can I count right now? Why do I care so much about impressing people? What is the harder choice I'm avoiding? How will today's difficulties reveal my character?[190]

Holiday describes the reflective activity of the solitude and silence space, a space of creating and responding to the professional world we live within.

Maybe you don't currently have a place of quietude as part of your professional wellness. You don't have an intentional time of the day either—the pace of life is too erratic and too noisy, and won't allow for it. And if you do make the time, sometimes you do not *want* to think about the deeper soul story stuff of your life.

And you won't, unless you build quietude into a daily *routine*.

New York Times best-selling author James Clear is someone to know. His book *Atomic Habits: An Easy and Proven Way to Build Good Habits and Break Bad Ones* is worth your time. In it, he writes about following the two-minute rule. He states, "When you start a new habit, it should take less than two minutes to do."[191]

Let's say you want to begin a new routine and make a habit of running, like me. You want to run a half marathon eventually. Clear suggests you need a "gateway habit" that leads you down a harder routine path. My two-minute gateway habit for running was to sit on my front curb in bare feet with my running socks and shoes in my hand.

I took a deep breath and put them on. That two-minute gateway habit was exactly how I started my routine for running, after taking more than a decade off from the routine. It was all I did the first day. And it was easy. Just put the shoes and socks on. I did not walk or run. I just felt the shoes on my feet again. That was the gateway to my new routine for running.

In the case of solitude, my two-minute rule now (after much experimentation) is to make a cup of coffee early in the morning. It is the trigger or gateway to everything that is next.

Clear indicates this is a sort of "mastering of the art of showing up,"[192] which leads to larger routines.

Consider a five-phase

routine for developing a new and improved personal habit for solitude. What might those phases look like for you?

_____

_____

_____

_____

_____

_____

_____

_____

_____

_____

_____

_____

_____

_____

_____

_____

_____

_____

_____

_____

Clear further indicates there are five phases for enlarging your routines, or what he refers to as "habit shaping."[193] Here is my example for developing the habit of *commitment to solitude and silence* using the five-phase idea from James Clear.

- **Phase 1:** Make coffee and sit alone for two minutes.
- **Phase 2:** Sit alone for five minutes, and then stop. Do this two days per week.
- **Phase 3:** Self-reflect on one question for ten minutes, and then stop. Do this three days per week.
- **Phase 4:** Write in a notebook during the silence for fifteen minutes. Do this four days per week.
- **Phase 5:** Get still, get silent, reflect, write, and renew for twenty minutes. Do this five days per week.

MY SOUL STORY

In an article in *Frontiers in Human Neuroscience*, Joseph M. Moran and colleagues indicate that our brains integrate external and internal information into a conscious workspace when resting quietly:

> Freedom from noise and our daily tasks unites the quiet without and within, allowing our conscious workspace to do its thing, to weave ourselves into the world, to discover where we fit in. That's the power of solitude and silence.[194]

Stillness built into our daily life is the gateway into the pursuit of the good for us and for the good we contribute to others each day. Do not try to escape the silence. Embrace it. Learn to listen and not speak.

Brené Brown reminds us that "stillness is not about nothingness; it is about creating a clearing. It's opening up an emotionally clutter-free space and allowing ourselves to feel and think and dream and question."[195]

Use the silence to weave yourself into the world. Find joy in the power and the solitude of the quietude life.

The PLC Life Is a Balanced, Unified Life

S   O   U   L

The *heart* of the PLC life is a story that does indeed unify and bring depth to our professional work together. It is a story that is complex, hopeful, and ever changing to meet the diverse needs of the students we serve.

The *soul* of the PLC life is built far beyond the depths of the selfish life, the acquiring life, and the first mountain life. The genius of the PLC life is in its culture of contribution and collaboration. It resides in the willingness of your team to make choices together and find interfusion with a much greater good for improved student learning, and in the reinforcing expectations of a culture of belonging, vulnerability, and validation.

To be a teacher is precisely to be responsible for and to do the good, *together*.

I asked my colleague Bob Eaker, one of the original architects of the PLC process, to speak to the final thoughts for this part of the book. I knew the soul story concepts of unity and community were close to who he is as a professor, teacher, education leader, and family man. The words that follow are what he had to say. The italics are his:

> The key [to a soul-filled school] is to constantly and consistently exhibit relentless pressure to do the right things, for the right reason, but *always, always* gracefully applied!
>
> When I was younger—much younger—I joined the U.S. Marine Corps in the early 1960s. One of my assignments while in the corps was to the marine detachment aboard the USS *Independence*, a CVA-class aircraft carrier. The year I spent aboard the *Independence* was amazing.
>
> I suppose most everyone knew this but me, but to launch or recover aircraft, the carrier must be heading into the wind. Often, this meant turning the aircraft

completely in the opposite direction. While this sounds simple enough, this is no small feat, and it takes much longer than one would think.

Think of an object with a flight deck that approximates five football fields, that houses eighty aircraft, along with fuel and ammunition that weigh roughly 105,000 tons, traveling at approximately thirty knots, suddenly directed to go the other way! The sheer inertia of such an object means it takes quite a while. (And, the supporting systems—the destroyers, refueling vessels, and other supporting systems—must change course too.)

Creating a unifying school or school district soul story is much the same. It takes time. One, you must have a clear sense of where and why you're changing direction. And two, you must have the passion and persistence (heart) to stay the course. Everything else is learning together, collaborating together, and creating together.

The motto of the U.S. Marine Corps is *semper fidelis* ("always faithful"). The question is, faithful to *what*? To the marines, it is clear from day one—to the Constitution of the United States, to the mission you are assigned, and to your fellow marines.

It has been more than five decades since I left the corps, and still, when I meet a fellow marine, or when I am wearing my Marine Corps lapel pin and a marine says, "Hello," the words to each other are always the same: "Semper fi."

That's what unifying cultures do. They transform the school culture from one of individual soul stories into a collective soul story whole. When you meet a fellow retired faculty member, there is an understanding about how special your common bond is with one another.

Creating a unifying soul story such as this is the most difficult challenge we face. It is not only worthwhile, it is necessary and goes to the very core of what it means to be a professional educator.[196]

MY SOUL STORY ♥

Reflect on the words of Bob Eaker and the seven chapters of part 3, "U Is for Unifying," as part of a fulfilled professional life. Describe your favorite takeaways from this part of the book.

In part 3, you looked closely at how to build a soul story culture in your schools and classrooms together, while maintaining a professional balance against the stress and strain of your daily emotional labor.

Looking ahead, in part 4, we come face to face with the harsh reality that we might be missing out on the joy of our professional life. We discover how to look forward and look back in order to maximize our soul story development and thrive in the moment of each day.

MY SOUL STORY ♥

Describe at least three possible actions you can take to better connect to the belonging, intimacy, vulnerability, and validation actions of your soul story journey. Write these actions as *I will* . . . statements, as you consider your professional soul story progress over time. Keep these statements close at hand as you act on and connect to your professional soul story.

DEVELOPING YOUR SOUL STORY

L

Is for Living

Essential Soul Story Question: Your soul story lives for contribution. Are you relentless?

> *We are not enemies but friends. We must not be enemies. . . . The mystic chords of memory, stretching . . . to every living heart and hearthstone all over this broad land, will yet swell the chorus of the Union, when again touched, as surely as they will be, by the better angels of our nature.*
>
> —Abraham Lincoln, First Inaugural Address

Part 4, "L Is for Living," is where you will discover how to live your soul story *today* to build your legacy for tomorrow.

We search, we overcome, we unify, and we live for a professional life fulfilled. We examine the view from our life on the second mountain and consider the defining moments and progress made so far, while also looking ahead to where the climb is taking us. From a professional life view, we will reach the end of our climb and wonder, "How did we do? Did we make it to the top?"

Perhaps. Only *you* can be the judge of your professional soul story journey.

In chapter 22, you examine the defining moments of your professional soul story timeline thus far. Whether you are a novice or a veteran of this profession, you will discover that your timeline is moving from zero to zero, and the proverbial clock is ticking on a finite number of days.

In chapter 23, you come face to face with *carpe diem* and the idea that you can simultaneously plan for spur-of-the-moment activities *and* plan for them to happen later, perhaps two or three school seasons down the road.

In chapter 24, I ask you to look deeply into the mirror and notice any drift from your professional soul story purpose. And there will be drift. There will be some not-so-fine defining moments. Our lives include regrets and moments in which perhaps we were not kind. We are, after all, human.

Chapter 25 offers a solution to the drift: *soul story courage*—a journey of courage toward the problem blindness you might be experiencing and a process to work your way through it to a life of few regrets. Moments of courage deserve credit on that soul story timeline.

Chapter 26 completes your professional journey with an understanding of the joy experienced through your actions of gratitude and grace as a professional. An essential question in this chapter is, Who will be the beneficiaries of your work life?

Chapter 27 is the final chapter of part 4 and also the book. We examine our school seasons, our "trips around the sun," as our professional life unfolds. We face the reality that the dates in our calendar always arrive, and we are often forced to ask, "Did I make a difference? Did I *pursue my moral good in order to create good in others?*"

The sum of all our actions each day ultimately becomes our teaching legacy. You create your path as you walk it. May it be one of joy, connection, love, hope, contribution, peace, and laughter.

The Date Always Arrives

S   O   U   L

Contribution is the sum of what grows when you are gone.
—Tom Rath

We were sitting together at a table in the Fieldhouse with lots of other tables and chairs spread about. It was part of a professional wellness day fair. "Let me show you your chart," he said. "Based on your current health, this is what your life will be like." I looked at my chart, and each successive year was looking good. Improving.

But I noticed at age eighty, my chart fell off the cliff and flatlined. I disappeared. I became a big zero.

"What is that?" I asked, pointing at my sudden drop in improvement.

He replied, "Well, that is when you are dead. You're reasonably healthy, so I gave you two extra years. Look, when you are born, you start at zero. When you die, you're back at zero again. And that date always arrives."

At the time, I was thirty-nine and in my seventeenth season of teaching. I have to admit, age eighty seemed far into the future, a long way down the road. The chart seemed to say to me, "You have a great and awesome future ahead, and then you are nothing."

It seemed a bit harsh.

Of course, he was a financial planner trying to convince me to invest in my future. When I make it to age seventy-nine, I will have money to spend until I am a zero once again.

I invested in my future. Maybe I'll surprise his statistics and make it past my second zero.

I remember driving home that afternoon and thinking my life is a *finite* timeline. Seriously. Seeing that chart back in 1991 reminded me that my *entire* life, not just my

Write about a recent professional contribution to the growth and positive well-being of your students or colleagues. Describe some details. What evidence of actions taken would you show a colleague?

_____

_____

_____

_____

_____

_____

_____

_____

_____

_____

_____

_____

_____

_____

_____

_____

_____

_____

_____

_____

_____

_____

_____

_____

_____

_____

professional life, would be done improving, living, and loving by 2031 if my financial planner's prediction was correct.

"It could also happen tomorrow," I thought. "Start preparing today."

And so it is. From the moment we start our professional life, we have a finite number of days and school seasons. The only question that matters is, What are we doing with that finite number of days to contribute to the growth, dignity, learning, and positive well-being of ourselves, our students, our colleagues, and most important, our families?

Exploring our soul story is about recognizing the moments we are in _today_, learning from the moments in our past, and using them to become more intentional about our future actions. The sum of our actions each day ultimately becomes the residue, and if we are not careful, a possible trail of regrets.

We create our professional life path as we walk it. Sometimes we wander; sometimes we take a few wrong turns. Most of the time, we learn from those wanderings and wrong turns to find our way back to a soul story path of contribution and good. Sometimes, in our quietude moments, we look back at the path we just created, at the view down that second mountain, and think, "Wow! We did all that! What a view!"

 # MY SOUL STORY

It is when we look back on the timeline of our professional life progress that we can consider, "How are we doing? What is the path we are leaving behind for others?" Our soul story is one big _formative_ experiment, season after season. It only becomes past tense when, as the accountant warned me, we become zero again.

And that date, the second zero, always arrives.

When I first got to Stevenson, my mentor and our principal at the time, Rick DuFour, had our leadership team (think guiding coalition) members each complete a timeline of significant events in our professional lives.

The idea was to go from zero to zero in our _professional_ life.

This was one month after my financial chart had predicted my death at age eighty. So I had that second big zero on my mind. Rick asked us to start the timeline with our first year of teaching. I suggested we think of this year as our *first* zero. We were to end our timeline with our predicted last year of teaching and leading. I suggested we write this date as our *second* zero.

We marked highlights or hash marks on the timeline when significant moments had happened to us professionally thus far, and predicted significant moments we hoped would happen down the road, as we got closer to that second zero.

At the time of the activity, my hash mark–worthy moments were more first mountain events (all about me) and fewer second mountain events (what I had done for others).

I had a hash mark at my 1973 graduation; at my first job at Stillman Valley; and at 1980, highlighting my master's degree and my second job at West Chicago. I had a hash mark at 1986 with two special moments: taking the job at Stevenson and going to the White House.

I had a hash mark at 1990 on my timeline, the year we had a significant reduction in student failures in the mathematics and science courses in our school, and we *partially* hit an unprecedented milestone goal (it would take another three years to fully hit the goal). Finally, I had one future hash mark at 1996, indicating my intent to go back to school to secure my doctorate.

By now, if you have read the previous twenty-one chapters, you know there is nothing wrong with my first mountain achievements and goals. But only my 1990 student-failure-reduction hash mark represented my *primary* purpose in this profession. The other memories and moments were nice, but they were merely personal achievements. The seventeen of us posted our professional timelines on the walls and did a gallery walk to learn more about one another.

It was in that moment I knew Stevenson was a different kind of culture. My colleagues had been with Rick a bit longer than I had, and they knew what he was driving at in this exercise. He was digging for our sense of *vocation*, not our career. The contributions we were making to the Stevenson community, not merely our achievements. Rick wanted to know our positive impact moments toward the dignity and learning of *every* student. What was our profession asking of us?

I still had a lot to learn.

Let's do the timeline exercise, reframed, updated, and adapted through the lens of Tom Rath. Rath calls his timeline idea *MILES* for "most influential life experiences."[197] It is part of an online inventory (called *Contribify*) he provides for his readers. You can learn more about it at the Contribify website (https://contribify.com). His work is designed to bring into focus the positive contributions we make to our team, peer group, and family.

To complete the MILES section of the Contribify profile, you "identify a few of the most formative experiences of your lifetime. What are the events, moments, or periods of time that most positively influenced who you are today?"[198]

> Try to think beyond common and expected life events like graduations and weddings. Think about some of the *signature stories* you tell others when describing why you do what you do today. Perhaps there were a few surprises that seemed unwelcome at the time but led to a great deal of personal growth.

> Start with experiences that had a decidedly positive influence on the trajectory of your work and life. Experiences that led to growth are the key.[199]

I asked special education teacher and colleague Corinne Howe to take Rath's online inventory about her specific professional life experiences listed in the MILES section. Corinne is part of the Lodi Unified School District in Lodi, California. Here is her observation:

> My first milestone occurred in my fourth year as a special education teacher for K–6 students with severe behavior problems. Without warning, I was being moved to a 7–12 setting for emotionally disturbed students and could not say goodbye to my K–6 students. I was upset.

> But this defining moment in my life shifted from negative to positive when a colleague, who knew my teaching passion well, suggested I transition to a grades 4–6 special education class in another district. I accepted this new position, to Lakewood School, where I stayed in the same special education classroom for the next twenty-seven years. The courage to make that move, to a job I loved, was a defining moment.

> My second milestone occurred in my fifteenth year as I extended my daily teaching to serve on various committees and train staff at several school sites and joined TAASA, a districtwide team that spent several years improving student access to educational services. I accepted the task and provided training to faculty throughout the district.

> In this vocation-defining moment, I had the opportunity to work with numerous colleagues and continue my growth as a teacher *and* a trainer, while still teaching full-time at the elementary school I loved. Eventually, my professional development work expanded to supporting school interns and substitute teachers with the testing of special education students and facilitating IEP meetings.

> I am now in season twenty-nine and my final transition as a professional educator. My current defining moment required

I leave the classroom and accept a full-time position with the district assessment team. I am now using my skills and abilities to help meet the needs of students and teachers across the entire district, which I find deeply rewarding. I can now more fully recognize and appreciate the story arc of my skills and abilities as a special educator.[200]

Now that you've read about Corinne's experiences, let's create a professional timeline! In the My Soul Story space, create a timeline from when you started your teaching profession to when you expect to retire. Be sure to also place a hash mark with the date you are completing the timeline. It will mark this moment in time. If you reflect on your timeline again, you can create a new mark shifted to the right.

MY SOUL STORY ♥

Use the lines provided to write the zero-to-zero timeline of your professional life by taking the following four steps.

1. On the far left, list the *year* you started (or will start) in our profession (first zero).
2. On the far right, list your best guess for the year you will retire from our profession (second zero).
3. In between those two marks, mark and label today's date.
4. Looking back from today, place marks at the years (and months, if you wish) when you had positive or negative professional experiences that ultimately positively influenced the trajectory of your professional life.

For each mark, use the lines and spaces provided to write briefly about the backstories that give context and meaning to your signature moments.

1st Zero   Today's Date   2nd Zero

As Rath indicates, did you mark timeline moments that *led to your own professional growth as well as the growth of others*? Also, did you provide some context and write some of the backstories behind the hash marks you chose to highlight?

There is a curious reality about professional timelines and highlight moments.

We don't always get to name the date of the second zero.

We know this, of course. When our professional life is in community with others, we have an awareness of the certain tragedy in this truth. I have shared with you in this book some of my colleagues who had abrupt and unplanned endings to their professional timelines.

Planned or not, we can plant the seeds *today* to live a life that matters *tomorrow*. By offering our singular purpose to the professional world we inhabit—*the positive creation of knowledge and the pursuit of good in others*—we leave a trail worth following.

When our beloved principal Dan Galloway retired after twenty-five years in the district (he got to name his second zero), our Stevenson faculty and staff created a video of pictures and highlights of funny and poignant moments in Dan's teaching and leading life at Stevenson. It was a photo and video highlight reel. Dan was one of those strong but humble leaders—decisive for the mission and students, yet modest in his approach.

The video was set to the lyrics of a song by Green Day ironically called "Good Riddance" (Dan could see the humor in that), but subtitled more fondly "Time of Your Life."[201]

Here are a couple of the lyrics:

"It's something unpredictable, but in the end it's right
I hope you had the time of your life."[202]

As time has passed, I wonder whether faculty and staff remember him. I wonder too how his impact lingers in the culture of the school. I watch the video once in a while. The words to the song pull you in. Our professional life is for sure a timeline that is something unpredictable. My memories of Dan and his impact are still strong but beginning to fade. Time waits for none of us.

This much I know for sure. The date always arrives.

How great would it be, when we hit that second zero, *not* to think and feel, "I hope *I* had the time of *my* life!" Rather, to be able to think and feel more deeply, beyond the self, "I hope *you* had the time of *your* life."

In the next chapter and those that follow, we write our own history as educators. That history will have its peaks and transitions, and ups and downs, but we can choose how to respond to events and write our soul story as we live it. Part of understanding our own professional wellness is managing the thousands of decisions and choices we make each day.

MY SOUL STORY 🩶

We can, if we want, create incredible moments in our professional life that are perhaps best appreciated while we are living them, but are worthy of hanging on to once the future becomes our past.

HOW do you use your quiet time to reflect on your progress and decision-making history as you walk through each school season?

_____

_____

_____

_____

_____

_____

_____

_____

_____

_____

_____

_____

_____

_____

_____

_____

_____

_____

_____

_____

_____

_____

_____

_____

Carpe Diem

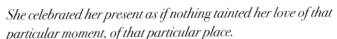

*She celebrated her present as if nothing tainted her love of that
particular moment, of that particular place.*

—Amanda Creasey

My journey with him began in song and, in many ways, ended in song.

The first time I met him was in a school hallway as I was walking to a school assembly in the gym. He ran by me and said, "I heard you can sing; follow me." And the next thing I knew, I was standing with him in front of two thousand screaming students, microphone in hand, singing, "Boom shaka-laka-laka, boom shaka-laka-laka," to the 1969 Sly and the Family Stone hit "I Want to Take You Higher."[203]

That was our beginning together.

Thirty-five years later, in the suffocating heat of a Tampa Bay summer, ten of us got on the local TECO Line streetcar after an end-of-the-day work dinner together, heading back to our downtown hotel. There were a few other people on the streetcar too.

The date was July 8, 2015, and it is hash-marked on my updated professional timeline (discussed in the previous chapter, page 187) as a defining moment in my life. Not one of those bigger defining moments, but one of those rare and unique, smaller, subtler unsuspecting moments that just stick in your memory.

There was silence on the streetcar. Few people were talking. We were a bit weary from the day's work, and our dinner together had left us with a vague awareness of our possible future without him.

But he was always a man of action. A carpe-diem, seize-the-day kind of guy. He loved to sing. By now, though, his singing voice was weak.

Cancer treatments will do that to you.

He sat across from me and asked, "What is that Bill Withers song we like to sing?"

"You mean 'Lean on Me'?" I said.

"Yes. That's it. Could you start it?"

"Start it here, now? On the streetcar?" I asked.

"Yes."

So I did.

Haltingly, shyly almost, I began with the help of others from our group, like Tim Brown, who quickly joined in, with voices much stronger than mine. You most likely know the 1972 tune and hear it often on the radio. The song starts out like this:

> Sometimes in our lives, we all have pain,
> We all have sorrow . . .[204]

The next thing we knew, all of us were belting out the song. And when I say *all of us*, I mean every passenger on that streetcar and the driver too. Two full renditions. As the streetcar would stop and pick up more passengers, they just joined in. We got louder and added harmony.

I saw his best friend, who was sitting behind him, grip his shoulders as they literally *leaned into* one another and sang that song together.

We had seized a defining moment we would not soon forget. Somehow, he just knew that music would naturally bring people together. The driver told me that streetcar ride was his best moment of the summer.

It was mine too.

We got off the train at the very last stop. There were people of color and multiple faiths, strangers mostly, looking at each other, high fiving, softly reminding us of our humanity. It was a night with him, a memory, a defining moment I will not forget.

That night also signaled what would become the beginning of the end of my incredible journey with him. The timelines of our personal and professional journeys were coming together in that singular moment.

∞

A lot is going on in my streetcar story.

First, why did the music, our singing together, make the moment so memorable? So emotional? So meaningful? We were not professional singers. Far from it. Yet we felt a deeper energy and connectedness to one another.

The answer is dopamine and oxytocin.

It turns out that music not only induces hormonal changes but also increases our sense of trust, love, and acceptance.[205] As mentioned in the Final Thoughts section of part 1 (page 53), dopamine is a neurotransmitter that feeds a curved structure (the striatal system) in the brain and signals the significance we assign to a given stimulus. Dopamine gets dumped into our brains when we hear a favorite song.[206]

Oxytocin moves through our brains when we sing or play instruments together as a group. Our social bonding is enhanced during these musical moments of togetherness.[207] No wonder it was such a stirring experience and has lasted as a defining professional moment in my memory.

Second, why did my streetcar experience, on what had been just another typical, long, and weary summer day, similar to many during my summer work season, suddenly change into a worthy defining moment in my memory?

MY SOUL STORY ♥

Brothers and authors Chip Heath and Dan Heath provide a hint. In *The Power of Moments*, they provide a road map for defining moments in our professional (and personal) timelines.[208] Those key hash-mark moments from the last chapter (page 187) are much more than mere happenstance, they claim. We can *create* them! Heath and Heath write:

> We all have defining moments in our lives— meaningful experiences that stand out in our memory. Many of them owe a great deal to chance. . . . But is that true? Must our defining moments just happen to us?

> Defining moments shape our lives, but we don't have to wait for them to happen. We can be the authors of them. . . . Why would you want to create them? To enrich your life. To connect with others. To make memories.[209]

We can be the authors of our best timeline moments!

Describe a favorite professional memory, represented by a defining moment, possibly built around some form of music. What was the name of the song, or instrumental, if there was one?

_____
_____
_____
_____
_____
_____
_____
_____
_____
_____
_____
_____
_____
_____
_____
_____
_____
_____
_____
_____
_____
_____
_____
_____
_____
_____

Describe a favorite

memory, a defining professional *carpe-diem* event in the classroom or with colleagues, when you *seized the day*. Was there someone or something that helped guide you to that moment? Explain.

_____
_____
_____
_____
_____
_____
_____
_____
_____
_____
_____
_____
_____
_____
_____
_____
_____
_____
_____
_____
_____
_____
_____

We can seize a moment and author that memory, and that is exactly what my close friend and colleague Rick DuFour did on that streetcar on July 8, 2015, when he asked the simple question, "What is that Bill Withers song?"

When we assess our experiences in life, we don't average our minute-by-minute sensations. Rather, we tend to remember defining moments that serve as flagship events: short experiences that are both memorable and meaningful.

Like that ride on the Tampa Bay streetcar.

There are many takeaways from *The Power of Moments*.[210] For me, one takeaway is the distinction between *creating* our professional life moments as we careen toward that second zero and just waiting for them to happen by chance.

We can create lifetime moments by seizing on them *spontaneously* when they present themselves. No advance planning needed. We can create the moment and not hope or wait to seize that moment.

Group singing on a quiet streetcar ride was not a planned event. It was this organic, spontaneous, carpe-diem, seize-the-day kind of moment fueled by the spark of just one person on that train.

Carpe diem is a phrase that comes from the Roman poet Horace. His full phrase was "carpe diem quam minimum credula postero," translated as "pluck the day."[211] Carpe-diem moments are generated by creating something unique, surprising, and uplifting, or off script, in your lessons or school activities with students and colleagues.

 # MY SOUL STORY

The Heath brothers also remind us that not all defining events on our professional timeline need be spontaneous.[212] You and I can *plan for* defining soul story moments on our zero-to-zero timeline of finite professional days as well.

We *target* a future date. We *create* a plan. We *take action* on the plan.

We say, "Let's make this special moment happen! Two weeks from now, or five months from now, or three years from now." We get excited!

And then, reality of the hard work and action to achieve the defining moment sets in. We drag a bit along the way. And then a funny thing happens with timelines.

The date. Always. Arrives. The future date we chose on our timeline? We blinked, and once again, that particular moment, that defining moment we planned so hard for, that we took action on and prepared for, zipped by and is now in our past.

And we can't take it back. The moment is over.

You and I can only learn from those moments, remember them, and then plan for our next defining professional moment. Until of course, we can't plan anymore.

Sometimes future defining professional moments require advanced planning with subsequent action. In one case for my professional life timeline, carpe diem had become *carpe annum*. Instead of seize the day, it became "seize the school year."

In the PLC life, teacher teams set goals or milestones for student achievement. At Stevenson, mathematics and science were my areas of teaching and leadership. Our mathematics and science faculty teams had set a future (defining moment) goal of increasing the student participation rate in our best programs to 50 percent and decreasing our D/F grade rate of student performance below 15 percent *without* reducing the curricular rigor of those programs.

This was a milestone goal at the time (1987) because only 10 percent of our students were allowed into our best math and science programs, and our D/F rate for student performance in mathematics and science was 49 percent. It took us eight years to reach those milestone moments and that goal. That date, August 22, 1995, is a date on my professional timeline. It took us eight years to stop placing quotas on student participation and create student success across the curriculum. It was, for our faculty, staff, students, and administrators, a well-planned, long-term moment of celebration.

The Heath brothers share some great advice and insight into how to turn an audacious future milestone into a well-planned defining moment.

To make sure a defining moment will measure up, they suggest four components. Their words are in bold, and my words follow.[213]

- **Elevation: Break the script of your normal routines and create a first—** We significantly changed our pedagogy, our interventions, and our access to all programs, especially for our students learning English as a second language and our special education students.

- **Insight: Stretch beyond your normal routines and expectations of each other—**This was the real beginning of shared practice, transparency with our routines, and teacher team collaboration. The PLC at Work life we know and live today at Stevenson.

- **Pride: Recognize and celebrate others as part of this moment—**We (students and teachers) had some small victory parties along the way, but on August 22, 1995, we had a big party to open the school year and publicly celebrate our team results.

- **Connection: Deepen ties with your students or colleagues and develop shared meaning in the moment—**During our August celebration, I had different teams of students and teachers tell their *stories of action* toward the mathematics and science achievement goals we had set. We told stories of achieving outcomes far beyond our reach just eight years prior. I gave every one of our mathematics and science faculty and staff a compass; on the back was inscribed *True North*, the direction of our student proficiency, access, and learning. It was a story revealed by our data and described by the beneficiaries of our effort and commitment as teachers—our students.

MY SOUL STORY 🩶

Describe a defining event or classroom or school-wide moment you or your team is planning. Maybe it will take a few weeks, months, or years. Maybe it will be a moment of elevation, insight, connection, or pride. How will you celebrate the milestone when you hit your target?

Go back to the My Soul Story timeline in chapter 22 (page 187). Looking *forward* from today, label hash marks on future weeks, months, or years where you are planning for future moments to be achieved and celebrated.

_____

_____

_____

_____

_____

_____

_____

_____

_____

_____

_____

_____

_____

_____

_____

_____

_____

August 22, 1995, eight years in the making, was a defining moment now deep in the past. Timeline moments are like that. They move by us like scenes in a movie.

It turns out that our firsts are an important part of creating defining moments. You might have noticed that, according to the Heath brothers' list, one of the ways to create meaningful moments is through *elevation by creating firsts*. They indicate that most of our significant events are firsts and take place between the ages of fifteen and thirty and during the early years of our teaching career. In addition, when we reflect back on our lives, we tend to give a *reminiscence bump* or memory preference to the same time period—ages fifteen through thirty.[214]

It's like we hit the age of forty, and all our firsts are over, except for those times we get on the metaphorical streetcar.

To paraphrase Kahlil Gibran: Do not measure time by saying there was a yesterday and there will be a tomorrow. The present moment contains all the time that can be hoped for, done, and realized.[215]

So, seize *this* day; keep those firsts coming in your professional and personal life. They will keep you engaged, stretched, and challenged in your work and life, as your tomorrows become your yesterdays.

Carpe diem, indeed.

— MY SOUL STORY ♥ —————————

HOW are you continuing to experience elevation in your professional life by creating firsts? Write about one or two examples.

Mirror, Mirror

What we possess is temporary, but what we become
is permanent.

—Devdutt Pattanaik

Remember part 1 of this book (page 5)? Part 1 was about *searching* for your soul story of social justice as you climb the second mountain of contribution to others.

It is a rough climb and comes with good and not-so-good moments. In addition, your professional soul story is *the pursuit of your moral good in order to create good in others.*

That is a lot to ask, season in and season out.

In part 1, I mentioned that sometimes your soul story comes searching for you when you least expect it and in the strangest of circumstances. Maybe it grabs you with a young child's innocent face and gap-toothed smile in your classroom. Maybe a teenager shows up at your classroom or office door seeking guidance and help. Maybe it reveals itself during a moment of clarity or vulnerability with a struggling colleague.

Or maybe in a moment of failure and frustration, when you're almost in tears, your soul story quietly touches you as you see, hear, and feel so much of the suffering, injustice, and lack of compassion for the children or young adults you serve.

"Why did I choose this profession?" you ask.

Whether in a moment of joy, doubt, pain, frustration, or sorrow, your soul story comes searching for you and answers the *why* question with force. The moment usually becomes one of those defining memories you can put on your zero-to-zero professional timeline.

And that is exactly what happened to me.

On a cold, windy, snowy, Midwest February morning, during my tenth school season, I rolled out of bed, made my much-needed morning coffee, took a hot shower, and like most mornings, used a towel to wipe steam off the mirror, too impatient to wait for it to clear.

But this morning was different. I was tired. I was cranky and irritable. My car often did not start in those cold winters. At 2:30 a.m. every morning, I would run out of my apartment to the open field parking lot with my winter coat over my pajamas, and start my car and let it run for fifteen minutes, hoping that at 6:00 a.m., it might have a chance as I headed to school.

Only I slept through my 2:30 a.m. alarm. Thankfully, I had run an electrical cord out of the balcony of my apartment and down to the car to place a light bulb on the battery overnight, but there were no guarantees with wind chills below 20 degrees Fahrenheit.

My car inconveniences, though, were not what was eating away at me.

As I looked in the mirror on that winter morning, I did not like what I saw. I did not like what I was becoming. I had lost my boundless enthusiasm and emotional moxie that had made me more dynamic during my earlier teaching years. And now, despite a deeper understanding of the content I was teaching, I had become dull and dry, disappointing, and selfish.

"I am their teacher! I am their inspiration! I am their role model. I am responsible for the joy and positive emotion of my classroom culture. It's not their fault I chose such a public profession and ended up as their teacher." These were the thoughts running through my head. Then out loud:

"Get your act together, Kanold!" I yelled at the face in the mirror.

I was in my tenth season of teaching and coaching, yet living the shallow teaching life described in chapter 9 (page 67). I was cutting corners on the quality of my daily lessons. My level of preparation and emotional connection to my students were under siege.

Unlike my advice to others, empathy and compassion were not on my current agenda. I was too trapped in my misery. Viewing my daily lessons from the perspective of my students was no longer on the preparation menu.

Worse yet, no one knew. Not one of my colleagues knew I was becoming unglued and giving less than my best as a professional. I was not yet working in community and unity with my colleagues, so I could hide. For far too long, I had been operating in a vacuum. No one other than possibly *some* of my students and parents suspected I was giving less than they deserved.

But kids adapt. Pretty soon they accepted the lowered expectations of their own performance, because I had lowered my expectations for their performance each day. And rest assured, they were observing everything I did and said, the cultural values I espoused but failed to act on, and my emotional state every day.

Looking back, I think I became like this because I *could*. I had not yet learned to stay connected to the soul story part of my work life. You know, the part of your professional life that knows you down deep. It is the *who you are when nobody but you is looking* self.

As I looked at that face staring at me in the mirror on that very cold morning, I knew I did not like what I saw of my very public self in front of my students. What on earth did my students think? No wonder they thought mathematics was a drag. I was the one dragging it all down. I was failing myself, much less them.

Sometimes the defining moments that you ultimately highlight and mark on your zero-to-zero professional timeline are not initially *positive* defining moments. This looking-in-the-mirror moment on that winter day was, for me, not my finest hour.

But it was a self-defining hour.

This long look in the mirror was a soul story moment of clarity that changed my teaching path. I don't know what made that morning different from all the others. Except, for whatever reason, on that morning, I could not stop staring at my face. I was overwhelmed by a sense of "this is what my students see every day." It was as if they were holding a mirror up to my face and saying, "This is what we see, Mr. Kanold."

My students, my classroom, and my lessons were *not* thriving. I was determined to be better. "I am better than this," I remember thinking.

MY SOUL STORY ♥

In that defining moment of clarity, I realized I was so much more to my students than just a role model (even if a poor one at the moment) or a teacher of mathematics. I was supposed to be a game changer in their lives!

Has there been a negative moment in your professional life when you took a "long look in the mirror"? What did you see? And how did you respond?

If there hasn't yet been such a moment, what can you do now to prevent such a moment on your professional timeline?

I was supposed to be the leader of the emotional culture expected in my classroom each day. I was the reason students would or would not learn with enthusiasm during the lesson. I knew I was not responsible for their motivation, but I was responsible for engaging them in a positive and validating learning environment, as described in chapter 19 (page 157). I intuitively knew what brain research would affirm many years later. "The fundamental condition for creating a thriving classroom is establishing emotional safety."[216]

I could at least *inspire* my students to learn.

I took my advice from chapter 21 (page 173). I got still and quiet and focused on a healthier response to the pressures I was facing (most of them self-induced). And, *I asked for help.* I had been slow in my life to take that necessary first step in the vulnerability loop described in chapter 18 (page 151).

The person I went to for help was a colleague I was just beginning to know. At the time, I took a risk. I asked him to meet me for coffee to share his instincts for sustaining such a positive and inspirational power as a teacher. He was fourteen years older than me, so he had certain wisdom I lacked. We met in Chicago for a lunch that lasted into the dinner hour and a shift change in the restaurant staff.

Three years later, he and I would coauthor our first textbook together (hash mark on the timeline). Thirty-three years later, I would deliver this incredible, soul-searching teacher and leader's eulogy to a packed house (a deeper hash mark on my timeline; a moment I can still feel today).

At the time, neither of us was very aware of brain research in the emerging field of neuroscience. Still, we had evidence from various techniques we personally used that engaging students in successful learning is a *social experience*. I needed him to teach me and remind me once again how to use the classroom as a positive *social and emotional* experience to create a more thriving learning environment for my mathematics classes.

We met weekly for seven years. And we became colleagues and friends for life. It would be correct to say we became mirror images of each other, laughing and finding joy in our professional and personal journey along the way.

Which brings me to a primary point of this chapter: mirror neurons.

Our brains have specialized cells called *mirror neurons*, which are activated when we perform an action and when students observe our action. Sometimes called *empathy neurons*, these cells help us understand the intentions of others and are active during social encounters in the classroom.[217]

Joan Y. Chiao, in the psychology department and the interdepartmental neuroscience program at Northwestern University, indicates:

> Several neural mechanisms have been identified as playing a key role in the creation and maintenance of cultural values, practices, and beliefs. Imitation or mirror neurons, sometimes implicated in empathy, facilitate the learning of cultural action, from simple gestures to complex artistic movement. . . . Sociocultural identity, such as race and gender, affects the degree of neural response when imitating similar and dissimilar others.[218]

Wow! What does this mean exactly?

Our emotions are a gateway to cognition and learning for students. When our curriculum, instruction, and assessments promote enjoyment, engagement, affirmation, elements of surprise, empathy, and personal relevance, student learning is likely to be retained more effectively. As our relationships respect the vast diversity of our students' traditions and beliefs, we become deeply human, and improved learning begins to occur.

MY SOUL STORY ♥

Educational thought leaders Carol Ann Tomlinson and David A. Sousa cite brain researcher Chai M. Tyng and colleague[219] as follows:

> Much recent research in neuroscience has focused on the influence emotion has on learning. Structures in the limbic system generate emotions, which are then moderated by the frontal lobe's control functions. Emotions have a strong influence on attention—and attention drives what the student's brain decides to learn or ignore. Emotions also modulate long-term memory, and thus can enhance or impair what is stored there. When new learning has minimal or no emotional component, the chances of long-term memory consolidation and storage are low.[220]

While our negative emotions shut down cognition and learning by our students, our positive emotions reinforce or strengthen memory, enhancing learning as a social interaction, as we develop empathy for others. Thus, developmental "foundations of cultural learning

Read the statement from Dr. Chiao carefully. Describe how your students (positively and negatively) imitate your values, practices, and beliefs.

_____

_____

_____

_____

_____

_____

_____

_____

_____

_____

_____

_____

_____

_____

_____

_____

_____

_____

_____

_____

_____

_____

_____

_____

_____

_____

within the prefrontal and motor regions may serve as neural precursors to compassionate feeling and actions during adolescence."[221]

So, what is the point? Look in the mirror every day. See what your students are seeing. See what your colleagues see. Although the mirror neuron research is relatively young, the reality is that you and I model one of two distinct daily emotional paths for our students.

Emotional Path 1 (Negative Emotions)

- Your negative emotions lead to no empathy or awareness of others . . .
  - Which leads to blame, shame, cognition breakdown, and low levels of student learning
  - Which leads to no compassion to relieve student suffering and lack of learning
  - Which leads to rare happiness and joy in the classroom culture for learning

Emotional Path 2 (Positive Emotions)

- Your positive emotions lead to awareness of the diversity of others; empathy modeled by you leads to mirror empathy by your students . . .
  - Which leads to a more compassionate classroom culture
  - Which leads to social structures for learning
  - Which leads to a classroom culture of happiness and joy for you and your students

MY SOUL STORY 💜

Which path is it for you this week—emotional path 1 or emotional path 2? Explain.

_____
_____
_____
_____
_____
_____
_____
_____

If you are on emotional path 1, how are you working toward emotional path 2? How can you mirror-model a more positive emotional state for your students and colleagues?

_____
_____
_____
_____
_____
_____
_____
_____
_____
_____

Practice empathy. Remember, empathy begins by making a personal connection with your students and colleagues—seeing their pain, knowing their suffering, and understanding who they are. Students' emotional safety is fundamental for creating a thriving classroom where risk taking is high, making mistakes is embraced, and anxiety toward learning is low.

Back to the rest of my mirror story and my professional colleague who modeled for me the type of teacher and leader I needed to reclaim so my students could experience a positive and emotionally safe space for learning. He brought me back to the best of my soul story self. And if he were still here with us, I know he would say I did the same for him over the years.

His name was Jerry Cummins.

His son Joel is a talented musician and founding member and keyboardist for the popular progressive rock band Umphrey's McGee. I asked Joel to share a specific memory he had about the mirror relationship between his dad and me. Here is what Joel had to say:

> As a young child, I remember my dad as a very cool, even-keeled, and smart man from whom I rarely saw much emotion except when it came to sports. When Tim came into my dad's life, I remember sensing a new energy that soon brought out a more exuberant side of his personality.
>
> By finding his mirror, I think mathematics and the concept of teaching immediately became a lot more fun for my dad. He had found a like-minded friend to confide in who also challenged him to think outside the box, be the best version of himself, and inspire others with his teaching and writing, all while having a good time doing it.
>
> From the power of a deep bond that Tim and Jerry (my dad) shared as close friends and colleagues in the world of mathematics education, creativity, passion, and joy emerged as the elements you felt emanating from them on a daily basis. I would argue their friendship and Tim's open-minded approach made my dad more open to embracing my career as a musician.
>
> Even though he couldn't play or sing, Dad witnessed how music stirred my soul (and eventually stirred others') by experiencing my music and celebrating it with me. He embraced it to the point that by 2012, my band's fans would occasionally chant his name when they saw him at shows. Life can be exciting and fun when you are empathetic, open-minded, and have a desire to keep learning. Through the way they lived, they taught me the journey *is* the destination, take it all in. Most important: be in the moment, be the best version of yourself, and be curious.[222]

Do you have a *mirror* colleague like Jerry? If so, name the person and thank him or her. Be specific. If not, who might be such a colleague down the road? Seek him or her out.

_____

_____

_____

_____

_____

_____

_____

_____

_____

_____

_____

_____

_____

_____

_____

_____

_____

_____

_____

_____

_____

_____

 # MY SOUL STORY

Jerry taught me to live today and let it just naturally build my legacy for tomorrow. He adopted the Kanold family motto, *carpe diem*, as his own. He reminded me that my only regret, as my timeline rolled along and the next season rolled past me, would be actions of kindness I did not or forgot to take.

"Have courage in the face of fear, take action toward hope, demonstrate grace toward others, and practice gratitude for the joy of life, despite hardships you have endured," Jerry would say to everyone he knew, not just me.

I hope you have a Jerry Cummins in your life. May you have a mirror friend who brings you back to your best professional self, season in and season out, only wanting to create good in you so you can live life today for your soul story timeline moments of tomorrow.

Soul Story Courage

S   O   U   L

Thomas Aquinas said that courage is the strength of mind capable of conquering whatever threatens the attainment of the highest good.

—Martin Luther King Jr.

Imagine you are a student in Socrates's class. The year is 420 BC. The following question is up for debate: *What is courage?* Use a picture or sentence or several short phrases, no more than eighteen words total, to give your answer. Remember Socrates is your teacher; he has high expectations for your answer!

MY HEARTPRINT

Courage has been studied, discussed, challenged, inspected, and dissected for centuries. On Amazon, as of this writing, there are three-thousand-plus books on courage with a broad range of viewpoints.

Courage is not wrapped up in a nice and neat how-to formula. It is much more complex.

Socrates and Aristotle thought of courage as the most important of the four cardinal virtues of a civil society. Socrates described courage as *wise* endurance of the soul, not foolish endurance or reckless endurance of the soul.[223]

What is courage?

_____
_____
_____
_____
_____
_____
_____
_____
_____
_____
_____
_____
_____
_____
_____
_____

Complete this sentence: *It took courage for me to . . .*

_____
_____
_____
_____
_____
_____
_____
_____
_____
_____
_____
_____
_____
_____
_____
_____
_____
_____
_____
_____
_____
_____

Aristotle described wisdom as *prudent* strength. He thought of courage as a *noble* act, an unselfish and morally good act.[224] Courage then is revealed within our professional soul story experiences and actions.

A more modern definition from *Merriam-Webster* claims courage to be "the mental or moral strength to venture, persevere, and withstand danger, fear, or difficulty."[225]

Socrates and *Merriam-Webster* share some courage commonalities: *strength, endurance, perseverance,* and *moral good.* They directly or indirectly indicate courage as an *action* in the face of fear or difficulty.

Courage is often a very tough choice. And what takes courage for me may not be a big deal for you. And vice versa. Most important, however, is that courage is considered a choice for morally *correct action* in the face of fear or loss.

As educators, courage begins with the decision to choose our profession, followed by the many actions to live and search for our soul story during our professional journey. Courage overcomes the obstacles, as described in part 2 (page 57), and seeks a culture of unity and community, as described in part 3 (page 121).

Courage lives in every action we take to eradicate the social injustices that attack everyday life.

Courage resides in our actions that educate the next generation of *all* children to become both smart and good, no matter their diversity or talents. Our students need us to be courageous.

We have each had defining moments of courage. Use the My Soul Story space to write about a moment of professional or personal courage. If you and a trusted colleague are comfortable, exchange your soul stories of courage with each other.

 # MY SOUL STORY

Our stories of courage are sometimes quiet and invisible to others. Courage manifests itself in the smallest personal and professional acts that help us overcome our fears. Courage emanates from our noble sense of correcting a wrong and our daily choices to take a stand for love and social justice for each student we teach. Our courage is more invisible to others.

As I was writing this chapter, I reread chapter 4 (page 23) and my story about Juan Gonzalez. Knocking on his sister's door in the middle of winter with a Spanish-speaking guidance counselor was a moment of courage. I was stretched out of my comfort zone.

Courage is usually a tough choice. Sometimes that choice is more public and out on social media. Those moments may seem bigger because there is a spotlight on what you say or do. "Do I speak or stay silent?"

This is a book about making choices—healthy choices for your professional wellness so you can make contributions to the moral good. A courageous choice is always a choice of dignity. It is never a choice of hate or harm. We are the defenders of social justice and equality.

Courage overcomes our blindness to a problem. Courage is the refusal to be indifferent and passive to a problem that can potentially cause enormous harm to others. Courage is ownership of the problem itself and then moving positively forward. The courageous advocate says, "I was not the one who created this problem, but I will be the one to fix it." It takes courage to *own* a problem that sits in front of you.

A first act of courage is to examine your current reality about student academic and social-emotional learning. What do the data tell us, and how can we own any problems revealed? The truth revealed by the student data guides the actions of our second mountain work life.

MY SOUL STORY ♥

Describe a current situation at school, on your team, or in your classroom in which there are student curriculum access or performance data issues revealed by you or your team.

Go deeper to examine data for students with disabilities, English learners (ELs), Black students, Latinx students, students of other races and ethnicities, students of poverty, and so on. Which group is most marginalized in your school and needs more of your attention in this school season?

Describe an area of problem blindness that might exist currently in your school or district.

_____
_____
_____
_____
_____
_____
_____
_____
_____
_____
_____
_____
_____
_____
_____
_____
_____
_____
_____
_____
_____
_____
_____
_____
_____
_____

During one decade of my professional life, I had the opportunity to work around the world with the U.S. Department of Defense Dependents Schools, or DoDDS as it was referred to at the time or DoDEA as of this writing.

I would work with the Department of Defense schools (usually these schools were on military bases for the children of the military personnel served by the base), helping teachers learn about the PLC process and the effectiveness research about teaching pedagogy. I would go to a base (school site) for a few weeks, observe the teaching in the school, provide professional development with the faculty and staff, and then debrief at the end of each visit.

In one specific school site based in Europe, I noticed the faculty's lethargy and lack of commitment to students and learning. There was a feeling of learned helplessness and little hope for improved student learning and progress in the school.

Although I did not know it at the time, I experienced what Dan Heath refers to as _problem blindness_, which he defines as:

> The belief that negative outcomes are natural or inevitable. Out of our control. When we're blind to a problem, we treat it like the weather. We may know it's bad, but ultimately we just shrug our shoulders. _What am I supposed to do about it? It's the weather._[226]

Heath further describes the malaise of problem blindness by the mindset, "It's a tough world, but that's the way it is, and I can't do anything about it."[227] Talk about abdicating our responsibility to own the culture we have created! _It's a tough world, but that's the way it is, and I can't do anything about it_ is not a soul story mindset.

MY SOUL STORY

And this was exactly the message I was receiving from the faculty and administration of this school during my site visit.

At the end of my two-week visit, I was in my room on the base writing up my exit notes for my final meeting with the faculty and staff. I had a decision to make. A coura-geous choice. I was unsure about what to say as I walked the perimeter of the base, rolling the details of my observations and discussions through my head.

I also had this feeling of insignificance. Who was I to tell the fac-ulty on this base what I thought? Who was I, a basic stranger, to take a stand on the social justice issues and racial bias I observed?

I would be gone by tomorrow night. Would I even make a dent in their understanding of how defeating their current cultural beliefs were to student learning and self-efficacy? When the adults of a system do not own the problem, then the system gets the results it gets. A self-fulfilling prophecy in a way.

And although at the time, I did not know it was called problem blindness, I knew in my heart that I must be the one to at least lift the blinders off the problem, and then let them decide what to do next.

Before I tell you what happened the next morning, I want to share the basic elements of a courageous act, and why I had such a struggle the night before my final meeting.

Business leadership authors James Kouzes and Barry Posner provide these elements of courage:

> It seems to us that we humans call upon our courage when . . .
>
> 1. Our lives present some significant challenge,
> 2. We feel fear when facing this adversity,
> 3. It requires personal initiative to overcome the fear and the challenge,
> 4. Something personally meaningful is at stake,
> 5. We might suffer loss in the process,
> 6. We have hope, and
> 7. Our life is transformed by the experience.[228]

Here is the rest of the story, examined against these seven elements of courage.

There was part of me that just wanted to leave it all alone, give the faculty a positive feedback report, and leave them blind to the prob-lem. Yet, I knew this would be my failure to *own the problem*.

My report would be a significant challenge. What if I was wrong about my observations? There was fear for me in this decision, because I knew it would cause anger directed at me (and it did). Yet, I decided to take the risk and to do so with grace, of course.

I have thought much about elements 4 and 5 in Kouzes and Posner's list. The fear for me was not life-threatening, but it was real. The commander of the base would be in the room. Once I was finished, he had the power to eliminate my DoDDS overseas assignment and send me home. The easy way out had much less risk.

I also feared (and I ended up being right) that the teachers would be so upset with me that I would get a letter of reprimand and an immediate demand in writing for an apology the next week. I could lose my reputation as an educator and lose future work with DoDDS, which I very much enjoyed.

"Keep silent," I thought. "Keep your real thoughts to yourself." I couldn't sleep.

At 8:00 a.m. the next day, I stood in the school auditorium in front of an assembly of laypeople (nonmilitary teachers and staff) and some military officers who also helped with the school administration and programs. Some of them had their own children in the school.

What follows is a summary of my one-hour exit report. I did my best to be a *warm demander*:

> I want to be completely transparent with you today. During my visit, I have encountered a school culture that lacks commitment to the care and well-being of every student.
>
> You have failed to adjust to the changes in your extended school community. This failure has caused some of you to stop trying, to stop giving your students the best of who you are every day. You live behind the belief: *This is not my fault.*
>
> Your lack of ownership to student learning has caused stagnant and declining student achievement results. It has caused a deeper learning gap for your students when they and their parents return home to the higher expectations for learning in the states.
>
> Worse, you have blamed your school's current performance on the students based on your own racial biases and prejudices. Last week, in an after-school meeting with many of you in this room, I asked you why a former high-performing school such as yours has had such incredibly low student academic performance for the past three years.
>
> Although you stated your beliefs using many different phrases, your answer to me was loud and clear.
>
> "Mr. Kanold, you don't understand our students and this place. This used to be an Air Force base, and now it is an Army base. What do you expect us to do?" At first, I did not understand what you meant. I have attended DoDDS military bases all over the world. I've encountered all different types of troops and families, and children of all colors, faiths, ethnicities, and languages. All parents want the best for their children, as they serve their country.

So I had to ask around. What does it mean that the base changed from the Air Force to the Army? Why is this a barrier to student learning? And the answer was appalling to me. Most of you sitting here are White.

Those of you with more than three years' experience on this base remember a time when this school had a majority of White students. Today your school is majority Black, and this is your excuse? Your students cannot learn as well as previous students because of the color of their skin?

Here is what my report is going to say. Every adult in this room needs to own this issue and remember you are professionals. Thus, you must overcome your complacency and indifference. Every adult in this room must change the narrative of your work life, stop making excuses, and stop blaming the children.

What must you do to fix this problem, the lack of student learning in this school? You need to better understand your students of color and listen to their parents, their fears, and their needs. And if you do not believe that increased levels of learning for your students are worthy of fixing, then don't stay here next year. These students, these Army families, deserve better than you are giving them.

I sat down as the principal dismissed everyone from the morning meeting. There was dead silence in the room. As a public speaker, I was used to applause and positive feedback, not dead silence. I'd like to tell you they broke into applause. They did not. Not that day. Perhaps their applause was silent, as I *know* some professionals in that room cared.

I was never invited back to that base, school, or city. I received a letter of reprimand, as I suspected I would. There were consequences to my actions, and it was almost ten years later before I was invited back to speak at a conference in the area. Imagine, however, my regret had I failed to live fearlessly on this soul story issue.

Is there anything in the path of your personal or professional life that requires courage? Requires personal risk, small or big? Needs something meaningful to be at stake for you? Love and lean into your students, including your most frustrating students, your most in need or marginalized students, *beyond reason*.

— MY SOUL STORY ♥ —————

Write your story of a courageous professional action you have taken in the past few years. It can be a private or public moment of professional courage. How did this action reflect the seven elements of courage?

It takes courage and fearlessness to become an educator. Would you agree? Inspirational teachers strive to integrate their lives upward in pursuit of continuous growth and learning. You pursue a life that brings your work up to the standards of your declared beliefs.

Living *today* so you can leave a legacy of inspiration and influence *tomorrow* is about making a difference and choosing to take a stand on things that really matter, such as your stand against racism, hatred, bigotry, bullying, lack of access, and all other forms of discrimination.

Sometimes, community events supersede all our hard work, focus, and effort as educators, and require a more public response. Like 1968 (when I was a teenager in Chicago), 2020 had a summer of protests and upheaval built on the constant stream of racial profiling and social injustices. Our extended communities were suffering, with all of it captured in real time on social media and cable news.

Add the relentless worldwide health crisis of the COVID-19 pandemic, when more than three hundred and forty thousand Americans lost their lives in 2020. Where is the hope?

Can courage, the wise endurance of the soul, win? Can courage win against the racial divide? Can courage win against a pandemic?

When you and I internally accept that we are not the ones who created these problems, but we will *own the problems* nonetheless—and we will be the ones who choose community and unity to solve the problems we face each day—*that* decision becomes our courage in action.

It is never too late to act with soul story courage, to create professional timeline moments that reflect wise endurance of the soul. Tomorrow is today. Live it wisely. Live it with love.

It is your timeline. Do not waste it.

Joy, Gratitude, and Grace

S   O   U   L

Without exception, every person I interviewed who described
living a joyful life or described themselves as joyful, actively
practiced gratitude and attributed their joyfulness to their
gratitude practice.

—Brené Brown

Let's start this chapter with a question: Who has been, who are, and who will be the *beneficiaries* of your professional soul story timeline of big and small defining moments?

Thus far in part 4, we have examined our professional timeline—our finite number of teaching and leading days—and some soul story–defining moments on that timeline. We have discussed how to create those moments during our professional journey—both spontaneously and with planning.

We have studied how to stop the slow drift away from our soul story timeline due to the relentless pressures of daily life by looking in the mirror when we get a bit lost. And we have examined the soul story courage required to attack our moments of problem blindness, and own the problems in front of our students, our colleagues, and ourselves.

This profession, I think, can take a lot out of us and yet be so rewarding and meaningful at the same moment and time. To some extent, this book has been about minimizing the former and maximizing the latter in order to find greater joy in the journey of our teaching profession.

In this chapter, we address one final action needed to stay connected to our soul story. Without it, all you have worked for will fade from memory as bitterness and burnout remove joy from the soul story of your work life. Your second mountain climb will descend quickly, and you will be left emotionally, physically, and spiritually bankrupt.

Who has been, are, and will be the beneficiaries of your professional soul story timeline of defining moments as an education professional?

_____
_____
_____
_____
_____
_____
_____
_____
_____
_____
_____
_____
_____
_____
_____
_____
_____
_____
_____
_____
_____
_____

To get started, let's first answer the *beneficiary* question.

MY SOUL STORY

This is an interesting question. Hang on to your answers for now. I promise, we will come back to this.

To describe this final yet vital soul story routine or practice, first consider two very similar, often interchanged, but different words with different meanings: *happiness* and *joy*.

Happiness and joy are essential aspects of our professional life. Although each can be elusive, if we work at it, we can experience them more often than not. I have often intermingled these two words, but there is a subtle difference within the context of our everyday moments.

Happiness is a "*state of well-being* and contentment, a pleasurable or satisfying *experience* [italics added]."[229] Happiness is a state of mind, a by-product of our experiences during our first and second mountain climbs.

Happiness is often the result of something more *external*—an award received, a big victory won, or a defining, small-win moment with your students or colleagues. After a long day at school, it's a sense of knowing that it was just a great day: "The learning rocked today; you could see it in their eyes! Light bulbs!" Or, "He did it! He passed that final class and will walk across the stage. Yes!"

Happiness is a high positive energy state. It is a place of self-efficacy, confidence, contentment, hopefulness, and helpfulness with others. The circumstances of the day, some you control and some you don't, serve that high positive energy state.

Yet just the right negative comment from someone, just the right set of bad or unexpected news or minor misunderstandings, can quickly tumble you out of that happiness state. It's elusive for sure.

Joy, on the other hand, is an "*emotion evoked by well-being*, success, or good fortune or by the prospect of possessing what one desires [italics added]."[230] Joy is an emotion we can choose even when the burdens of life make it very difficult to be happy.

Joy, or joyfulness, tends to be more *internal*, an integral aspect of your professional wellness and your soul story. Joy is the result of your *intentional practice* of gratitude.

Happiness is based more on the external circumstances in your life, whereas joy directly connects to internally *practicing gratitude* today, tomorrow, and forever.

Yes, it is your choice to answer the gratitude call to action, or not.

There are days where you might be thinking, "Really? Have you seen what my day or week has been like? And you want me to feel and demonstrate joy? You want me to practice gratitude? Do you *know* what my life is like right now?"

Yes and *no*. I can't possibly know your professional or personal life from your point of view, in the moment you are in today. But I can want joy for you. No matter the circumstances, as humans, we should each know the blessing of joy.

Brené Brown reveals this joy–gratitude connection in the epigraph for this chapter. She indicates in her research that we attribute our joyfulness to our *gratitude practice*.[231]

She further concludes, "People were quick to point out the differences between happiness and joy as the difference between human emotion that's connected to circumstances and a spiritual way of engaging with the world that's connected to practicing gratitude."[232]

So, joy is the residue of *practicing gratitude*. Got it.

If we are to develop our soul story timeline with ordinary moments of internal joy, then how do we practice gratitude daily?

Education thought leader and colleague Tim Brown is the most joyful, inspiring, grace-filled person I know. Here is what he has to say about how we can practice gratitude in our daily life:

> Motivate, inspire, teach!
>
> My wife occasionally texts me those three words right before I deliver a keynote address or engage educators in a professional learning day. Her gentle reminder provides a boost of energy.
>
> When I was a building principal, I developed routines that would put my heart and soul into the right frame of mind for an "A game" day. I felt the students and colleagues I worked with deserved my best every day.
>
> I discovered I'm not the only educator who sings on their way to work! I may be the only one making up attendance songs and school theme songs to sing with my students, but I love knowing that so many educators understand the importance of showing their colleagues and students they are happy, positive, and joyful as they enter the schoolhouse.

Complete the following sentence: *Today, I am so grateful for . . .*

_____

_____

_____

_____

_____

_____

_____

_____

_____

_____

_____

_____

_____

_____

_____

_____

_____

_____

_____

_____

_____

_____

_____

_____

_____

_____

_____

_____

When I was a first-year teacher, Joe Freeman, in his beautiful baritone voice, would belt out a song as he entered the school building. I figured if this twenty-eight-year veteran teacher was still singing every morning, then I had chosen the right profession! I'm convinced that sharing your positivity influences attitudes, and therefore the approach others take.

Yet, the soul story of a school is never about one heroic individual. In our case, it was about a community of educators who intended to change the world for the students they served. It was not hard to show my gratitude by writing a weekly letter to the staff or speaking about our school story to members of our community. It was time for our stakeholders to feel the joy I felt as I witnessed our mission, vision, and collective commitments for improved student learning in action.[233]

We can develop several routines or habits to practice gratitude and experience more joy, especially during difficult and challenging times.

We begin with a gratitude routine that is not too time-consuming. Brené Brown provides an activity in order to get into the habit of practicing gratitude more often (see chapter 21, page 173, for more on habits and routines). She says:

> When I am flooded with fear and scarcity, I try to call forward joy and sufficiency by acknowledging the fear, then transforming it into gratitude. I say this out loud: "I'm feeling vulnerable today. That's okay. I'm so grateful for _____." Doing this has absolutely increased my capacity for joy.[234]

Let's try it!

 # MY SOUL STORY

Was that easy or hard to do? Could it become part of your quietude time every day?

A second routine for practicing gratitude will take a few days. I'll explain it, and after you complete the activity, write about it in the My Soul Story space provided.

Think of this as an experiment.

Day 1: Share Complaints

Go to work, and as you greet people, share with them a small complaint or grumbling. Don't direct it at anyone or be mean spirited; just complain about little details of your life. If you are not used to complaining, and your colleagues will wonder what is wrong with you, then space out the complaints a bit in terms of time and vary who you are complaining to.

Some examples to help you get started:

- "I just could not get any sleep last night; I was so restless!"
- "I'm so busy, so exhausted, I don't know how I'm going to make it through the day."
- "What's up with this weather?"
- "My leg has really been bothering me lately."
- "My hair is such a mess today."
- "This unit is such a drag to teach."

At the end of the first day, write two or three sentences describing how you felt spending the day complaining about the conditions of life around you.

Day 2: Share Gratitude

Start every conversation you have with others at work, including your students, by practicing some words of gratitude. Remember the advice from chapter 16 (page 131): *Overdo your thank-yous on this day!*

You could say things such as:

- "I am so thankful for the rain today."
- "Did you see those stars last night? I am so thankful I stepped outside."
- "Thank goodness for (insert name of colleague or staff member)! What a tech guru and so kind and thoughtful too!"
- "I love my classroom layout; thanks for helping me."
- "I am so grateful for our special education team; we really need their support."

At the end of the second day, write about how you feel in just a few sentences.

MY SOUL STORY ♥

Compare your
emotional experiences from the first day (share complaints) and the second day (share gratitude). What do you notice about the presence of joy in each day?

Describe how you
might use *the best part of my
day* . . . idea with family, friends,
students, or colleagues.

_____
_____
_____
_____
_____
_____
_____
_____
_____
_____
_____
_____
_____
_____
_____
_____
_____
_____

A third routine for practicing gratitude is called *the best part of my day*. A good time to practice this routine is with family and friends at dinnertime. Special education teacher and leader Corinne Howe, whom you met in chapter 22 (page 187), first introduced me to this practice.

To practice this routine, rotate the conversation clockwise around the table. One at a time, each person reveals the best part of his or her day. Although responses are often not surprising, sometimes the responses reveal a greater depth and understanding into the person sharing.

♥ MY SOUL STORY

A fourth routine for practicing gratitude takes a bit more time, but it is well worth it during your professional lifetime.

While I was writing this book, I ran into Matthew DuFour. Matt is Rick DuFour's son and also one of my former students. Matt was kind enough to share with me a letter I had written to his dad during our early days of working together. It was at a time in Rick's life when professional changes were taking place, and a time in my life when I was becoming more aware of the need to write letters of thanks to people—both professional and personal—who were important to me.

We tend to take for granted those closest to our inner circle, and I was trying to fight that tendency and be more appreciative of those around me.

The letter Matt gave me had been in a file box Rick kept of important moments in his life. The letter had meant something special to him. And I had no idea. I remember at the time I wrote that letter, I felt a need to tell him thank you and let him know how valuable he was to me as a friend, colleague, and mentor. And to let him know that I was grateful for some of the specific actions he had taken to contribute to my professional life.

When I read my handwritten letter from so many years ago, it was as if Matt was giving me a gift. It reminded me of my connection with Rick. It reminded me of the day I gave it to Rick in a McDonald's restaurant in Evanston, Illinois, and it reminded me of my love and respect for him.

We can never overdo our thank-yous.

So, here is what you do.

Sometime in the next week, choose someone in your professional life to whom you want to demonstrate gratitude. Write this person a letter, typed or handwritten.

Then, ask this person for thirty minutes of his or her time. Maybe you can meet for a cup of coffee or a glass of wine, or just sit in an empty classroom without any specific reason as to why, just to chat.

Sit with this person, and when you are ready, ask him or her to let you read your letter aloud, without interruption. Give him or her a copy of your letter when your time together ends. Not only will you both find joy in this moment, but that moment of vulnerability will build trust.

I received deep and meaningful feedback on my early writing of this book from a colleague of mine, Denise Walston, whom I have known a long time. I sent her an email in which I thanked her and told her she was like a sister to me. I mentioned how her grace and wisdom have always inspired me. We live on opposite sides of the United States, so my meeting with her could not be face to face. Yet, I have her email response, and I printed it out. There is a subtle joy in that exchange.

MY SOUL STORY ♥

Gratitude, I believe, allows for the extension of grace.

Throughout this book, I have shared the story of my colleague Becky DuFour. In chapter 1 (page 7) and again in chapter 11 (page 83), I shared not only her daily practice of gratitude but also her way of moving through life with such demonstrated *grace toward others*.

Grace is the "disposition to or an act or instance of kindness, courtesy, or clemency."[235] More than thoughtfulness, kindness, consideration, and courtesy, grace is also a disposition toward clemency—forgiveness at some level.

Decide who should be the recipient of your gratitude letter. Write the letter. Meet with this person. When your interaction is over, reflect on how it went in this space.

_____

_____

_____

_____

_____

_____

_____

_____

_____

_____

_____

_____

_____

_____

_____

_____

_____

_____

_____

_____

_____

_____

_____

_____

_____

Kouzes and Posner write:

> The people we work with and count on are also human. We
> need to give them the chance to be the best they can be,
> even to be better than they thought they could be . . . Let's
> all have the humility to remember where we started and the
> humanity to offer others the same opportunities.[236]

Grace is a demonstrated action. I can choose to act with grace toward
you or not. There are many times when I do not feel like demonstrating grace toward others. It feels to me like they don't deserve grace
from me. It is in those moments that I have lost connection to my
soul story—*to become good in order to create good in others.*

Grace wins when we set down the grudges we are carrying around
toward others, accepting they too are human.

Grace wins when we use forgiveness to help others become better
than they thought they could be.

Grace wins when we offer opportunities to create good in others by
understanding our failures and humanity.

What follows is a partial description of the life of grace demonstrated
toward others by Becky DuFour. This is part of my eulogy message at
her memorial service described in chapter 1 (page 7).

> One of the blessings you taught us was to see others with-
> out judging. You were so genuinely humble that each person
> you met became an object of wonder.
>
> What grace!
>
> How often did you patiently speak with and listen to one
> PLC associate or one event attendee after another and help
> them to feel more valued in that moment than anyone else
> in the room?
>
> What grace!
>
> St. Augustine refers to a loftier life pursuit of *doing the right
> thing, to the right degree, in the right way, and with the right
> kind of love*. We want you to know that is the gift you gave us.
>
> You lifted up each of us just by being a mentor, patiently
> answering our emails, lending a kind and thoughtful ear,
> always with grace, always with kindness, always with the right
> kind of love.
>
> What grace!
>
> I know you would not want us to sit in sadness, but rather, you
> would want us to be grateful and find new joy in the mourn-
> ing after this day. We promise you, we will. It will be part of
> our commitment to you. To honor you with joy in our lives as
> a tribute for the joy you offered us during yours.

So, remember the My Soul Story question at the beginning of this chapter (page 219)? What did you write down? Who are the *beneficiaries* of your soul story work life?

Well, first, *you* are one of them. Your soul story timeline starts to fill in as you practice moments of gratitude, including during difficult times and circumstances that might make happiness more elusive.

Your soul story timeline currently is and will be filled with other beneficiaries—the students and colleagues of your work life. Your zero-to-zero professional timeline needs thousands of hash marks on it to list every child or teenager who benefits from your joy, your courage, and your decision to choose this profession and act *in loco parentis*.

And what about your past, current, or future beneficiaries? What will they become?

They become adults who, because of you, learned to *create good in themselves*. They, in turn, can now *create good in others*. Their soul story journey perhaps began because of you. Eventually, their children and their work-life colleagues become, in a way, the *secondary* beneficiaries of your lifetime of work.

Like much of your soul story journey, joy is an internal choice and action, even though today's circumstances may not always bring you the experience of happiness tomorrow.

Don't let the joyful persons in your life be the exception. Join them.

May you always stay close to the flame of joy, knowing you made the heartprint choice of being part of our incredible profession. Your work life, your professional soul story effort, day in and day out, has been and will be always be a choice of *pursuing your moral good in order to create good in others*. Your beneficiaries are and will be many.

I, for one, am grateful for *you* in *this* day.

One More Trip Around the Sun

S   O   U   ♥

Celebrating what I should have done
With these souvenirs of my trip around the sun.
—Jimmy Buffett and Martina McBride[237]

This chapter has come a long way from my beginning drafts for this book. I had been struggling with how to end the book since I started writing it. In my original manuscript, the title to this chapter was "alrightokuhhuhnowwhat." That Twitter-style hashtag title held on through four months of drafts.

The next title was Your Choice, Your Soul Legacy. That title did not last long and was replaced with Life Is Short, also short lived (no pun intended). During my twenty-third draft of the book, I finally gave up. I would figure it out when I got there.

Eventually, I settled on Beginnings and Endings. It seemed fitting. It met the zero-to-zero concept of our professional timeline. But the title felt incomplete to me. What about our life in between those zeros?

I felt pressure to provide a meaningful ending. I figured if you worked your way through this book chapter by chapter, and did so with colleagues, then you would arrive, like me, a little exhausted. Add to it the happiness circumstances (or not) of your current or previous school season, and I wanted this final chapter to have a deeper meaning, or maybe give you a bit of a boost!

My final choice for the title of this chapter arrived during a run (my quietude space) and a brief daily break from the manuscript. I was listening to a Jimmy Buffett and Martina

Describe your trip
around the sun *this* school year.
What are some of the souvenirs
you are collecting from your trip?

_____
_____
_____
_____
_____
_____
_____
_____
_____
_____
_____
_____
_____
_____
_____
_____
_____
_____
_____
_____
_____
_____
_____
_____

McBride song "Trip Around the Sun."[238] As soon as I heard it, I thought, "This is the perfect metaphor to end the book."

By the time I heard the song, my work on *SOUL!* had literally been two trips around the sun of my professional life. There was a year of research and interviews, and then a year of writing, reviews, and rewriting; more edits; more rewrites; more research; and fine-tuning.

A trip around the sun is exactly how I felt about the general timeline of our professional life, only our trips start sometime in late summer and into a fall of new beginnings. The trip drags through a long slog of learning together, often defined by our winter weather and seasonal changes.

After the slog, we travel into spring and closure as we wrap up the school season, say goodbye to relationships built with so many students and colleagues, and move into a summertime of rest, repair, and renewal, only to start another trip around the sun the following season.

And every one of those trips is unique. They stack up. They become our soul story. You build that story as you live it. Some of you are just starting construction and have a lot of trips ahead of you. Others are in the middle of your trips around the sun, starting to build the *souvenirs* of your trips (as Jimmy Buffett would say).[239]

Others are getting close to the end. If you are like me, you are holding out for just one more trip around the sun. We do not want our vocation to end. Not quite yet. And that is the way it should be.

MY SOUL STORY

I asked my colleague Linda Reusch to respond to this My Soul Story prompt.

Linda reached her second zero as I was writing this chapter. The year 2020 was her final season as a teacher, and the COVID-19 pandemic will for sure mark it as unique and memorable. Linda is also unique, powerful, humble, and incredible as a teacher in many ways, not the least of which is her thirty-five seasons of inspirational teaching to thousands of students.

In full disclosure, I asked Linda to share her response to this prompt because I was there for her first zero. I was her cooperating teacher in 1985 as student teaching began her journey into teaching as a vocation.

We blinked, and it is thirty-five school seasons later, one trip around the sun stacked on top of the other.

I asked Linda, a second mountain climber, if she could identify, share, and describe her feelings as her second zero was closing in. Linda showed me what grace, gratitude, joy, and community look like in times of tough circumstances. Here is what Linda had to say (using fictional names for students to protect their privacy):

> Due to the pandemic, on March 12, 2020, we all received an email stating that school would switch to e-learning starting the following Monday for at least three weeks. At that moment, it simply wasn't "real" to any of us. Teachers reported back to school on March 13 to learn how our role in teaching was about to change.
>
> We learned how to implement Zoom meetings. We had conversations about how to assess students in a setting in which integrity and honesty were questionable. Most important, we talked about how flexibility and grace would have to be at the forefront of all our decision making.
>
> As educators, we really had no idea how students and their families were coping with so many uncertainties. Had parents lost jobs? Were family members sick? Did siblings need care? Were students simply missing their peers? The thought "old dog, new tricks" crossed my mind several times in the following weeks.
>
> My students and I actually cherished our time on Zoom over the next few weeks as an outlet to the craziness going on in the world. Although most of my students were present on Zoom, the one aspect of teaching that I was truly missing during this time was my personal connection with students. Seeing them remotely was acceptable to teach; however, I needed more.
>
> When we realized that remote learning was going to be a way of life through the end of the semester, a flood of emotion overtook me. How was I going to encourage my students to fight for every point on their AP exam? I wouldn't be there on exam day to give them a high five and remind them, "You got this!"
>
> Could they feel my passion over the computer screen? This was my very last year in the classroom, and I had so many expectations of how I saw my senior year playing out. We had looked forward to our last pep assembly and last Spring Fling together. I had promised to high five seniors at graduation as

they were walking back from receiving their diplomas. None of this was going to happen, and I needed to find a way to connect with each one of my students personally.

At first, I felt the need to write a few of my students a letter during this remote learning time, expressing something personal to them. "Thanks for always working so hard." "I've missed you in Zoom this past week. Is everything okay?" "You were such a great addition to first period this year!" "Do you know that your peers really appreciate you?"

As I started thinking about who I would write to, my list continued to get longer. I was seriously considering writing each of my 140 students a letter. I posed this idea to my husband and one other colleague. I was certain that they would think I was crazy, but both immediately supported my decision.

I ordered notecards and stamps and began my quest to write each of my students a letter, letting them know that they were important to me. I couldn't not write these letters any more than I could stay away from teaching students all these years! Connecting with teens is in my DNA.

As the letters started arriving in my students' mailboxes, I started to receive some thank-you emails. Students were excited to get personal acknowledgment from their teacher. Honestly, I secretly expected some responses from students who were more outspoken all year.

I did not expect how many of my students responded to my letter who had not spoken up all year. Maguire had been absent in many, many Zoom classes. . . . and all of a sudden, he was present and working again. Gary wrote me a beautiful email telling me how he always enjoyed coming to my class because it was a comfortable place to be. Abby expressed that at the beginning of the year, she was very anxious being a junior in a mainly senior class and appreciated how welcoming I made her feel.

Luis wrote back and shared how he and his family had a good laugh over dinner about a homework story that I had shared in his letter. Rohita hadn't spoken all year, and she emailed to say how prepared she felt for the AP exam, and she appreciated all the extra time I had spent working with her individually.

As teachers, we never know when or how we are impacting a life. It happens every day and often in the most unlikely places. For me, connecting to the students *is* teaching. We teach so much more than the subject area that we went to school to master. For me, mathematics is just the subject that I love and the means to connect with the students. I sincerely hope that my students learn so much more in my classroom about life, and about being a good, honest, and respectable person.[240]

I read Linda's words and sat quietly for a bit. It struck me how she has lived her professional life exactly for the purpose of *creating good in others*.

She finished her last trip around the sun with such a relational elegance, similar to how she finished every trip, every year. I have so much respect for her. I am so happy for her.

MY SOUL STORY ♥

No matter how many professional trips we have taken around the sun, this is the question we ask: "Did we *pursue our moral good in order to create good in others?*"

I have held back from sharing the following words of wisdom from my colleague Luis Cruz until now. I could have placed his words anywhere but felt this was just the right spot. I feel blessed to know this man who has dedicated his life to become good in order to create good in others.

Luis brings into focus how our trips around the sun, those defining moments we mark on our timeline, should be chosen by the spirituality of our expanding *goodness*. He writes:

> I believe that for those of us whose souls have been activated with the power to enthusiastically search for joy, liberation, and optimal success (in whatever way we define success), continuously re-energizing our souls to "keep striving" is only possible when we commit to helping others find the switch that activates *their* souls.
>
> Herein lies the power of our profession, the continuous pursuit to empower our souls by empowering others to do the same. You cannot complete the soul story of your professional life alone. It is all about relationships. It is about overcoming failure and celebrating the highs, *together*. Surround yourself with people you love, and love what they do.[241]

And so, as this chapter and the book come to an end, there is one final challenge for you: in one sentence, what do you want your professional soul story legacy to be?

HOW are you connecting with your students during your current trip around the sun?

_____
_____
_____
_____
_____
_____
_____
_____
_____
_____
_____
_____
_____
_____
_____
_____
_____
_____
_____
_____
_____
_____
_____

What do you hope your soul story legacy will be when your professional timeline hits that second zero?

_____

_____

_____

_____

_____

_____

_____

_____

_____

_____

_____

_____

_____

_____

_____

_____

_____

_____

_____

_____

_____

_____

_____

_____

_____

_____

 # MY SOUL STORY

I also asked many of my colleagues this My Soul Story question. Their answers were varied, yet focused on some common themes: giving to others, doing the good, acting with kindness, making a difference in the lives of students and colleagues, living with courage, and sacrificing for the improvement of others.

Looking back at my own professional life, and looking forward at my promise for tomorrow, I hope my soul story will continue to be one of perseverance in face of failure as I serve a good much greater than myself. That seems to be a reasonable legacy.

And so, it is: *we live today to build our legacy for tomorrow.*

Enjoy your ride during each trip around the sun. I hope this book has helped.

No matter how you hope to be remembered, keep exploring and learning each school season. Make the most of your human potential, and use our profession to help others to do the same. Like Linda and her final trip around the sun, if you dare to look, that second zero is staring back at you in the mirror.

You are on top of the second mountain.

The date *always* arrives.

Only time will tell if it is time well spent, indeed.

The PLC Life Is a *Bene* Life

To implement the PLC process requires a culture-care shift into the themes of part 4. It takes courage, a deep look into the proverbial mirror, and a *carpe-diem* mentality to decide to work together, examine the reality of the story told by your data, and set and plan for future moments of celebration on your professional timeline. Living today, so there are no regrets tomorrow. And yet, joy can be elusive if we are too exhausted to practice intentional routines of gratitude and grace each day.

As we have journeyed through this book, I realize we each respond to our professional "call of contribution" differently. We are each fractured a bit differently. We all sit at the professional table, so to speak, with a diversity of experiences and personalities that shape us as educators.

Yet, we are part of the human experience too, no matter how refracted our lens might be. Our professional and very human life is a shared experience through our common humanity, dignity, and decency.

At the end of chapter 26, Joy, Gratitude, and Grace (page 219), I brought to a close the *benes* of our professional journey. The words *bene*ficiary and *bene*fit show up in the book more than fifty times! I am not surprised, as our contributions to others in this profession make us *bene*factors, creating a trail of beneficiaries along our teaching and leading timeline of meaningful moments.

We seek to be both benefactors and also beneficiaries during our teaching and leading journey. And yet, if we aren't careful, constant contributions to others can come with a personal price to our professional wellness and well-being. So we seek to live a balanced professional life.

In short, we search for and try to find our *slack tide*.

For about forty-five minutes after high tide and low tide, there is a period of time called *slack tide*, or more accurately *slack water*. "Slack water is a short period in a body of

Reflect on the idea of finding time in your day that is completely unstressed. What can you do, starting today, to find your personal slack tide time?

_____
_____
_____
_____
_____
_____
_____
_____
_____

Reflect on the six chapters of part 4. What are your primary takeaways? Keep these statements close at hand as you act on and connect to your personal and professional soul story timeline today and tomorrow.

_____
_____
_____
_____
_____
_____
_____
_____
_____

tidal water when the water is *completely unstressed*, and there is no movement either way in the tidal stream, which occurs before the direction of the tidal stream reverses."[242]

Sounds good, does it not? A time twice a day that is completely unstressed. A time when calm replaces chaos, when quiet replaces the noise. A time when we swim without stress in the ebbs and flows of our teaching and leading life. A time when we disengage from our professional life and benefit from time that allows for "claiming my heart and soul, taking away the stress of the day."[243]

MY SOUL STORY

Whatever you do, don't squander your life on things that don't matter. Don't let your life drift into the shallows, allowing life's joys and mysteries to pass by you on your timeline.

As educators, we cannot underestimate the power of our daily actions; and we cannot run away from them either. This is our vocation. This is our professional life story. Do what you can between the zeros, give yourself some grace each day, practice self-care and collective care, and make room for your personal slack tide for a better version of you tomorrow. And I'll do the same.

May the wake of your walk be filled with images of kindness and care, compassion and love, and joy and laughter as you pour into the hearts and the souls of others. This is the true benefit of your professional life.

From the bottom of my heart and soul to yours.

Acknowledgments

I first want to thank my FamBam, as we call it. During the writing of this book, FamBam expanded by two with our grandchildren, Abigail and Maguire, and a third grandchild is on his way. They represent the next generation, and my wife Susan and I worry and wonder what is ahead for them. We can only hope they will be fortunate enough to have teachers and leaders who thought the idea of a book about your soul story was worthy of your time.

Like many families, we face our obstacles and challenges with determination and joy on most days, and I cannot thank our children Anna, Jess, Jaclyn, Tim, and Adam enough for reminding me that my greatest sources of joy, on the most difficult of days, reside within them. Susan is my rock. I am fortunate she chose to walk through life with me. My debt, love, and thanks to her, always.

SOUL! is now my twenty-fourth authored or coauthored book for Solution Tree Press. I am pretty sure Douglas Rife (president and publisher of Solution Tree International) could not have imagined we would produce twenty-four books in the past thirteen years together, when we sat for coffee in an Indianapolis airport in late 2008. I know I could not have envisioned that future on my timeline, as my writing was very raw. I thank him for his professional impact and support, his belief to push me and pull me forward, as well as his personal strength to display his own deep and heartfelt soul story every day. My life is enriched because he has crossed my path.

Yet, that airport meeting with Douglas would not have been possible without the unconditional support and friendship of Jeff Jones, who leads and believes in the heart and soul mission of improving the educational lives of children. Thank you for the giving of your time and treasure to my work.

As an author, you quickly realize the process of writing a book is like being part of a family that does not always agree. And it is easy to become defensive. Yet, when I am willing to really listen, I also realize we share the common goal of producing something that works for you, the reader. This is where the Solution Tree editorial team becomes such an invaluable aspect of my work. I was once again fortunate to work with Christine Hood, Kendra Slayton, and Amy Rubenstein, and receive additional support from Jessi Finn, Elisabeth Abrams, Laura Cox, Sarah Ludwig, and Elijah Oates. Christine especially was of invaluable support and guidance once again. Sarah Payne-Mills is this bright light of positivity, optimism, and wisdom. Her support knows no bounds as she directs the publications team and is patient with all of the nuances for such a book as this. She made sure I had the space and opportunity to collaborate at a deep level through every stage of this book. Thank you all!

A funny thing happened on the way to writing this book. It explains the dynamic and privilege of working with the Solution Tree family. Not only did I have the support of Solution Tree leaders, such as Shannon Ritz, Renee Marshall, and Erica Dooley-Dorocke, but so many of the Solution Tree staff pitched in and voiced their support directly to me during the writing process. Thank you!

In addition, every educational colleague I asked for input into the book as a contributor, interviewee, or reviewer, said *yes*. *SOUL!* became so much stronger because their voices are either directly or indirectly found in these pages. They believed enough in this project to help me shape the message for you. And, despite crazy busy schedules, they said *yes* and met deadlines.

My deep thanks to these super reviewers, who read every page of the manuscript and took time to not only respond, but to push me to dig deeper. These reviewers represent every part of our country from all walks of educational life and volunteered to review all four parts of the book, respond to dozens of inquiries from me over an eight-month period, and provide the kind of wisdom and feedback, in a way I could hear, understand, and embrace as each iteration of the manuscript became stronger. *SOUL!* has for sure been a collective-care writing experience for me. To each of you, I am so deeply grateful: Brian Butler, Bob Eaker, Jenn Deinhart, Martha Bruckner, Lucy Van Scyoc, Dan Cohan, Scott Carr, Julie Schmidt, Georgina Rivera, Jasmine Kullar, and Denise Walston. My thanks to one and all.

And, of course, thanks to so many school teachers and leaders, who were swamped by the pandemic of 2020, and yet still managed to provide deep feedback on one or two major sections of the book. These reviewers include outstanding educators I am honored to call colleagues: Luis Cruz, Mark Weichel, Judy Middleton, Grace Kelemanik, Claudia Wheatley, Aaron Hansen, Regina Owens, Ken Williams, Kim Bailey, Brandon Jones, Bob Sonju, Bill Barnes, Jaclyn Kanold, Anthony Muhammad, Chris Jackicic, Bill Ferriter, Mike Mattos, Sarah Schuhl, Mona Toncheff, Darwin Spiller, Becky Walker, Jessica McIntyre, Katie White, Dave Ebert, Tim Brown, Janel Keating, and Thomasenia Lott Adams. I do not know how to thank you. I am so honored that you would give your time and wisdom to this effort.

In addition, a special thanks to the educators and leaders who, in the summer of 2019, sat with me time and again as I asked questions and bugged them to let me either tell a part of their story or place their wisdom into the book. They allowed me to interview them, provided much-needed feedback on my early sketch of ideas, and in the end, gave me a small piece of themselves to place into the book. My thanks to these authors, teachers, and leaders: Julie Schmidt and her District 96 leadership team in Buffalo Grove, Illinois; Paul Kelly and his Elk Grove High School leadership team in Elk Grove, Illinois; Janel Keating and her White River School District leadership team in Buckley, Washington; Bob Eaker; Luis Cruz; Mark Weichel; Tim Brown; Mona Toncheff; Sarah Schuhl; Brian Butler; Regina Owens; Aaron Hansen; Linda Reusch; Katie Graves; Jenn Deinhart; Bill Ferriter; Mike Mattos; Jasmine Kullar; Denise Walston; Lucy Van Scyoc; Corinne Howe; Joel Cummins; Ken Williams; and Bill Barnes. Your words of wisdom were and are compelling.

And finally, my thanks to each of you, the readers. You are the ones in the full stream of educational waters, helping make every day a success for the next generation of young adults. Thank you for caring enough about reflecting on your own professional soul story and your personal and professional wellness. May we all benefit from knowing you along the way of our soul story journey.

Notes

Foreword

1 Kanold, T. D. (2017). *HEART! Fully forming your professional life as a teacher and leader.* Bloomington, IN: Solution Tree Press.

A Note to Readers

2 Kanold, T. D. (2017). *HEART! Fully forming your professional life as a teacher and leader.* Bloomington, IN: Solution Tree Press.

Introduction

3 Carmichael, H., & Loesser, F. (1934). *Heart and soul.* Accessed at https://secondhandsongs .com/work/117450/all on October 15, 2020.

4 Willard, D., Porter, S. L., Preston, A., & Ten Elshof, G. A. (Eds.). (2018). *The disappearance of moral knowledge.* New York: Routledge, pp. 367–370.

5 Internet Encyclopedia of Philosophy. (n.d.). *Socrates: Priority of the care of the soul.* Accessed at www.iep.utm.edu/socrates/#SSH2bii on August 25, 2020.

Part 1: S Is for Searching

Chapter 1

6 Kanold, T. D. (2018, October 9). *The "now what?" of life: Celebrating Rebecca DuFour* [Blog post]. Accessed at www.allthingsplc.info/blog/view/373/the-now-what-of-life-celebrating -rebecca-dufour on November 4, 2020.

7 Brooks, D. (2019). *The second mountain: The quest for a moral life.* New York: Random House, p. 48.

Chapter 2

8 Shawiak, R. V. (n.d.). *Claiming my heart and soul.* Accessed at www.poemhunter.com/poem /claiming-my-heart-and-soul on November 4, 2020.

9 Carmichael, H., & Loesser, F. (1934). *Heart and soul.* Accessed at https://secondhandsongs .com/work/117450/all on October 15, 2020.

10 Brooks, D. (2019). *The second mountain: The quest for a moral life.* New York: Random House, p. 46.

11 Ibid., p. 47.

12 Kanold, T. D. (2017). *HEART! Fully forming your professional life as a teacher and leader.* Bloomington, IN: Solution Tree Press, p. 2.

13 In loco parentis. (n.d.). In *Merriam-Webster.* Accessed at www.merriam-webster.com /dictionary/in%20loco%20parentis on July 20, 2020.

Chapter 3

14 In loco parentis. (n.d.). In *Merriam-Webster*. Accessed at www.merriam-webster.com /dictionary/in%20loco%20parentis on July 20, 2020.

15 IDEA: Individuals with Disabilities Education Act. (n.d.). *About IDEA*. Accessed at https://sites.ed.gov/idea/about-idea on October 14, 2020.

Chapter 4

16 Social justice. (n.d.). In *Oxford reference*. Accessed at www.oxfordreference.com/view/10 .1093/oi/authority.20110803100515279 on July 20, 2020.

17 Ferguson, R. F. (2016). *Aiming higher together: Strategizing better educational outcomes for boys and young men of color*. Washington, DC: Urban Institute. Accessed at www.urban.org /research/publication/aiming-higher-together-strategizing-better-educational-outcomes-boys -and-young-men-color on July 20, 2020.

18 Ibid.

19 Washington, J. M. (Ed.). (1986). *A testament of hope: The essential writings and speeches of Martin Luther King Jr.* New York: HarperCollins, p. 237.

20 Delpit, L. (2013). *"Multiplication is for white people": Raising expectations for other people's children*. New York: New Press, p. 77.

21 Muhammad, A., & Cruz, L. F. (2019). *Time for change: 4 essential skills for transformational school and district leaders*. Bloomington, IN: Solution Tree Press.

22 L. Cruz, personal communication, September 15, 2019.

23 Ibid.

24 Ibid.

25 Ibid.

26 Washington, J. M. (Ed.). (1986). *A testament of hope: The essential writings and speeches of Martin Luther King Jr.* New York: HarperCollins, p. 230.

Chapter 5

27 William Stafford, excerpt from "Ask Me" from *Ask Me: 100 Essential Poems*. Copyright © 1977, 2014 by William Stafford and the Estate of William Stafford. Reprinted with the permission of The Permission Company, LLC on behalf of Graywolf Press, Minneapolis, Minnesota, graywolfpress.org.

28 Palmer, P. J. (2000). *Let your life speak: Listening for the voice of vocation*. San Francisco: Jossey-Bass, pp. 4–5.

29 Brooks, D. (2019). *The second mountain: The quest for a moral life*. New York: Random House.

30 Ibid., p. xiv.

31 Stafford, K. (Ed.). (2014). *Ask me: 100 essential poems—William Stafford*. Minneapolis, MN: Graywolf Press, p. 6.

32 Palmer, P. J. (2000). *Let your life speak: Listening for the voice of vocation*. San Francisco: Jossey-Bass.

33 Brooks, D. (2019). *The second mountain: The quest for a moral life*. New York: Random House.

34 Ibid., pp. 89–90.

35 Ibid., p. 91.

36 Ibid., p. xvi.

37 M. Weichel, personal communication, March 16, 2020.

Chapter 6

38 Suffering. (n.d.). In *Merriam-Webster*. Accessed at www.merriam-webster.com/dictionary /suffering on July 20, 2020.

39 Compassion. (n.d.). In *Merriam-Webster*. Accessed at www.merriam-webster.com/dictionary /compassion on July 20, 2020.

40 Goetz, J. L., Keltner, D., & Simon-Thomas, E. (2010). Compassion: An evolutionary analysis and empirical review. *Psychological Bulletin, 136*(3), 353.

41 Seppälä, E. M., Simon-Thomas, E., Brown, S. L., Worline, M. C., Cameron, C. D., & Doty, J. R. (Eds.). (2017). *The Oxford handbook of compassion science*. New York: Oxford University Press.

42 Trzeciak, S., & Mazzarelli, A. (2019). *Compassionomics: The revolutionary scientific evidence that caring makes a difference*. Pensacola, FL: Studer Group, pp. 300–301.

43 Ambady, N., Koo, J., Rosenthal, R., & Winograd, C. H. (2002). Physical therapists' nonverbal communication predicts geriatric patients' health outcomes. *Psychology and Aging*, *17*(3), 443–452.

44 Doherty, C., Kiley, J., & Johnson, B. (2016). *A divided and pessimistic electorate*. Washington, DC: Pew Research Center. Accessed at www.pewresearch.org/politics/wp-content/uploads /sites/4/2016/11/11-10-16-election-release.pdf on October 7, 2020.

45 Neff, K., & Germer, C. (2017). Self-compassion and psychological well-being. In E. M. Seppälä, E. Simon-Thomas, S. L. Brown, M. C. Worline, C. D. Cameron, & J. R. Doty (Eds.), *The Oxford handbook of compassion science* (pp. 371–386). New York: Oxford University Press.

46 Ibid., p. 371.

47 Trzeciak, S., & Mazzarelli, A. (2019). *Compassionomics: The revolutionary scientific evidence that caring makes a difference*. Pensacola, FL: Studer Group.

48 Ibid.

49 Ibid., pp. 299–300.

50 Ibid., p. 301.

51 Ibid., p. 304.

52 Jazaieri, H. (2018). Compassionate education from preschool to graduate school: Bringing a culture of compassion into the classroom. *Journal of Research in Innovative Teaching and Learning*, *11*(1), 22–66.

53 Chödrön, P. (2018). *The places that scare you: A guide to fearlessness in difficult times*. Boulder, CO: Shambhala Publications.

54 Ibid., p. 50.

55 Kanold, T. D. (2017). *HEART! Fully forming your professional life as a teacher and leader*. Bloomington, IN: Solution Tree Press.

56 Neff, K., & Germer, C. (2017). Self-compassion and psychological well-being. In E. M. Seppälä, E. Simon-Thomas, S. L. Brown, M. C. Worline, C. D. Cameron, & J. R. Doty (Eds.), *The Oxford handbook of compassion science* (pp. 371–386). New York: Oxford University Press, p. 371.

57 Chiao, J. Y. (2017). Cultural neuroscience of compassion and empathy. In E. M. Seppälä, E. Simon-Thomas, S. L. Brown, M. C. Worline, C. D. Cameron, & J. R. Doty (Eds.), *The Oxford handbook of compassion science* (pp. 147–158). New York: Oxford University Press, p. 148.

58 Saturn, S. R. (2017). Two factors that fuel compassion: The oxytocin system and the social experience of moral elevation. In E. M. Seppälä, E. Simon-Thomas, S. L. Brown, M. C. Worline, C. D. Cameron, & J. R. Doty (Eds.), *The Oxford handbook of compassion science* (pp. 121–132). New York: Oxford University Press, p. 125.

Chapter 7

59 B. Butler, personal communication, February–March 2020.

Part 1: Final Thoughts

60 Cable, D. M. (2018). *Alive at work: The neuroscience of helping your people love what they do*. Boston: Harvard Business School Press, p. 6.

61 Ibid.

62 Ibid., p. 7.

63 Ibid., p. 8.

64 Ibid.

65 Glaude, E. S., Jr. (2017). *Democracy in black: How race still enslaves the American soul.* New York: Crown, p. 47.

Part 2: O Is for Overcoming

Chapter 8

66 Mental map. (n.d.). In *APA dictionary of psychology.* Accessed at https://dictionary.apa.org/mental-map on July 20, 2020.

67 Achor, S. (2010). *The happiness advantage: The seven principles of positive psychology that fuel success and performance at work.* New York: Penguin Random House, p. 108.

68 B. Barnes, personal communication, May 15, 2020.

Chapter 9

69 Palmer, P. J. (2009). *A hidden wholeness: The journey toward an undivided life.* San Francisco: Jossey-Bass, p. 20.

70 K. Graves, personal communication, May 20, 2020.

71 Holiday, R. (2015). *The obstacle is the way: The ancient art of turning adversity to advantage.* London: Profile Books, p. 130.

Chapter 10

72 R. DuFour, personal communication, October 19, 1991.

73 Anwar, Y. (2017, September 8). *How many different human emotions are there?* [Video file]. Accessed at https://greatergood.berkeley.edu/article/item/how_many_different_human_emotions_are_there on October 8, 2020.

74 Anwar, Y. (2017, September 8). *How many different human emotions are there?* [Video file]. Accessed at https://greatergood.berkeley.edu/article/item/how_many_different_human_emotions_are_there on July 20, 2020.

75 Emotion. (n.d.). In *Merriam-Webster.* Accessed at www.merriam-webster.com/dictionary/emotion on July 20, 2020.

76 Mayer, J. D., & Salovey, P. (1997). What is emotional intelligence? In P. Salovey & D. J. Sluyter (Eds.), *Emotional development and emotional intelligence: Educational implications* (pp. 3–31). New York: Basic Books, p. 10.

77 Mersino, A. (2013). *Emotional intelligence for project managers: The people skills you need to achieve outstanding results* (2nd ed.). New York: AMACOM, pp. 22–23.

78 Willard, D. (2002). *Renovation of the heart: Putting on the character of Christ.* Colorado Springs, CO: NavPress, p. 13.

Chapter 11

79 Anger. (n.d.). In *Merriam-Webster.* Accessed at www.merriam-webster.com/dictionary/anger on July 20, 2020.

80 Kanold, T. D. (2017). *HEART! Fully forming your professional life as a teacher and leader.* Bloomington, IN: Solution Tree Press, p. 34.

81 Piercy, M. (1982). To be of use. In *Circles on the water: Selected poems of Marge Piercy.* New York: Gallup Press, p. 106.

82 Ibid.

83 Anger. (n.d.). In *Merriam-Webster.* Accessed at www.merriam-webster.com/dictionary/anger on July 20, 2020.

84 Grant, A. (2016). *Originals: How non-conformists move the world.* New York: Viking Penguin, p. 248.

85 MindTools. (n.d.). *How good is your anger management? Controlling your anger before it controls you.* Accessed at www.mindtools.com/pages/article/newTCS_88.htm on July 20, 2020.

Chapter 12

86 Perfectionism. (n.d.). In *Merriam-Webster.* Accessed at www.merriam-webster.com/dictionary/perfectionism on July 20, 2020.

87 Envy. (n.d.). In *Merriam-Webster.* Accessed at www.merriam-webster.com/dictionary/envy on July 20, 2020.

88 Jealousy. (n.d.). In *Merriam-Webster*. Accessed at www.merriam-webster.com/dictionary/jealousy on July 20, 2020.

89 Holiday, R. (2019). *Stillness is the key*. New York: Portfolio/Penguin, p. 115.

90 Holiday, R. (2016). *Ego is the enemy*. New York: Portfolio/Penguin, pp. 116–117.

91 R. Owens, personal communication, March 31, 2020.

92 Brown, B. (2012). *Daring greatly: How the courage to be vulnerable transforms the way we live, love, parent, and lead*. New York: Penguin Random House, p. 10.

93 Brown, B. [BreneBrown]. (2020, March 7). *1. Don't look for confirmation that you don't belong or that you're not good enough. You'll always find it. 2. Remember you* [Twitter moment]. Accessed at https://twitter.com/BreneBrown on March 7, 2020.

94 Holiday, R. (2019). *Stillness is the key*. New York: Portfolio/Penguin, p. 124.

95 Burnett, B., & Evans, D. (2020). *Designing your work life: How to thrive and change and find happiness at work*. New York: Penguin Random House, pp. 19–20.

Chapter 13

96 Hard-hearted. (n.d.). In *Merriam-Webster*. Accessed at www.merriam-webster.com/dictionary/hard-hearted on July 20, 2020.

97 Neff, K., & Germer, C. (2017). Self-compassion and psychological well-being. In E. M. Seppälä, E. Simon-Thomas, S. L. Brown, M. C. Worline, C. D. Cameron, & J. R. Doty (Eds.), *The Oxford handbook of compassion science* (pp. 371–386). New York: Oxford University Press, p. 371.

98 Seppälä, E. M., Simon-Thomas, E., Brown, S. L., Worline, M. C., Cameron, C. D., & Doty, J. R. (Eds.). (2017). *The Oxford handbook of compassion science*. New York: Oxford University Press.

99 Neff, K., & Germer, C. (2017). Self-compassion and psychological well-being. In E. M. Seppälä, E. Simon-Thomas, S. L. Brown, M. C. Worline, C. D. Cameron, & J. R. Doty (Eds.), *The Oxford handbook of compassion science* (pp. 371–386). New York: Oxford University Press, p. 371.

100 Neff, K. (2011). *Self-compassion: The proven power of being kind to yourself*. New York: HarperCollins.

101 Germer, C., & Neff, K. (2013). Self-compassion in clinical practice. *Journal of Clinical Psychology*, *69*(8), 856–867, p. 857.

102 Gardner, J. W. (1992). The secret ailment. *Across the Board*, *12*(8), 47–50, p. 47.

103 Society of Classical Poets. (2012, August 20). *Five greatest poems by Robert Frost*. Accessed at https://classicalpoets.org/2012/08/20/five-greatest-poems-by-robert-frost on July 20, 2020.

Chapter 14

104 Loehr, J. (2007). *The power of story: Rewrite your destiny in business and in life*. New York: Free Press, p. 79.

105 Holiday, R. (2015). *The obstacle is the way: The ancient art of turning adversity to advantage*. London: Profile Books.

106 Centers for Disease Control and Prevention. (n.d.). *COVID-19: Cases in the U.S.* Accessed at www.cdc.gov/coronavirus/2019-ncov/cases-updates/cases-in-us.html#epi-curve on January 1, 2021.

107 L. Van Scyoc, personal communication, June 19, 2020.

108 J. Kullar, personal communication, June 29, 2020.

109 Levine, D. (2020, March 25). Turning social distancing into a positive. *U.S. News & World Report*. Accessed at https://health.usnews.com/conditions/articles/turning-social-distancing-into-a-positive#expert-sources on July 20, 2020.

110 Neff, K., & Germer, C. (2017). Self-compassion and psychological well-being. In E. M. Seppälä, E. Simon-Thomas, S. L. Brown, M. C. Worline, C. D. Cameron, & J. R. Doty (Eds.), *The Oxford handbook of compassion science* (pp. 371–386). New York: Oxford University Press, p. 125.

111 Ibid.

Part 2: Final Thoughts

112 Simpson, A. [PBS NewsHour]. (2018, December 7). *George H. W. Bush "never hated anyone. He knew what his mother and my mother always knew: Hatred corrodes the container* [Twitter moment]. Accessed at https://twitter.com/newshour/status/1070369145311510528?lang=en on April 10, 2020.

113 Hatred. (n.d.). *The list of world proverbs*. Accessed at www.listofproverbs.com/keywords/hatred on October 18, 2020.

114 Washington, J. M. (Ed.). (1986). *A testament of hope: The essential writings and speeches of Martin Luther King Jr.* New York: HarperCollins, p. 514.

Part 3: U Is for Unifying

115 Kanold, T. D. (2017). *HEART! Fully forming your professional life as a teacher and leader.* Bloomington, IN: Solution Tree Press.

Chapter 15

116 Great Seal. (2016). *E pluribus unum: Origin and meaning of the motto carried in the beak of the bald eagle on the Great Seal.* Accessed at www.greatseal.com/mottoes/unum.html on July 20, 2020.

117 E pluribus unum. (n.d.). In *Merriam-Webster*. Accessed at www.merriam-webster.com /dictionary/e%20pluribus%20unum on October 9, 2020.

118 Community. (n.d.). In *Merriam-Webster*. Accessed at www.merriam-webster.com/dictionary /community on July 20, 2020.

119 Com. (n.d.). In *Merriam-Webster*. Accessed at www.merriam-webster.com/dictionary/com on July 20, 2020.

120 Unity. (n.d.). In *Merriam-Webster*. Accessed at www.merriam-webster.com/dictionary/unity on July 20, 2020.

121 Mineo, L. (2017, April 11). Good genes are nice, but joy is better. *Harvard Gazette*. Accessed at https://news.harvard.edu/gazette/story/2017/04/over-nearly-80-years-harvard-study-has-been -showing-how-to-live-a-healthy-and-happy-life on July 20, 2020.

122 Ibid. Accessed on October 9, 2020.

123 Washington, J. M. (Ed.). (1986). *A testament of hope: The essential writings and speeches of Martin Luther King Jr.* New York: HarperCollins, p. 122.

124 A. Muhammad, personal communication, April 19, 2020.

125 Rath, T. (2020). *Life's great question: Discover how you contribute to the world.* San Francisco: Silicon Guild Books, p. 12.

126 GreatSeal.com. (n.d.). *E pluribus unum*. Accessed at http://greatseal.com/mottoes/unum.html on January 24, 2021.

Chapter 16

127 Hills, J. (2018). *How an understanding of neuroscience can help create inclusion.* Accessed at https://headheartbrain.com/resources/how-an-understanding-of-neuroscience-can-help-create -inclusion on July 20, 2020.

128 Stanford Medicine Department of Psychiatry and Behavioral Sciences. (n.d.). *The Belonging Project at Stanford.* Accessed at https://med.stanford.edu/psychiatry/special-initiatives /belonging.html on July 20, 2020.

129 Cole, R. W. (2008). Educating everybody's children: We know what works—and what doesn't. In R. W. Cole (Ed.), *Educating everybody's children: Diverse teaching strategies for diverse learners* (Revised and expanded 2nd ed., pp. 1–40). Alexandria, VA: Association for Supervision and Curriculum Development.

130 Coyle, D. (2018). *The culture code: The secrets of highly successful groups.* New York: Penguin Random House.

131 Ibid., pp. 74–88.

132 Ibid., p. 75.

133 Ibid., pp. 76–77.

134 Ibid., p. 78.

135 Ibid., p. 80.

136 Ibid., p. 81.

137 Ibid., p. 85.

138 Ibid., p. 87.

139 J. McGrath, personal communication, August 17, 1992.

Chapter 17

140 Rath, T. (2020). *Life's great question: Discover how you contribute to the world.* San Francisco: Silicon Guild Books, p. 12.

141 De Pree, M. (1989). *Leadership is an art.* New York: Dell.

142 Ibid., p. 60.

143 Reeves, D., & DuFour, R. (2016, March). *The futility of PLC lite.* Accessed at https://kappan online.org/the-futility-of-plc-lite on September 29, 2020.

144 S. Carr, personal communication, July 3, 2020.

145 M. Mattos, personal communication, July 6, 2020.

146 Rath, T. (2020). *Life's great question: Discover how you contribute to the world.* San Francisco: Silicon Guild Books, p. 12.

147 Catalyst. (2015, March 2). *Infographic: Inclusion matters.* Accessed at www.catalyst.org/research /infographic-inclusion-matters on July 20, 2020.

148 Ibid.

149 Kasmirli, M. (2019, February 11). *Tools for thinking: Isaiah Berlin's two concepts of freedom.* Accessed at https://aeon.co/ideas/tools-for-thinking-isaiah-berlins-two-concepts-of-freedom on July 20, 2020.

150 Professional. (n.d.). In *Merriam-Webster.* Accessed at www.merriam-webster.com/dictionary /professional on July 20, 2020.

151 Heller, R. (2020). Organizing schools so teachers can succeed: A conversation with Susan Moore Johnson. *Phi Delta Kappan, 101*(6), 35–39, p. 35.

152 Ibid., p. 37.

153 Kasmirli, M. (2019, February 11). *Tools for thinking: Isaiah Berlin's two concepts of freedom.* Accessed at https://aeon.co/ideas/tools-for-thinking-isaiah-berlins-two-concepts-of-freedom on July 20, 2020.

154 C. Jackicic, personal communication, May 23, 2020.

Chapter 18

155 A. Hansen, personal communication, May 15, 2020.

156 Vulnerable. (n.d.). In *Merriam-Webster.* Accessed at www.merriam-webster.com/dictionary /vulnerable on July 20, 2020.

157 Zak, P. J. (2017). The neuroscience of trust. *Harvard Business Review.* Accessed at https://hbr .org/2017/01/the-neuroscience-of-trust on July 20, 2020.

158 Ibid.

159 J. Schmidt & Kildeer Countryside School District 96 team, personal communication, June 10, 2020.

160 Ibid.

161 Coyle, D. (2018). *The culture code: The secrets of highly successful groups.* New York: Penguin Random House, p. 104.

162 Ibid., pp. 104–105.

163 Ibid., p. 112.

164 S. Schuhl & M. Toncheff, personal communication, June 15, 2020.

165 Reis, H. T., & Carmichael, C. L. (2006). *Perceived Partner Responsiveness Scale.* Accessed at www.sas.rochester.edu/psy/people/faculty/reis_harry/assets/pdf/reisetal_2018_pprs.pdf on July 20, 2020.

166 Coyle, D. (2018). *The culture code: The secrets of highly successful groups.* New York: Penguin Random House, p. 113.

Chapter 19

167 Validation. (n.d.). In *Merriam-Webster*. Accessed at www.merriam-webster.com/dictionary/validation on July 20, 2020.

168 Burns, M. (2019, February 19). I'm a neuroscientist. Here's how teachers change kids' brains. *EdSurge*. Accessed at www.edsurge.com/news/2019-02-19-i-m-a-neuroscientist-here-s-how-teachers-change-kids-brains on July 20, 2020.

169 Saphier, J. (2017, November 30). *High expectations teaching*. Presented at the annual conference of the Association of Educational Service Agencies, San Antonio, TX. Accessed at www.aesa.us/annualconference/2017presentations/Jon%20Saphier-High%20Expect%20Teaching.pdf on July 20, 2020.

170 W. Ferriter, personal communication, July 22, 2019

171 Ibid., April 29, 2020.

172 Tolerance. (n.d.). In *Merriam-Webster*. Accessed at www.merriam-webster.com/dictionary/tolerance on July 20, 2020.

Chapter 20

173 Morgan, G. (1997). *Images of organization* (2nd ed.). Thousand Oaks, CA: SAGE.

174 Ibid.

175 Ibid.

176 Hypocrisy. (n.d.). In *Merriam-Webster*. Accessed at www.merriam-webster.com/dictionary/hypocrisy on July 20, 2020.

177 A. Muhammad, personal communication, May 15, 2020.

178 Chappell, B. (2020, April 9). "This is not humanity's first plague," Pope Francis says of coronavirus. *NPR*. Accessed at www.npr.org/sections/coronavirus-live-updates/2020/04/09/830759485/this-is-not-humanity-s-first-plague-pope-francis-says-of-coronavirus on July 20, 2020.

179 J. Deinhart, personal communication, May 4, 2020.

Chapter 21

180 Holiday, R. (2019). *Stillness is the key*. New York: Portfolio/Penguin, pp. xv–xvi.

181 Quietude. (n.d.). In *Merriam-Webster*. Accessed at www.merriam-webster.com/dictionary/quietude on July 20, 2020.

182 Holiday, R. (2019). *Stillness is the key*. New York: Portfolio/Penguin, p. xv.

183 Turkle, S. (2012). *Alone together: Why we expect more from technology and less from each other*. New York: Basic Books.

184 Turkle, S. (2012, February). *Connected, but alone?* [Video file]. Accessed at www.ted.com/talks/sherry_turkle_connected_but_alone/transcript on July 20, 2020, 14:22.

185 Holiday, R. (2019). *Stillness is the key*. New York: Portfolio/Penguin, p. 215.

186 Artist. (n.d.). In *Merriam-Webster*. Accessed at www.merriam-webster.com/dictionary/artist on July 20, 2020.

187 Holiday, R. (2019). *Stillness is the key*. New York: Portfolio/Penguin, p. 61.

188 Gross, D. A. (2014, August 21). *This is your brain on silence*. Accessed at http://nautil.us/issue/16/nothingness/this-is-your-brain-on-silence on July 20, 2020.

189 London, J. (1999). Getting into print (1903). In D. L. Walker & J. C. Reesman (Eds.), *"No mentor but myself": Jack London on writing and writers* (2nd ed.). Stanford, CA: Stanford University Press, p. 57.

190 Holiday, R. (2019). *Stillness is the key*. New York: Portfolio/Penguin, p. 55.

191 Clear, J. (2018). *Atomic habits: An easy and proven way to build good habits and break bad ones*. New York: Random House, p. 162.

192 Ibid., p. 164.

193 Ibid., p. 166.

194 Moran, J. M., Kelley, W. M., & Heatherton, T. F. (2013). What can the organization of the brain's default mode network tell us about self-knowledge? *Frontiers in Human Neuroscience, 7*, 391. Accessed at www.frontiersin.org/articles/10.3389/fnhum.2013.00391/full on July 20, 2020.

195 Brown, B. (2010). *The gifts of imperfection: Let go of who you think you're supposed to be and embrace who you are.* Center City, MN: Hazelden, p. 108.

Part 3: Final Thoughts

196 R. Eaker, personal communication, May 10, 2020.

Part 4: L Is for Living

Chapter 22

197 Rath, T. (2020). *Life's great question: Discover how you contribute to the world.* San Francisco: Silicon Guild Books, p. 45.

198 Ibid.

199 Ibid., p. 45.

200 C. Howe, personal communication, June 4, 2020.

201 Songfacts. (n.d.). *Lyrics for "Good Riddance (Time of Your Life)" by Green Day.* Accessed at www.songfacts.com/lyrics/green-day/good-riddance-time-of-your-life on July 20, 2020.

202 Ibid.

Chapter 23

203 Wang, O. (2016). *Sly and the Family Stone: 20 essential songs.* Accessed at www.rollingstone .com/music/music-lists/sly-and-the-family-stone-20-essential-songs-79782/the-beau-brummels -laugh-laugh-1965-39243 on October 14, 2020.

204 soulbrothanumbahone. (2016, July 19). *Bill Withers—Lean on me* [Video file]. Accessed at www.youtube.com/watch?v=qkaexjc-1os on October 14, 2020.

205 Medina, J. (2014). *Brain rules: 12 principles for surviving and thriving at work, home, and school.* Seattle, WA: Pear Press.

206 Ibid.

207 Ibid.

208 Heath, C., & Heath, D. (2017). *The power of moments: Why certain experiences have extraordinary impact.* London: Bantam Press.

209 Ibid., pp. 4–5.

210 Heath, C., & Heath, D. (2017). *The power of moments: Why certain experiences have extraordinary impact.* London: Bantam Press.

211 Carpe diem. (n.d.). In *Merriam-Webster.* Accessed at www.merriam-webster.com/dictionary /carpe%20diem on July 20, 2020.

212 Heath, C., & Heath, D. (2017). *The power of moments: Why certain experiences have extraordinary impact.* London: Bantam Press.

213 Ibid., pp. 12–14.

214 Heath, C., & Heath, D. (2017). *The power of moments: Why certain experiences have extraordinary impact.* London: Bantam Press.

215 Gibran, K. (1960). *Thoughts and meditations* (A. R. Ferris, Trans.). New York: Citadel Press.

Chapter 24

216 Beach, H., & Strijack, T. N. (2020). *Reclaiming our students: Why children are more anxious, aggressive, and shut down than ever—and what we can do about it.* Vancouver, British Columbia, Canada: Page Two Books, p. 236.

217 Tomlinson, C. A., & Sousa, D. A. (2020). The sciences of teaching. *Educational Leadership, 77*(8), 14–20.

218 Chiao, J. Y. (2017). Cultural neuroscience of compassion and empathy. In E. M. Seppälä, E. Simon-Thomas, S. L. Brown, M. C. Worline, C. D. Cameron, & J. R. Doty (Eds.), *The Oxford handbook of compassion science* (pp. 147–158). New York: Oxford University Press, p. 148.

219 Tomlinson, C. A., & Sousa, D. A. (2020). The sciences of teaching. *Educational Leadership*, *77*(8), 14–20, p. 18.

220 Tyng, C. M., Amin, H. U., Saad, M. N. M., & Malik, A. S. (2017). The influences of emotion on learning and memory. *Frontiers in Psychology*, *8*(1454).

221 Chiao, J. Y. (2017). Cultural neuroscience of compassion and empathy. In E. M. Seppälä, E. Simon-Thomas, S. L. Brown, M. C. Worline, C. D. Cameron, & J. R. Doty (Eds.), *The Oxford handbook of compassion science* (pp. 147–158). New York: Oxford University Press, p. 153.

222 J. Cummins, personal communication, June 15, 2020.

Chapter 25

223 Southern Illinois University. (n.d.). *In the virtue of courage in Plato's Laches 1*. Accessed at www.siue.edu/~evailat/el6.html on July 4, 2020.

224 Ibid.

225 Courage. (n.d.). In *Merriam-Webster*. Accessed at www.merriam-webster.com/dictionary /courage on July 20, 2020.

226 Heath, D. (2020). *Upstream: The quest to solve problems before they happen*. New York: Simon & Schuster, p. 23.

227 Ibid., p. 24.

228 Kouzes, J. M., & Posner, B. Z. (2006). *A leader's legacy*. San Francisco: Jossey-Bass, p. 140.

Chapter 26

229 Happiness. (n.d.). In *Merriam-Webster*. Accessed at www.merriam-webster.com/dictionary /happiness on July 20, 2020.

230 Joy. (n.d.). In *Merriam-Webster*. Accessed at www.merriam-webster.com/dictionary/joy on July 20, 2020.

231 Brown, B. (2010). *The gifts of imperfection: Let go of who you think you're supposed to be and embrace who you are*. Center City, MN: Hazelden.

232 Ibid., p. 78.

233 T. Brown, personal communication, June 23, 2020.

234 Brown, B. (2010). *The gifts of imperfection: Let go of who you think you're supposed to be and embrace who you are*. Center City, MN: Hazelden, p. 84.

235 Grace. (n.d.). In *Merriam-Webster*. Accessed at www.merriam-webster.com/dictionary/grace on July 20, 2020.

236 Kouzes, J. M., & Posner, B. Z. (2006). *A leader's legacy*. San Francisco: Jossey-Bass, p. 162.

Chapter 27

237 Buffet, J. (2004). *Trip around the sun*. Accessed at www.azlyrics.com/lyrics/jimmybuffett/trip aroundthesun.html on October 14, 2020.

238 Ibid.

239 Ibid.

240 L. Reusch, personal communication, May 27, 2020.

241 L. Cruz, personal communication, February 21, 2020.

Part 4: Final Thoughts

242 Bowditch, N., & Bowditch, J. I. (2018). *The American practical navigator*. Bethesda, MD: National Imagery and Mapping Agency, p. 139.

243 Shawiak, R.V. (n.d.). *Claiming my heart and soul*. Accessed at www.poemhunter.com/poem /claiming-my-heart-and-soul on February 12, 2020.

Index

Praise for

SOUL!

Fulfilling the Promise of Your Professional Life as a Teacher and Leader

"In *SOUL!*, Timothy D. Kanold has created a compelling and timely companion to his best-selling book *HEART!* Dr. Kanold connects our journey as educators to our inherent desire for purpose and impact. His personal stories and reflections shine a light on the importance of investing in our purpose. While *HEART!* shows us how to have a positive impact on others and leave our 'heartprint,' *SOUL!* encourages us to turn inward and check our own healthy and sometimes unhealthy reactions and decisions that drive the *why* behind our impact. Dr. Kanold uses an effective balance of research and relatable personal experiences to help readers develop strategies to cope with obstacles that can block their ability to be effective at building personal and professional relationships. As a school leader, I will encourage my staff to use *SOUL!* as a tool to improve their professional collaboration with peers and improve their impact with students."

—Scott Carr
Principal, Heritage Middle School, Liberty, Missouri

"*SOUL!* by Timothy D. Kanold is one of those books that will truly make you think and reflect, not just as an educator but also as a person. Throughout the book, I paused and reflected on how I've grown over the years but more importantly how much I still need to grow. The personal stories embedded throughout this book will resonate with every reader because we have all had similar experiences, whether it's losing a loved one or experiencing a failure. Dr. Kanold brings those personal stories back to the message of each chapter. This book is definitely worth reading and sharing with colleagues in order to help each of us grow as educators and as people."

—Jasmine K. Kullar
Assistant Superintendent, Cobb County School District, Georgia

"*SOUL!* will resonate with every educator, as it deeply goes to the heart of why we entered this profession. It is quite simply a masterpiece of storytelling. Author Timothy D. Kanold challenges readers to write their own soul stories, which gives them a mirror to who they are and a window into the opportunities still out there. Dr. Kanold's focuses on grace, compassion, empathy, vulnerability, and equity are woven throughout the book as uniting and powerful themes, reminding educators to hold firm to these qualities and continue their beautiful but challenging journey through this profession. *SOUL!* is quite simply the best educational book of its kind that I have ever read!"

—Brian K. Butler
Author and Educational Consultant

"*SOUL!* asks readers to embark on a journey that guides them toward a more purpose-driven professional life. During this journey, readers are catapulted to the promise and reality of a life that results from embracing compassion, empathy, equity, and joy, leaving a lasting imprint that benefits students, parents, and colleagues. Through personal stories and opportunities for reflection, Timothy D. Kanold makes readers conscious of the things they do not see about themselves. This amazing book touches the core of our being and helps us fulfill the promise of our professional lives."

—Denise M. Walston
Director of Mathematics, Council of the Great City Schools

"The work of successful educators and professionals is hard. It takes passion, dedication, and sacrifice. *SOUL!* is a must-read for school and district staff, but it also contributes to fields outside of education. It encourages readers to reach their full potential by engaging deeply in the best practices of their work and to create strong connections with colleagues, students, and families. *SOUL!* navigates readers through this overarching question: 'What drives us to find complete fulfillment in our vocation?' Like Dr. Kanold's prequel, *HEART!*, this book serves as a guide along this important and impactful journey."

—Daniel Cohan
Chief of Secondary Schools, Jeffco Public Schools, Jefferson County, Colorado

"In *SOUL!*, Timothy D. Kanold takes us on a powerful journey that encourages us to reflect on both our personal stories and our impact on others. He recognizes that as educators, we dedicate incredible amounts of our time, energy, and talents in service to our school communities. As educators, we will undoubtedly connect to the real and relatable accounts of his soul story and feel empowered by his guidance as we seek to understand our own journeys. *SOUL!* is engaging, emotionally healing, and truly a gift for all educators."

—Jennifer Deinhart
K-8 Mathematics Specialist and Solution Tree Author and Associate

"When Timothy D. Kanold's *HEART!* was published in 2017, I remember how deeply it spoke to me, and how desperately I needed to focus on the very essence of the book as an educator. Four years later, my sense of urgency has escalated beyond belief. Who in education doesn't need to develop his or her soul story by searching, overcoming, unifying, and living? In *SOUL!*, Dr. Kanold gives us yet another opportunity to learn, listen, reflect, and record our journey during a time of disruption, resilience, and challenge, not only in education but in society. We need to take this journey for ourselves, for our students, and for each other."

—Julie A. Schmidt
Superintendent of Schools, Kildeer Countryside
Community Consolidated School District 96, Buffalo Grove, Illinois

"In *SOUL!*, author Timothy D. Kanold asks us to reflect on the very *soul* of what it means to be an educator. He is one of those people who asks questions and then listens intently to the answers. He shows you that he is interested in and cares about you and your answers. You leave the conversation feeling heard and feeling confirmed. Dr. Kanold's book *SOUL!* makes you feel the same way. He reminds us of why we chose education as our profession and digs deep into the source of what ignites us. *SOUL!* is a must-read for all educators!"

—Janel Keating Hambly
Superintendent, White River School District, Buckley, Washington